Justice Scalia

Justice Scalia

Rhetoric and the Rule of Law

EDITED BY BRIAN G. SLOCUM
AND FRANCIS J. MOOTZ III

The University of Chicago Press
Chicago and London

The University of Chicago Press, Chicago 60637
The University of Chicago Press, Ltd., London
© 2019 by The University of Chicago
For more information, contact the University of Chicago Press, 1427 E. 60th St., Chicago, IL 60637.
Published 2019
Printed in the United States of America

28 27 26 25 24 23 22 21 20 19   1 2 3 4 5

ISBN-13: 978-0-226-60165-6 (cloth)
ISBN-13: 978-0-226-60182-3 (paper)
ISBN-13: 978-0-226-60179-3 (e-book)
DOI: https://doi.org/10.7208/chicago/9780226601793.001.0001

Chapter 1, "Scalia as Procrustes for the Majority, Scalia as Cassandra in Dissent,"
first published in *Jahrbuch des öffentlichen Rechts der Gegenwart* 65 (2017): 765.

Library of Congress Cataloging-in-Publication Data
Names: Slocum, Brian G., editor. | Mootz, Francis J., editor.
Title: Justice Scalia : rhetoric and the rule of law / edited by Brian G. Slocum and Francis J. Mootz III.
Description: Chicago ; London : The University of Chicago Press, 2019. | Includes bibliographical
references and index.
Identifiers: LCCN 2018030219 | ISBN 9780226601656 (cloth : alk. paper) | ISBN 9780226601823
(pbk. : alk. paper) | ISBN 9780226601793 (e-book)
Subjects: LCSH: Scalia, Antonin. | Law—Interpretation and construction. | Constitutional law—
United States—Interpretation and construction. | Rhetoric.
Classification: LCC KF8745.S33 J87 2019 | DDC 347.73/2634—dc23
LC record available at https://lccn.loc.gov/2018030219

♾ This paper meets the requirements of ANSI/NISO Z39.48–1992 (Permanence of Paper).

For Leticia Saucedo, who keeps my passion for the law and justice alive.
FJM III

To Jennifer Slocum, for her loyalty and support.
BGS

Contents

Introduction

FRANCIS J. MOOTZ III
AND BRIAN G. SLOCUM

Justice Antonin Scalia is universally acknowledged to be the single most important figure in the emergence of the "new textualist" approach to statutory interpretation and the "new originalist" approach to constitutional interpretation. He authored numerous opinions during his thirty years as associate justice of the Supreme Court, and published articles and books that defended his judicial practice. He was well known for his vigorous advocacy, particularly in his many stinging dissents that challenged the Court's jurisprudential methodology. Notably, he achieved some measure of victory in his 2008 majority opinion in *District of Columbia v. Heller*, in which a majority of the Court nominally adopted an originalist approach to interpreting the Second Amendment. Even if he did not persuade the majority of the Court to fully embrace his legal philosophy expressly for all cases, he has strongly influenced the manner in which lawyers argue cases and judges write their opinions.

There have been many efforts to delineate and assess Justice Scalia's jurisprudence with regard to its legitimacy and effects on American law. This volume takes a decidedly different tack. The contributors embody broad and diverse perspectives, including those from rhetoric, philosophy, linguistics, politics, and legal theory and jurisprudence, and the chapters focus on the rhetorical strategies in Justice Scalia's opinions rather than the logic or validity of his legal arguments. Justice Scalia has been criticized for the harsh and biting style that he often directed at people, including his colleagues. Others have lauded him for his uncompromising principles, erudite references, and clever *bon mots*. In this volume, the contributors consider Justice Scalia's rhetoric in the full classical sense of the term *rhetoric*, and not simply as a reference to style or ornamentation. As defined by Aristotle, rhetoric is "an ability, in each [particular] case, to see the available means of persuasion."[1] The guiding theme of this book is that Justice Scalia enacts his vision of the rule of law through his rhetorical framing. The medium is the message, and the form is the substance.

Part 1 addresses Justice Scalia's rhetoric of constitutional adjudication and part 2, his rhetoric of statutory textualism, but the arguments developed in the two parts coalesce around a few key themes. The most important, perhaps, involves the dichotomous nature of Justice Scalia's jurisprudential legacy. In a meta sense, Justice Scalia's influence is widely recognized. Justice Elena Kagan, no jurisprudential ally of Justice Scalia, has acknowledged the profound effect he has had on legal argumentation and judicial practice.[2] Yet a consistent theme in the chapters is that Justice Scalia's rhetorical victories (and rhetorical excesses) belie his failure to frame a coherent narrative of the rule of law and its necessary connection to textualism and originalism.

Part of Justice Scalia's rhetorical framing of the requirements of the rule of law involved a certain view of rules and language as highly determinate and inflexible. The consequences made him influential in ways that he did not anticipate (or appreciate). Mary Anne Case argues in chapter 1 that what distinguishes Justice Scalia as a writer of majority opinions is less his adherence to interpretive approaches, such as originalism or textualism, and more his commitment to "the rule of law as a law of rules."[3] This commitment was characterized by a procrustean forcing of prior precedent into the rigid form of "the best rule of law to govern the case at hand." The result was often that subsequent decisions, whether by courts or legislators, backed away from the implications of the categorical rule Scalia had fashioned. Yet, his dissenting opinions, which tended to warn of the consequences that would follow from the logic of the decision just taken or the rule just articulated by the majority, often painted a prophetic picture which in time came true. The result is that Justice Scalia's common-law, analogical reasoning had more of an effect on his colleagues on the Court than his efforts to fashion determinate decision rules.

Rhetorical victories or defeats aside, Justice Scalia's desire for determinate rules of decision undoubtedly motivated his need to emphasize the determinate nature of language. The problem, which Scott Soames explains in chapter 2, is that Justice Scalia's view of language is at odds with current thinking about language. In particular, Justice Scalia's version of textualism seeks to identify the original linguistic meaning of the legal text, but linguistic meaning does not always capture what the original lawmakers asserted in adopting the text. Furthermore, Justice Scalia's view of language as highly determinate ignores situations where judges need to precisify vague legal contents to reach definite results. Justice Scalia thus failed to develop a framework for the various constitutional cases where the original linguistic meaning could not determine the interpretive dispute.

Operationalizing a rhetorical framing of language, and thus interpretation, as highly determinate requires defining the constituent question of interpretation as a search for the linguistic meaning of the text instead of what lawmakers or ratifiers originally used it to assert or stipulate, as Soames explains, but it also involves acontextual interpretation of a different sort. Victoria Nourse explains in chapter 3, through the historic *Morrison v. Olson* case involving the power of the president to remove an independent counsel, that there were often three stages to the process. First, a specific word is isolated. Second, the word is rhetorically isolated from the rest of the relevant text. Finally, through a process of pragmatic enrichment, meaning that is not lexically encoded is implicitly added to the word in order to bolster the chosen interpretation.

The tripartite interpretive method identified by Nourse was part of Justice Scalia's "fair-reading" method (although not officially, of course), which he claimed would narrow the range of acceptable judicial decision-making and argumentation. In order to sell his interpretive philosophy, Justice Scalia attempted to create "communion" between himself and the audience, which involved appealing to the critics of textualism. Brian Slocum, in chapter 4, explains that Justice Scalia, in his 2012 book (his final and most comprehensive opus on interpretation), repeatedly emphasized the importance of context to interpretation and conceded that language is "notoriously slippery." Yet he simultaneously asserted that "variability in interpretation is a distemper" that could be avoided through his interpretive method. He attempted to demonstrate the determinacy of his interpretive method through an analysis of H. L. A. Hart's famous no-vehicles-in-the-park hypothetical, but he only confirmed its enduring message about the fuzziness of language and, even more damaging to his vision, the ineliminable influence of extratextual considerations on legal interpretations. Like his prophetic dissents, Justice Scalia's analysis convincingly illustrated the position against which he was arguing.

Despite the certainty of the interpretive vision expressed in Justice Scalia's scholarly writings, the justificatory rhetoric used by him in actual cases was sometimes more equivocal. For instance, as Larry Solan describes in chapter 5, at times Justice Scalia espoused an objective, public-meaning approach to interpretation as being based on constitutional principles relating to the role of the judiciary. At other times, though, Justice Scalia argued that his methodology was most likely to ascertain the communicative intent of the legislature. Justice Scalia considered only a restricted range of determinants of legislative intent, however, refusing to consult legislative history. On the basis of recent empirical studies, it is questionable whether his favored interpretive principles accurately reflect the realities of legislative drafting, and thus legislative intent.

The very nature of our legal system's treatment of textual interpretation undermined Justice Scalia's vision of determinate decision rules, determinate interpretive rules, and, as a consequence, determinate results. As Abbe Gluck describes in chapter 6, Justice Scalia ultimately could not accurately deem himself an interpretive formalist. For instance, there are too many available interpretive rules (more than a hundred presumptions!) for statutory interpretation to properly be regarded as formalist. Many of the rules may point to different interpretations in any given case, and there are no ordering rules regarding which interpretive rules should be given priority in case of conflict. Furthermore, judges do not treat interpretive rules as real law that is binding on them or others, perhaps because judges themselves create most of the interpretive rules. The result, contrary to formalist ideals, is that judges have enormous discretion in selecting interpretations.

It may seem counterintuitive to us now, but Justice Scalia's more extreme views of rules and language do not follow ineluctably from some of his earliest decisions on the Supreme Court. In fact, early in his tenure on the Court, Justice Scalia could skillfully balance equities when he deemed it necessary, as Jay Mootz explains in chapter 7, Justice Scalia was an effective spokesperson and a skilled jurist who effectively challenged conventional accounts and patterns of decision-making, while recognizing some of the practical limitations of his theoretical approach. Only later did Justice Scalia become more strident as his vision failed to become reality. He refused to accept defeat, undoubtedly frustrated that the Court was disregarding his earlier articulations of the way to avoid a jurisprudential cataclysm. Ultimately, Justice Scalia recognized that the jurisprudential apocalypse had occurred around him, and his angry (often embarrassing) opinions in his later years obscured the promise of his earlier vision.

Part 3 of the volume applies various philosophical approaches and methodological techniques to examine the opinions authored by Justice Scalia. Steven Mailloux describes in chapter 8 the slippage between Justice Scalia's formal theory and his substantive holdings, as exhibited in his scathing expressions of shock and disgust at his colleagues' opinions. Drawing on Kenneth Burke's investigation of religious rhetoric, Mailloux explores how Justice Scalia's reconciliation of (nonbinding) Catholic social teaching and the death penalty exhibits the intermingling of content and form in his thought.

In chapter 9, Darien Shanske argues that Justice Scalia's rhetorical presentation betrays commitments at odds with his judicial philosophy. One might assume that a textualist would embrace a dry and technical style of exegesis, but nothing could be less true of Justice Scalia. Shanske claims that Justice Scalia's robust rhetoric amounts to an outward-facing, public-engaging effort to persuade on the basis of political philosophy, and that his approach serves to demonstrate the durability of law despite heated disagreement. Ultimately, Justice Scalia's performance undermines his claim about what the rule of law requires, because he provides a model of how rhetorical engagement in the creation of law can satisfy the presuppositions of democratic principles.

The contribution by Taylor, Jockers, and Nascimento in chapter 10 utilizes rhetorical theory to uncover the genuine interpretative instability at the heart of Justice Scalia's judicial practice. Although he claims to follow a constrained practice, the authors focus on how his characterization of opposing views as "absurd" in fact expands the scope of discretion. Intriguingly, they use *Bush v. Gore* as an exemplary case, even though Justice Scalia did not nominally author the opinion, based on a sophisticated rhetorical analysis that reveals his role in the opinion. Finally, in chapter 11 Brian Bix illuminates how Justice Scalia's rhetorical construction of "the family" is a driver of his opinions regarding the scope and limits of the Constitution's application to families and matters of intimate relations. Bix argues that all interpreters have preconceptions and heuristics similar to those exhibited by Justice Scalia but that Justice Scalia appeared to be unmindful of his.

The chapters in part 3 demonstrate the vitality of a rhetorical critique of Justice Scalia's opinions. One of Justice Scalia's most important opinions is his majority opinion in the *Heller* case. Part 4 focuses on Justice Scalia's opinion by stepping outside doctrinal analysis to consider the lessons of rhetorical theory. Gene Garver in chapter 12 undermines Justice Scalia's claim to employ a neutral method of interpretation by exploring the role of the preamble in the Second Amendment. Looking to music, Garver explains that the very purpose of a preamble is to contextualize the song that follows, which disrupts Justice Scalia's practice in *Heller* of isolating the preamble to render the text into a statement of a decontextualized and universal right. This is not a constrained deduction, but a polemical strategy by the justice. In a related vein, Peter Brooks in chapter 13 argues that the incoherent tension between originalism and textualism is on display in Justice Scalia's effort in *Heller* to cabin interpretive choice. It is not just the inability of a modern interpreter to recover pristine original meanings, but also the recalcitrance of the Latin-inspired text to definitive analysis. Brooks criticizes the crude nature of Justice Scalia's opinion, including his refusal to credit an amicus brief by various professors of linguistics. Garver and Brooks thus provide complementary critiques of the rhetoric of inevitability.

Finally, in part 5 three contributors address the element of time in Justice Scalia's judicial rhetoric. In response to Justice Scalia's charge that the Court had embraced a separate, abridged edition of the First Amendment, Colin Starger in chapter 14 demonstrates that Scalia's opinions express anti-abortion sentiments through an epideictic strategy of opposing the erosion of values and celebrating the pro-life perspective. In a detailed accounting of cases unfolding through time, Starger provides a deep reading of Justice Scalia's rhetoric as instructive for the potential of epideictic speech. In a similar vein, Linda Berger in chapter 15 charts how Justice Scalia constructed the precedent of past cases in his Free Exercise Clause opinions. Using a combination of close and distant reading techniques from literary theory, Berger uses Justice Scalia's opinion in *Smith* to uncover the determinants of precedential staying power by focusing on his creation of, and the ultimate reception of, the relevant legal rules. There is perhaps no more important temporal consideration at work in judicial interpretation than the decision to overrule a precedent previously accorded stare decisis weight. Clarke Rountree in chapter 16 describes a tripartite approach used by Justice Scalia when he considered the competing needs of past, present, and future in deciding whether to overrule precedent. In the end, Justice Scalia's acerbic rhetoric probably cost the institution some credibility in cases in which he urged the Court to overturn incorrectly decided precedent.

PART 1

The Rhetoric of Constitutional Adjudication

Scalia as Procrustes for the Majority,
Scalia as Cassandra in Dissent

MARY ANNE CASE

The late U.S. Supreme Court Justice Antonin Scalia was infamous for the prose style of his dissenting opinions, frequently described with adjectives such as "vitriolic," "derisive," and, putting it mildly, "colorful." In a single, not unrepresentative, dissent—that in the Affordable Care Act (Obamacare) case of *King v. Burwell*—Scalia characterized the majority opinion, written by Chief Justice John Roberts, as "quite absurd,"[1] "with no semblance of shame," "feeble," full of "interpretive jiggery-pokery," and "pure applesauce."[2] His description of opinions written by more liberal and more junior justices could be even more intemperate.[3]

In this essay, I want to focus on another, less frequently remarked upon quality of Scalia's dissents, which is their tendency to warn prophetically of the consequences that would follow from the logic of the decision just taken or the rule just articulated by a majority of his fellow justices, consequences denied or ignored at the time by the majority. In these dissents, Scalia behaves somewhat like the Trojan princess Cassandra, whose gift of prophecy came with the curse that she would not be believed, and whose clear-eyed warnings as a consequence went unheeded until the time when what they predicted came to pass. Like Cassandra, Scalia is on the losing side of many of his prophecies—what he is predicting is the exact opposite of what he wants to see happen. Every battle, however, is necessarily both "lost and won,"[4] so that what is bad news for the Trojans is good news for the Greeks, and what Scalia sees as the catastrophic consequences of a decision are most welcome from the perspective of his ideological opponents. In describing what for him are the horrors that will follow from the majority's logic, he often paints a prophetic picture which in time comes true, perhaps in part because of rather than in spite of his dramatic articulation of an opinion's implications.

The essay then uses another Greek myth, that of Procrustes, to shed light on a tendency in Scalia's majority opinions. Just as Procrustes forced his guests to fit snugly into an iron bed, stretching out their bodies or chopping off their limbs as necessary, so Scalia frequently forced all prior doctrine in a given area of law into the shape he needed for the new rule he announces in a majority opinion. As with Procrustes's unfortunate guests, so with Scalia's procrustean majority opinions: the result, I shall argue, is often that the operation is a success, but the patient dies. Subsequent decisions, whether by courts or legislatures, tend to back away from the implications of the categorical rule Scalia had gone through such pains to fashion. The paradoxical result is that Scalia as Cassandra dissenting has sometimes been more effective in illuminating the path to results he deplores than Scalia as Procrustes has been in bringing about results he favors. This is so notwithstanding that Scalia in procrustean mode does his rhetorical best to minimize the innovative or controversial character of his holding for the majority, whereas Scalia in dissent seeks rhetorically to maximize the unprecedented and revolutionary character of the majority position to which he objects.

The Cassandra of Gay Rights

The clearest example of Scalia as Cassandra is in the progression of the U.S. Supreme Court's gay rights cases from *Romer v. Evans* through *Obergefell v. Hodges*,[5] and I use these to illustrate the phenomenon.[6] In *Romer*, the Supreme Court struck down an amendment to the Colorado constitution that disadvantaged gays, lesbians, and bisexuals, without so much as mentioning its own prior precedent of *Bowers v. Hardwick*,[7] which had upheld criminal penalties for homosexual sex. For Scalia, this was a "contradict[ion]" because "[i]f the Court [in *Bowers*] was unwilling to object to state laws that criminalize the behavior that defines the class, it is hardly open . . . to conclude that state sponsored discrimination against the class is invidious. After all, there can hardly be more palpable discrimination against a class than making the conduct that defines the class criminal.'"[8] Although there were good reasons for the Court to see Colorado's Amendment 2 as constitutionally problematic, even with respect to a class whose behavior could be criminalized,[9] within a decade the Court, in *Lawrence v. Texas*,[10] agreed with Scalia that the "foundations of *Bowers* have sustained serious erosion from . . . *Romer*,"[11] and the decision should be overruled. While it held in *Lawrence* that private, consensual, adult homosexual sex could no longer constitutionally be criminalized, the Court insisted its decision "[did] not involve whether the government must give formal recognition to any relationship that homosexual persons seek to enter."[12] Scalia's responded in dissent:

> Do not believe it. More illuminating than this bald, unreasoned disclaimer is the progression of thought displayed by an earlier passage in the Court's opinion, which notes the constitutional protections afforded to "personal decisions relating to *marriage*, procreation, contraception, family relationships, child rearing, and education," and then declares that "persons in a homosexual relationship may seek autonomy for these purposes, just as heterosexual persons do." . . . Today's opinion dismantles the structure of constitutional law that has permitted a distinction to be made between heterosexual and homosexual unions, insofar as formal recognition in marriage is concerned.[13]

He was proven right by degrees. In *United States v. Windsor*, the Court struck down the federal Defense of Marriage Act (DOMA), holding that the federal government could not constitutionally withhold recognition from those same-sex marriages recognized under state law, but ending by insisting, "This opinion and its holding are confined to those lawful marriages."[14] Scalia responded,

> I have heard such "bald, unreasoned disclaimer[s]" before. Lawrence, 539 U.S. at 604. When the Court declared a constitutional right to homosexual sodomy, we were assured that the case had nothing, nothing at all to do with "whether the government must give formal recognition to any relationship that homosexual persons seek to enter." . . . Now we are told that DOMA is invalid because it "demeans the couple, whose moral and sexual choices the Constitution protects," . . . —with an accompanying citation of *Lawrence*. It takes real cheek for today's majority to assure us . . . that a constitutional requirement to give formal recognition to same-sex marriage is not at issue here.[15]

Scalia did acknowledge that the "scatter-shot rationales" of the majority opinion left many bases for distinguishing the right upheld in *Windsor* from a more general federal constitutional right to marriage for same-sex couples and urged lower courts to "take the Court at its word and distinguish away."[16] But, unlike Chief Justice Roberts, who devoted a substantial portion of his own dissent to shoring up those possible distinctions,[17] Scalia went on to dismantle them. In *Lawrence*, he had already engaged in some suggested editing of the language of Justice O'Connor's concurring opinion, to show how easily an argument about the criminalization of sodomy could be transformed into one concerning the recognition of same-sex marriage.[18] In his *Windsor* dissent, Scalia goes so far as to use the strikeout function to show how easily whole paragraphs of the majority's opinion could be edited to form part of an opinion constitutionalizing a nationwide right to same-sex marriage. For example,

> Consider how easy (inevitable) it is to make the following substitutions in a passage from today's opinion . . . :
>
>> "~~DOMA's~~ *This state law's* principal effect is to identify a subset of ~~state-sanctioned marriages~~ *constitutionally protected sexual relationships,* see *Lawrence,* and make them unequal. The principal purpose is to impose in-equality, not for other reasons like governmental efficiency. Responsibili-ties, as well as rights, enhance the dignity and integrity of the person. And ~~DOMA~~ *this state law* contrives to deprive some couples ~~married under the laws of their State~~ *enjoying constitutionally protected sexual relationships,* but not other couples, of both rights and responsibilities."
>
> Similarly transposable passages—deliberately transposable, I think—abound.[19]

Lower-court judges were quick to take up Scalia's editorial suggestions[20] and more generally to adopt the view propounded in his dissent as to the logi-cal inevitability of an extension of the holding of *Windsor* to state marriage laws,[21] leading one scholar to suggest that Scalia's *Windsor* dissent paradoxi-cally "might be remembered as the most influential opinion of his career."[22] Indeed, nearly half of the many lower-court decisions that struck down state same-sex marriage bans in the immediate aftermath of *Windsor* explicitly cited Scalia's dissent and treated its reasoning as more persuasive than the qualifying language of the majority or of Roberts's dissent. Within two years, the Supreme Court proved Scalia's prophecies true, holding in *Obergefell* that the constitution did indeed require states "to license same-sex marriages [and] to recognize same-sex marriages performed out of State,"[23] for the rea-son that he predicted: to wit, that "[i]t demeans gays and lesbians for the State to lock them out of a central institution of the Nation's society."[24]

Scalia's comparatively dispassionate elaborations of the worrisome impli-cations he sees in majority opinions such as those in the gay rights cases have had a much better track record in moving the Court in a direction he deplores than any of his more vitriolic dissents have had in moving the Court in a di-rection he favors. One might ask why Scalia engaged in this apparently per-verse behavior—repeatedly drawing a road map to precisely the destination he does not want his colleagues on the Court to reach. Many have similarly asked why Scalia over time did not tone down, but only ratcheted up the level of invective in his dissents, [25] despite evidence it had never persuaded but may rather have alienated his colleagues.[26] Here again, he resembles Cassandra, a prophet possessed, lacking full control of either the substance or the tone of utterances, but impelled to speak truth regardless of its consequences.

Formulating Categorical Rules While Leaving No Case Behind

Whether they are passionate raging or more dispassionate prediction, Scalia's dissents may have more lasting influence than his majority opinions. As long-time Court watcher Linda Greenhouse observed, even on those occasions when he did have the opportunity to "come close to achieving one of his jurisprudential goals, his colleagues have either hung back at the last minute or, feeling buyers' remorse, retreated at the next opportunity."[27] The two principal examples Greenhouse discusses are the Court's backing down from the proposition, articulated in Scalia's majority opinion in *Lucas v. South Carolina Coastal Council*,[28] that even temporary restrictions on a land owner's right to develop property can amount to a taking for which the owner is entitled to compensation, and its similar retreat from his expansive interpretation of the Confrontation Clause in *Crawford v. Washington*.[29] Associated with the buyers' remorse in each of these cases may be precisely what Scalia himself was likely most proud of in each of them—that he used his majority opinion not simply to decide the particular case but to formulate a new categorical rule for a whole line of cases, together with newly formulated categorical exceptions to this rule.[30]

Indeed, what distinguishes Scalia as a writer of majority opinions, I would argue, is less his adherence to interpretive approaches such as originalism or textualism, and more his commitment to "the rule of law as a law of rules,"[31] and his consequent aversion to the use of case-by-case adjudication or multi-factor balancing tests in constitutional law.[32] As he explained, "When one is dealing, as my Court often is, with issues so heartfelt that they are believed by one side or the other to be resolved by the Constitution itself, it does not greatly appeal to one's sense of justice to say: 'Well, that earlier case had nine factors, this one has nine plus one.' Much better, even at the expense of the mild substantive distortion that any generalization introduces, to have a clear, previously enunciated rule that one can point to in explanation of the decision."[33] His willingness to tolerate an error, even injustice, in an individual case in the interests of enunciating and abiding by clear rules[34] even led him so far as to suggest that the actual innocence of a criminal defendant under sentence of death might by itself be an insufficient basis for a court to reopen his case.[35] This puts him squarely at one extreme of the arc of a pendulum that has swung for a millennium in Anglo-American law between rules and

standards, law and equity, the forms of action and the Chancellor's foot.[36] Far
from seeing the charge of formalism as a criticism, Scalia exclaimed, "Long
live formalism. It is what makes a government a government of laws and not
of men."[37]

For Scalia, textualism facilitated formalism, and he was quick to point
out that "[e]very issue of law [he] resolved as a federal judge is an interpretation of text—the text of a regulation, or of a statute, or of the Constitution."[38]
He therefore inveighed against carrying over into the judicial interpretation
of legislative texts, including constitutions, "the *attitude* of the common-
law judge—the mindset that asks, 'What is the most desirable resolution of
this case, and how can any impediments to the achievement of that result be
evaded?'"[39]

For what he saw as the regrettable persistence of this common-law mindset, Scalia blamed, in the first instance, American legal education, which continued to inculcate in law students an "image of the great judge" as

> the man (or woman) who has the intelligence to know what is the best rule
> of law to govern the case at hand, and then the skill to perform the broken-
> field running through earlier cases that leaves him free to impose that rule—
> distinguishing one prior case on his left, straight-arming another one on his
> right, high-stepping away from another precedent about to tackle him from
> the rear, until (bravo!) he reaches his goal: good law. That image of the great
> judge remains with the former law student when he himself becomes a judge,
> and thus the common-law tradition is passed on and on.[40]

What Scalia here characterizes as heroic "broken-field running through
earlier cases" is precisely the phenomenon I would characterize instead as
procrustean fitting of prior precedent into the rigid form of "the best rule
of law to govern the case at hand."[41] If I am describing this phenomenon in
a constitutional rather than a common-law case, am I being more true to
Scalia's own commitments by characterizing it negatively, as analogous to the
destructive work of a villain like Procrustes rather than to the heroic success
of a star athlete?[42] If I am right that Scalia's majority opinions in constitutional
cases frequently do what he deplores, is he suffering from the delusion of
which he accuses other American lawyers and judges, whom he sees as failing
to take account of the changed nature of their tasks in what he characterizes
as their new, democratically determined, civil-law system? Perhaps, but the
situation is somewhat more complicated, because Scalia's procrustean ten-
dencies are most clearly on display in cases that, although they may be constitutional, do not, by his own account, involve the interpretation of consti-

tutional text, because they depend on the incorporation doctrine, a doctrine he sees as having developed without a legitimate basis in constitutional text.

To make this clear requires spelling out something that most American lawyers, including Supreme Court justices, tend to gloss over, although they know it perfectly well: When the U.S. Constitution was ratified in the eighteenth century, its Bill of Rights (including the First Amendment, with its protections for speech, religion, and press, the Fifth Amendment's protections for property, and the various protections for criminal defendants) was seen to operate only as against the federal government. To the extent the several states also were under a constitutional obligation to protect, for example, the freedom of speech, this obligation would only derive from their respective state constitutions. Only over the course of the century and a half since the ratification of the Fourteenth Amendment in the aftermath of the Civil War did the Supreme Court come to hold that most of the provisions of the Bill of Rights also applied to the states. The process by which this was done was not wholesale, but piecemeal and gradual, with separate cases over time considering each provision and occasionally rejecting incorporation of a particular right as against the states. While First Amendment free-speech protections were recognized as incorporated early in the twentieth century,[43] for example, it took until the new millennium for the same to be held true of the Second Amendment right to keep and bear arms.[44]

The textual hook for incorporation of provisions of the Bill of Rights against the states became the Due Process Clause of the Fourteenth Amendment. This technically makes the incorporation of Bill of Rights protections a form of substantive due process, the same doctrinal category which led to such controversial protections as those for economic liberties in the *Lochner*[45] era and for abortion in *Roe v. Wade*[46] and its progeny. Scalia was in general no fan of substantive due process, seeing it as oxymoronic because, "by its inescapable terms," the Due Process Clause "guarantees only process."[47] "To say otherwise," according to Scalia, "is to abandon textualism, and to render democratically adopted texts mere springboards for judicial lawmaking."[48] Yet he "acquiesced in the Court's incorporation of certain guarantees in the Bill of Rights 'because it is both long established and narrowly limited.'"[49]

Because neither text nor original meaning, but only stare decisis, the cumulative weight of precedent, grounds the law applying provisions of the Bill of Rights to the states, a judge deciding a case involving an incorporated provision is necessarily acting as a common-law judge, without access to a civil-law-style alternative to the methodologies of the common law. Such a judge must of necessity "distinguish precedent[s] . . . until (bravo) he reaches

his goal: good law,"[50] even if this means "attacking the enterprise with the Mr.
Fix-it mentality of the common-law judge," which Scalia warned was "a sure
recipe for incompetence and usurpation."[51]

Fitting Free-Exercise Doctrine into a Procrustean Bed

With these background considerations in mind, let me now turn to a detailed
analysis of one major Scalia opinion that fits the procrustean pattern I have
identified,[52] the free exercise of religion case *Employment Division v. Smith*,[53]
in which he goes to heroic lengths to leave no case behind on his path to announcing a categorical rule. *Smith* involved the incorporation of the First
Amendment's religion clauses as against the states, an incorporation so thoroughly accomplished that despite the technical inaccuracy of such a classification, it is typically referred to without qualification as a First Amendment
case. Indeed, the very first sentence of Scalia's opinion reads simply, "This case
requires us to decide whether the *Free Exercise Clause of the First Amendment*
permits the State of Oregon to include religiously inspired peyote use within
the reach of its general criminal prohibition on use of that drug, and thus permits the State to deny unemployment benefits to persons dismissed from their
jobs because of such religiously inspired use."[54]

Smith, a Native American drug counselor, lost his job because he had engaged as a member of the Native American Church in the ritual sacramental consumption of the hallucinogen peyote, whose use the state of Oregon
had criminalized without providing an exemption for religious use, although
a number of other states and the federal government had provided such an
exemption in their own drug laws. Over the course of the quarter-century
before the *Smith* case, the free-exercise cases decided by the U.S. Supreme
Court applied a test first set out in another unemployment compensation
case, *Sherbert v. Verner*,[55] requiring that "governmental actions that substantially burden a religious practice must be justified by a compelling governmental interest." If the action could not be so justified, the Court had held,
a religiously motivated objector would be constitutionally entitled to an exemption from the government action. Although few who brought exemption
claims before the Supreme Court were ultimately successful, standard-like
language requiring narrow tailoring to achieve a compelling governmental
interest suffused the cases during this quarter-century period.

Scalia preferred rules to standards; he hated balancing tests, and he took
the occasion of having been assigned the majority opinion to set out a categorical rule for free-exercise claims. Reaching back to *Reynolds v. United
States*,[56] a foundational nineteenth-century case involving unsuccessful at-

tempts by Mormons in the Utah territory to claim a religious exemption from laws criminalizing polygamy,[57] Scalia declared that, from the time of *Reynolds*, "subsequent decisions have consistently held that the right of free exercise does not relieve an individual of the obligation to comply with a 'valid and neutral law of general applicability on the ground that the law proscribes (or prescribes) conduct that his religion prescribes (or proscribes).'"[58] This was the constitutional rule he held to be applicable to all free-exercise exemption claims. Scalia's characterization of *Reynolds* itself was indisputably correct. That case had proclaimed that laws "are made for the government of actions, and while they cannot interfere with mere religious belief and opinions, they may with practices. . . . [To permit] a man [to] excuse his practices to the contrary because of his religious belief . . . would be to make the professed doctrines of religious belief superior to the law of the land, and in effect to permit every citizen to become a law unto himself."[59]

But to support the proposition that "the record of more than a century of our free exercise jurisprudence" had established "that an individual's religious beliefs [do not] excuse him from compliance with an otherwise valid law prohibiting conduct that the State is free to regulate,"[60] he began, bizarrely, not with *Reynolds*, but with a quotation from a case that had been overruled on other grounds within a few years of having been decided, *Minersville School District v. Gobitis*.[61] Indeed, citations to *Gobitis* bracketed Scalia's discussion of *Reynolds*, without any mention by Scalia that *Gobitis* had been in so many words "overruled,"[62] let alone that it is "widely . . . viewed as one of the Court's great constitutional mistakes."[63] Although the Court in *Gobitis* had upheld a compulsory flag salute by schoolchildren against a claim for religious exemption by young Jehovah's Witnesses in 1940, by 1943, with the United States in the throes of the Second World War and concerns raised about the similarity of the pledge gesture to the "Nazi-Fascist salute,"[64] the Court had reversed course and held it to be a violation of free-speech protections to compel students to salute the flag and recite a pledge of allegiance, regardless of whether their objections to doing so were religiously grounded.

Scalia was able to take the bulk of the text of his own rule, categorically requiring even the religious objector to "comply with a 'valid and neutral law of general applicability,'" verbatim from a recently decided case, *United States v. Lee*,[65] which had denied an Amish employer's claim for exemption from the Social Security tax. The difficulty Scalia faced was that, while Lee may have lost, the Court had upheld the constitutional claim of another Amish claimant, Yoder, to be exempt from a neutral and generally applicable law requiring him to send his young children to school until the age of sixteen.[66] Moreover, among the previously successful free-exercise claimants before the

Supreme Court in the decades immediately preceding *Smith* had been three raising claims to unemployment compensation, including *Sherbert*, the very first Supreme Court case to mandate as a constitutional matter an accommodation for those whose religious exercise is burdened by government.[67] To make good his categorical rule, Scalia had either to overrule or to distinguish these cases. He chose a procrustean fitting of these cases into his framework, making the startling claims that the Supreme Court had "never held that an individual's religious beliefs excuse him from compliance with an otherwise valid law prohibiting conduct that the State is free to regulate"[68] and had "never invalidated any governmental action on the basis of the *Sherbert* test except the denial of unemployment compensation."[69] Unemployment compensation schemes, he argued, involved "individualized governmental assessment of the reasons for the relevant conduct" and the Court's "decisions in the unemployment cases stand for the proposition that where the State has in place a system of individual exemptions, it may not refuse to extend that system to cases of 'religious hardship' without compelling reason." Particularly because *Smith* was itself an unemployment compensation case, this distinction was far from persuasive, so Scalia emphasized that Smith lost his job because Oregon criminalized peyote use, whereas the successful claimants' conduct had all been legal.

This still left Scalia with a need to distinguish *Wisconsin v. Yoder*, which had not only "excused [the Yoders] from compliance with the otherwise valid" school attendance law, but "invalidated [the] governmental action" of imposing a fine on the Yoder parents for the misdemeanor of not continuing to send their children to school. Scalia's solution was to invent a new category of "hybrid rights" claims. He insisted that just as some other successful free-exercise claimants had paired their religious claims with free-speech claims, Yoder's victory depended on a combination of religious and parental rights claims. Scalia's emphasis on the parental rights component of Yoder's case was particularly odd, given his view that the "theory of unenumerated parental rights underlying [*Yoder* and the two other parental rights cases cited in *Smith*] has small claim to *stare decisis* protection."[70]

His efforts did not impress the lower courts, which, in the decades since *Smith*, have been presented with a number of cases making "hybrid rights" claims and not only rejected all of them, but even rejected the very notion that such a claim could ever be viable. The contrast between the lower-court judges' receptivity to the Cassandra-like case for same-sex marriage in Scalia's *Windsor* dissent and their complete dismissal of his procrustean hybrid rights analysis, which one representative lower-court opinion called "completely illogical,"[71] could not be more stark.

Courts did apply the categorical rule Scalia proclaimed in *Smith*, but academic commentators, activists, and practitioners raised so many objections to it that *Smith* became "one of the most heavily criticized constitutional decisions of recent times."[72] Within three years of the decision, a broad coalition of civil liberties and religious rights groups representing a vast variety of faith traditions and political persuasions, from the American Civil Liberties Union to the Traditional Values Coalition, persuaded a nearly unanimous U.S. Congress to pass a statute dubbed the Religious Freedom Restoration Act of 1993 (RFRA) whose announced "purpose" was "to restore the compelling interest test as set forth in *Sherbert* . . . and . . . *Yoder* . . . and to guarantee its application in all cases where free exercise of religion is substantially burdened."[73] The Court, which did not take kindly to what it saw as a usurpation of its prerogatives, saw RFRA as violative of both the separation of powers and the principles of federalism and held that Congress lacked power to impose RFRA on the states.[74] Nevertheless, RFRA remains applicable to the federal government, approximately half the states have additionally passed so called mini-RFRAs of their own, and aspects of RFRA have successfully been imposed by Congress on the states through the Religious Land Use and Institutionalized Persons Act (RLUIPA).

Scalia had warned prophetically in *Smith*,

> The rule respondents favor [deeming presumptively invalid, as applied to the religious objector, every regulation of conduct that does not protect an interest of the highest order] would open the prospect of . . . required religious exemptions from civic obligations of almost every conceivable kind—ranging from compulsory military service, to the payment of taxes; to health and safety regulation such as manslaughter and child neglect laws, compulsory vaccination laws, drug laws, and traffic laws; to social welfare legislation such as minimum wage laws, child labor laws, animal cruelty laws, environmental protection laws, and laws providing for equality of opportunity for the races."[75]

Although it took the better part of two decades for anything like his parade of horribles to come marching in with full force, the past several years have seen RFRA mobilized as a new front in the sexual culture wars. Hundreds of successful cases, including several to have reached the Supreme Court, were brought on behalf of for-profit corporations and religious nonprofits[76] challenging as a burden on free exercise the Affordable Care Act mandate that employers include full coverage of contraceptives among the health insurance benefits they provide their employees. At the state level, objectors to same-sex marriage, from cake bakers and florists to county clerks such as Kentucky's Kim Davis, have raised RFRA claims or lobbied for new state RFRAs. In her dissenting opinion in *Hobby Lobby*, the first of the contraception mandate cases to reach the Supreme Court, Justice Ruth Bader Ginsburg mustered a parade of horribles under RFRA even longer than Scalia's in *Smith*.[77] As Scalia himself pointed out at the oral argument of *Hobby Lobby*, one reason for this longer list was that RFRA had gone beyond the "pre-*Employment Division v. Smith* law" in that the "compelling State interest test in the prior cases was never accompanied by a least restrictive alternative" as it was under RFRA.[78]

In light of RFRA, how should we evaluate the success of Scalia's procrustean efforts to impose a rigid rule on free-exercise cases in *Smith*? On the one hand, in rejecting a constitutional right to religious exemptions from generally applicable laws in *Smith*, Scalia made clear that he was not ruling out the possibility of exemptions, merely "leaving accommodation to the political process," even though this would "place at a relative disadvantage those religious practices that are not widely engaged in."[79] Scalia's willingness to leave the rights of minorities to the political process (and perhaps his expectation that they will lose in this process) unites his announced approach in both the gay rights cases discussed above and the religious accommodation cases. But in neither set of cases does he get what he wants. As to gay rights, over Scalia's protests that the result is a "threat to American democracy,"[80] the Court constitutionalized the vision his dissents conjured up. As to religious accommodation, Scalia expected that the legislature would at most enact rule-like categorical exemptions for certain narrowly specified, religiously motivated activities.[81] He thought he had killed the compelling governmental interest test for religious exemptions by contorting it to fit in his procrustean bed in *Smith*. But far from remaining safely dead, the test rose up again stronger than ever, this time with democratic warrant and well nigh limitless scope in the form of RFRA. The legislature from which he had hoped for clear rules had now commanded the very thing he found "horrible to contemplate": to wit, "that federal judges will regularly balance against the importance of general laws the significance of religious practice." To borrow a metaphor Scalia used concerning another judge-made test used in religion clause cases, "[l]ike some ghoul in a late-night horror movie that repeatedly sits up in its grave and shuffles abroad, after being repeatedly killed and buried,"[82] the compelling interest test for religious exemptions rose up to haunt him.

In evaluating Scalia's legacy, then, one must take account of what for him were the perverse consequences of both his procrustean majority opinions and his Cassandra-like dissents, each of which can ultimately be reckoned failures in that, despite his best efforts, the approaches he wished to suppress prevailed, and the law moved in exactly the opposite direction from the one in which he was seeking to drive it.

Justice Scalia's Philosophy of Interpretation: From Textualism to Deferentialism

SCOTT SOAMES

The opening sentence in Justice Scalia's "Common-Law Courts in a Civil-Law System" announces his attempt "to explain the currently neglected state of *the science of construing legal texts*" (my emphasis).[1] The use of the word *science*, with its air of precision and objectivity, contrasts with his description of the role played by the common law in the education provided by American law schools. "The overwhelming majority of courses taught in the first year . . . teach the substance, and the methodology of the common law. . . . To understand what an effect that must have, you must appreciate that the common law is not really *common law*. . . . That is to say it is not 'customary law,' but is rather law developed by the judges."[2] Since, in Scalia's view, common-law judges were, essentially, legislators, he finds it unsurprising that law professors, legal scholars, and many educated in law schools are so enamored with judicial legislation. "What intellectual fun all of this is! It explains why first-year law school is so exhilarating: because it consists of playing common-law judge, which in turn consists of playing king—devising, out of the brilliance of one's own mind, those laws that ought to govern mankind. . . . [N]o wonder so many law students . . . aspire for the rest of their lives to be judges."[3]

This is the stage Scalia sets. Before giving arguments, he sets up a rhetorical contrast. On one side, we have the neglected science of interpreting legal texts—presumably vital to a country with a constitution that vests all legislative power in Congress and none in the judiciary, and with state constitutions that do the same. On the other side, we have a legal culture dominated by institutions that reject the conception of law that our founding documents put in place. Although the message isn't explicitly stated, Scalia's language and imagery drive it home. Sober and respectable science versus the passion of youth and their misguided mentors, who thrill at the prospect of playing king.

Scalia's rhetoric—with its echo of 1776—isn't a trick. It is the work of a master of political persuasion preparing the ground for intellectual battle. Although his ideal judge is more of a textual scientist than a political campaigner, he couldn't confine himself to expounding the principles of objective, scientific judging. He had to persuade the culture first to allow and then to demand it. He believed that American judges should be textualists, where we may think of a legal text as a linguistic object, like a novel. The law enacted is the content of the lawmakers' use of that linguistic object. It is what they asserted or stipulated in adopting it. The job of the judge is to discern that assertive content and apply it to cases—not to alter it to reach desirable political results.

That was Scalia's doctrine of the judicial interpretation. He believed that textualism is enshrined in the Constitution and hence that judicial departures from it are pieces of judicial legislation that violate Article 1, Section 1: "All legislative powers herein granted shall be vested in the Congress of the United States." If he is right, then American judges who willfully legislate from the bench violate their legal duty. He further believed the robust separation of legislative, executive, and judicial power in American democracy to be normatively superior to variants that would enhance the power of the judiciary at the expense of the other two branches.

Being a textualist, Scalia developed a remarkable intuitive grasp of the messages conveyed by spoken or written words. Being not only a legal scholar but also a legal polemicist, he became a master of political persuasion, whose rhetoric was aimed as much at the general educated public as it was at legal professionals. In what follows, I try to illustrate both of these remarkable abilities. But I also argue that Scalia was neither a linguistic theoretician nor a systematic legal philosopher. Because of this, it is important to identify and correct certain of his errors and to reformulate and unify some of his most important insights in order to advance his project of developing a workable version of originalism. In what follows I try to do that.

From Original Meaning to Original Asserted Content

Although Scalia's textualism officially identifies the law enacted by adopting a legal text with its *original linguistic meaning* at the time of enactment, in practice, he implicitly identifies the law with *what the original lawmakers asserted* in adopting the text. Since linguistic meaning and assertive content are different, this was a mistake. *What a speaker uses a sentence S to assert* in a given context is, roughly, *what a reasonable hearer or reader who knows the linguistic meaning of S, and is aware of all relevant intersubjectively available features of the context of utterance, would rationally take the speaker's use of S to be intended to commit the speaker to.* Usually all parties know the meanings of the sentences used and the purpose of the communication, as well as what previously has been asserted or agreed upon. Because of this, what is asserted can often be identified with what *the speaker* means and *the hearers* take the speaker to mean by the use of a sentence. But how is *what S means* related to *what a speaker means* by a particular use of S? Often, when S *means* that so-and-so, *speakers mean* that so-and-so by uses of S. In many, but not all, contexts, the converse is also true; *when speakers ordinarily mean* that so-and-so, often S *does too*. But the exceptions to these rough and ready rules are important.

The sentence "*I am finished*" is grammatically complete but interpretively incomplete. When it is used, the completion can be provided by the nonlinguistic situation of use, the larger discourse, or the presuppositions of speaker/hearers. This isn't linguistic ambiguity arising from several linguistic conventions, it is linguistic underspecificity. Another example is "*Susan will go to a nearby restaurant.*" Nearby what? Our present location, her present location, a location she or we will be visiting next week? It depends on the context of utterance.

Next consider possessive noun phrases *NP's N*. Interpreting them requires identifying the possession relation R holding between the referent of the possessor *NP* and the individual designated by the phrase. When N is a relational noun, it provides a default possession relation. The default designation of "Tom's teacher" is someone who bears the teaching relation R to Tom; the default designation of "Tom's student" is one who bears the converse of that relation to Tom. Similar remarks apply to "Tom's mother," "Tom's boss," and "Tom's birthplace." Crucially, however, the default choice can be overridden. Imagine that two journalists, Tom and Bill, have each been assigned to interview a local student. When this is presupposed, one can use "Tom's student" to refer to the student *interviewed by* Tom, and "Bill's student" to refer to the one *interviewed by* Bill. In these cases what is asserted isn't fully determined by the linguistic meanings of the sentences used.

The lesson extends to uses of possessive noun phrases involving nonrelational nouns, like *car* and *book*, to which a potential possessor may bear many different relations. "Tom's car" can be used to designate a car he owns, drives, is riding in, or has bet on in the Indianapolis 500; "Pam's book" may be used to designate a book she wrote, plans to write, is reading, or has requested from the library. As before, this isn't ambiguity; it is nonspecificity. The meaning of *NP's N* requires it to designate something to which N applies that stands in R to what *NP* designates. But the meaning doesn't determine R. Hence, linguistic meanings of sentences containing possessive noun phrases often aren't what they are used to assert.

Matters like these can be legally important. The phrase *attorney's fees* occurs in a case that came before Justice Scalia in 1988 that involved reimbursements of plaintiffs expenses in a civil right's case. The controlling legal language specified that plaintiffs could recover *attorney's fees* as part of the costs in bringing the case. What does the use of that phrase in this context designate? Does it include expenses an attorney charges her client for all aspects of the defense, including those paid to witnesses? Or does it include only fees paid for her services alone? You can ponder the linguistic meaning of "attorney's fees" forever and come up with nothing because the answer must come from context. According to some commentators, Scalia missed this when he opted for the narrower interpretation.[4]

Another example is Scalia's dissent in *Smith v. United States* concerning what the Congress used the following clause to assert:[5] "Whoever . . . uses or carries a firearm [in committing a crime of violence or drug trafficking], shall, in addition to the punishment provided for such [a] crime . . . be sentenced to imprisonment for five years,"[6] The question was whether to trade a gun for drugs was to use a firearm in committing a crime. Scalia thought not.

> To use an instrumentality ordinarily means to use it for its intended purpose. When someone asks, "Do you use a cane?," he is not inquiring whether you have your grandfather's silver-handled walking stick on display in the hall; he wants to know whether you walk with a cane. Similarly, to speak of "using a firearm" is to speak of using it for its distinctive purpose, i.e., as a weapon.[7]

> The Court asserts that the "significant flaw" in this argument is that "to say that the ordinary meaning of 'uses a firearm' includes using a firearm as a weapon" is quite different from saying that the ordinary meaning "also excludes any other use." The two are indeed different—but it is precisely the latter that I assert to be true. The ordinary meaning of "uses a firearm" does not include using it as an article of commerce. *I think it perfectly obvious, for example, that the objective falsity requirement for a perjury conviction would not be satisfied if a witness answered "no" to a prosecutor's inquiry whether he had ever "used a firearm," even though he had once sold his grandfather's Enfield rifle to a collector.*[8]

Scalia correctly identifies *what question is asked* by one who says "Do you use a cane?" and *what is asserted* when one answers "No" to the prosecutor's question, "Have you ever used a firearm?" Applying his reasoning to the Smith case, he correctly concluded that in adopting the text cited above, Congress *asserted* that using a firearm as a weapon in committing a crime is subject to additional punishment. However, he misstated his conclusion, stating that the *ordinary meaning* of "uses a firearm" pertains only to the uses of a firearm as a weapon.[9]

The majority rightly pointed out that this was false, but not for the right reason. The linguistic meaning of "uses an *N*" is *silent* about how *N* is used. So, when "uses a firearm" occurs in a sentence, the assertion must be *completed*, either by a qualifying phrase—for example, "as a weapon," or "as an item of barter"—or by extracting needed content from the shared presuppositions of the language users, in this case Congress and its audience, which includes public officials plus reasonable, informed members of the public. Like the agents in Scalia's hypothetical examples, Congress should be seen as relying on obvious presuppositions in the communicative context. The job of the Court was to infer *what Congress asserted* from the semantically unspecific linguistic meaning of the statutory language plus the context of use.

This result requires revising textualism by identifying the content of a legal text with what the lawmakers asserted in adopting it. This isn't a retreat from originalism; it is an adjustment that brings it into line with current thinking about language. It is now common in linguistics and the philosophy of language to distinguish the meaning of a sentence from what is asserted by ordinary uses of the sentence in particular contexts. Although the two sometimes coincide, often they don't. In every legal case in which they don't, originalism demands fidelity not to original linguistic meaning but to what was originally asserted or stipulated.[10]

In some of his formulations Scalia implicitly recognized this. Many passages in his "Common-Law Courts in a Civil-Law System" describe the law as what lawmakers *said* or *promulgated*. For example, in describing the widely accepted rule "that when the text of a statute is clear, that is the end of the matter," he asks, rhetorically, "Why should that be so, if what the legislature *intended*, rather than what it *said*, is the object of our inquiry."[11] His insight is correct; it shouldn't be muddied with misleading talk about meaning.

What Does Originalism Tell Us about Applying the Law in Hard Cases?

When it is clear what the lawmakers asserted in adopting a text, the duty of judges is to deduce an outcome from that asserted content plus the facts of the case. Sometimes, however, no determinate outcome is deducible because the law is vague, and so neither determinately applies nor determinately fails to apply to the relevant facts. Judges must then *precisify* vague legal contents to reach definite results. In other cases, relevant laws plus new facts determine inconsistent outcomes. In both types of cases, judges must modify legal content, thereby creating new law. Since Scalia believed that judges shouldn't legislate, he needed a way of grounding *judicial rectification* in some form of deference. However, he never articulated such a principle and sometimes seemed to reject using the intent of the legislature to formulate one.

In "Common-Law Courts," speaking of legislative intent, he says, "You will find it frequently said . . . that the judge's objective in interpreting a statute is to give effect to 'the intent of the legislature.' This principle . . . does not square with some of the (few) generally accepted concrete rules of statutory construction. One is the rule that when the text of a statute is clear, that is the end of the matter. Why should this be so, if what the legislature *intended*, rather than what it *said*, is the object of our inquiry?" (16), The expected answer, "It should not be so," is correct as far as it goes, but it wasn't Scalia's last word. He also distinguished subjective intent (as an aggregate of the aims and motives of individual legislators) from objective intent, inferable from the content of a law and its place in the larger body of law. "[W]e do not really look for subjective legislative intent. We look for a sort of 'objectified' intent—the intent that a reasonable person would gather from the text of the law, placed alongside the remainder of the *corpus juris*. . . . '[T]he primary object of all rules for interpreting statutes is to ascertain the legislative intent; or, *exactly, the meaning which the subject is authorized to understand the legislature intended*'" (17).[12] Scalia doesn't here consider whether legislative intent might aid in precisifying vague original content or eliminating inconsistencies created over time. But he does identify a potentially useful notion of objectified intent—something rationally inferable from the legislature's action—that is distinct from "subjective intent." In an age in which major pieces of legislation routinely contain thousands of pages of text written by small armies of staffers, typically no member of the legislature is familiar with the whole text, and many haven't seen any of it. To imagine that one could ask each member what he or she intended in adopting the text, and, by aggregating, converge on a meaningful result is, as Scalia rightly suggests, absurd.

Objective intent is another matter. Scalia gives two examples. One involves resolving ambiguities: "Another rule of construction is that ambiguities in a newly enacted statute are to be resolved in such fashion as to make the statute, not only internally consistent, but also compatible with previously enacted laws" (16). When the text contains an expression governed by linguistic conventions generating multiple meanings, resolution of the ambiguity is needed to determine what the legislature asserted. Since allowing *what the legislature meant* or *intended to say* to play this role doesn't threaten the identification of law with *what was said* in adopting the text, Scalia doesn't contest it. He also appeals to objective intent in correcting scrivener's errors.

> I acknowledge an interpretive doctrine of what the old writers call *lapsus linguae* (slip of tongue), and what our modern cases call 'scrivener's error,' where on the very face of the statute it is clear to the reader that a mistake of expression (rather than of legislative wisdom) has been made. For example, a statute may say 'defendant' when only 'criminal defendant' (i.e., not 'civil defendant') makes sense. The objective import of the statute is clear enough, and I think it not contrary to sound principles of interpretation, in such extreme cases, to give the totality of context preference over a single word. (20–21)

In both cases—resolving linguistic ambiguity and correcting scrivener's errors—the interpreter uses the text as a whole to determine what the legislature *intended to say or assert*, which is then identified with what the legislature *did say or assert*, despite inartfully doing so. This is natural, and it fits our ordinary treatment of slips of the tongue and other harmless errors of articulation. What Scalia doesn't do is use such intent-based disambiguation or correction to *substitute* what the legislature intended to say for what it actually did say. It was this harmony between original intent and original assertion that allowed him to acknowledge legislative intent as sometimes useful.

But why shouldn't objective legislative intent be more broadly useful? If objective intent can help decide which of two different things *the legislature said or asserted* in adopting an ambiguous or incorrectly articulated text, why shouldn't *what the legislature objectively intended the law to do* help us precisify vagueness or resolve inconsistencies? If the objective *intent* of the legislature is often rationally inferable, despite not being an aggregate of intentions of individual legislators, then surely the objective *goals, beliefs,* and *assertions* of the legislature are often rationally inferable, despite not being aggregated sums of the subjective attitudes of individual legislators. Scalia himself maintains that the legislature, like other collective bodies, does *assert* or *stipulate* that so-and-so. Presumably he would agree that it also sometimes *asks* or *investigates* whether such-and-such is so, and, after *gathering evidence*, it sometimes *concludes* that it is. If, like other collective bodies, it can *assert, stipulate, ask,* and *conclude*, then surely it must also *believe* some things and *intend* others. An originalist bent on discovering *what the legislature said or stipulated* is in no position to reject all claims about *what the legislature believed or intended.*

In "Common-Law Courts," Scalia offers two reasons for distrusting judicial appeals to intent. The theoretical reason is that the law is what the legislature asserts it to be, not what they intended to assert. The practical reason is that substituting what judges surmise the legislature must, or should have, intended to say for what it did say invites judicial subversion of American democracy (17–18). Though laudable, these sentiments deprive originalists of crucial resources when rectifications of original asserted contents are needed to precisify vague content or amend inconsistent content. In these cases, the goal is to supplement, not supplant, original content to reach a verdict that comports with original intent.

The Need for Intent-Based, Gap-Closing Constitutional Interpretation

Scalia recognized that constitutional cases pose special difficulties. In "Common-Law Courts," he says, "There is plenty of room for disagreement as to what original meaning was, and *even more so as to how that original meaning applies . . . to new and unforeseen phenomena.* How, for example, does the First Amendment guarantee of 'the freedom of speech' apply to new technologies that did not exist when the guarantee was created. . . . In such new fields, the Court must follow the trajectory of the First Amendment" (45; my emphasis). Scalia identifies two loci of controversy: the originally stipulated content of the First Amendment guarantee of freedom of speech (and of the press), and the application of that content to new technologies. This suggests that the latter controversy might persist even if the former is resolved. This will be so if the originally stipulated content is vague and so neither determinately applies nor determinately fails to apply to some new technologies today. Scalia needs a principle, which he never stated, to govern the search for acceptable outcomes in such cases.

The point is illustrated by his concurring opinion in *Citizens United v. Federal Election Commission*.[13] At issue was the 2002 McCain-Feingold campaign finance law prohibiting corporations and unions from funding "electioneering communication" advocating defeat of a candidate for federal office sixty days before a general election or thirty days before a primary. The law was used to stop the nonprofit corporation, Citizens United, from airing *Hillary: The Movie* within thirty days of a Democratic presidential primary in 2008. The Supreme Court decided 5–4 in favor of Citizens United that the ban violated the First Amendment free-speech guarantee.

Scalia's concurrence asked, *Whose freedom is guaranteed—only individuals and newspapers, or groups of individuals, including those that are legally incorporated?* Noting that the speech of religious, educational, social, and political groups organized under general incorporation statutes was unregulated at the founding, he argued that to restrict such speech now would be to *abridge* the freedom of speech that then existed. His evidence supports the thesis that the common understanding of the assertion made by using of the free-speech clause was roughly the following: Originally Asserted Content: *Congress shall not abridge—that is, truncate or diminish—freedoms of the kind currently enjoyed by individuals, groups, or organizations of individuals to speak or communicate (e.g., in pamphlets, letters, newspapers, and books)*. Although this originalist result is satisfying, it raises a further, more troubling, issue. How, if the original content of the First Amendment guarantee is as austere as this, do originalists reach the robust results they often do in First Amendment cases? In *Citizens* the route is easy to see.

Note the italicized parts of the final paragraph in Scalia's opinion:

> The Amendment is written in terms of "speech," not speakers. Its text offers no foothold for excluding any category of speaker, from single individuals to partnerships of individuals, to unincorporated associations of individuals, to incorporated associations of individuals . . . We are therefore simply left with the question *whether the speech at issue in this case is "speech" covered by the First Amendment*. No one says otherwise. *A documentary film critical of a potential Presidential candidate is core political speech*, and its nature as such does not change simply because it was funded by a corporation.[14]

The question was, "Would banning *a movie* critical of a presidential candidate count as *abridging* the freedoms *of the kind* enjoyed at the founding *to speak and communicate?*" To answer it, Scalia had to precisify the vague notion *the kinds of freedom to speak or communicate* enjoyed at the founding. This wasn't deciding what the original asserted content was; it was deciding how to extend that content to new circumstances. Scalia's description of the movie as *core political speech* reflects a conception of how the content of the First Amendment had already been extended long before the case was heard.

Was that extension justified? The originalist answer must be that it correctly identifies a critical component of *what the framers and ratifiers of the First Amendment were trying to achieve*—namely, to protect free speech and communication by individuals, groups, and organizations about matters of public or political importance. The writings of these men, and much of the public discourse at the time, indicate that they judged free speech and communication on matters of public or political importance to be a right of free citizens and a necessary feature of a self-governing republic.

Was Scalia a First Amendment Originalist?

If the rationales for Scalia's other opinions regarding the First Amendment guarantee of free speech and a free press were this clear, it would be easier to reconcile his stated originalist principles of interpretation with the body of his free-speech jurisprudence. His opinion in *Citizens United* was originalist. Some others appear not to be.

One borderline case is Scalia's dissent from the decision in *Hill v. Colorado* upholding a law restricting the attempts of opponents of abortion to dissuade individual women from going through with their plans to have abortions.

> Colorado's statute makes it a criminal act knowingly to approach within 8 feet of another person on the public way or sidewalk area within 100 feet of the entrance door of a health care facility for the purpose of passing a leaflet to, displaying a sign to, or engaging in oral protest, education, or counseling with such person. . . . [T]he regulation as it applies to oral communications is obviously and undeniably content-based. A speaker wishing to approach another for the purpose of communicating *any* message except one of protest, education, or counseling may do so without first securing the other's consent. Whether a speaker must obtain permission before approaching within eight feet—and whether he will be sent to prison for failing to do so—depends entirely on *what he intends to say* when he gets there.[15]

This provocative first paragraph of the dissent sets the tone of what is meant to be both a legal argument aimed at his fellow justices and their successors, and a rhetorically powerful indictment of the Court aimed at a broader public audience. The legal argument is that the limitation on speech isn't content-neutral, and so the restriction on personal counseling and conversation should be stricken from the statute. The political message is that the Court's obsessive insistence on constitutionalizing abortion robbed opponents of their democratic rights to play a role in determining abortion policy and is now restricting their First Amendment right to freedom of expression. Hence the rhetoric of the final section of the dissent (note the rhetorical force of the words I have italicized).

> [T]he public spaces outside of health care facilities [have] become, . . . by virtue of this Court's decisions, *a forum of last resort for those who oppose abortion.* The possibility of limiting abortion by legislative means—even abortion of a *live-and-kicking child that is almost entirely out of the womb*—has been rendered impossible by our decisions. . . . Those whose concern is for the physical safety and security of clinic patients . . . should take no comfort from today's decision. Individuals or groups intent on *bullying or frightening women* out of an abortion, or doctors out of performing that procedure, will not be deterred by Colorado's statute; *bullhorns and screaming* from eight feet away will serve their purposes well. But those who would accomplish their moral and religious objectives . . . by trying to persuade individual women of the rightness

of their cause, will be deterred. . . . As I have suggested, . . . today's decision is not an isolated distortion of our traditional constitutional principles, but is one of many *aggressively pro-abortion novelties* announced by the Court in recent years. Today's *distortions*, however, are particularly *blatant*. . . . "Uninhibited, robust, and wide open" debate is replaced by the power of the state to protect an unheard-of "right to be let alone" on the public streets. I dissent.[16]

Stripped of this final rhetorical flourish, the originalist credentials of Scalia's legal argument are questionable. The key premise of the argument, expressed in the first paragraph, is that if the statute's restriction on speech isn't content-neutral, it violates the First Amendment. Although that assumption is supported by precedent, it is not clearly supported by the original assertive content or the original intent of the amendment. A statute regulating organized attempts in restricted and well-defined environments in which women are seeking medical treatment to dissuade them from doing something legal that one believes to be immoral isn't, on its face, a law restricting core political speech on a matter of public importance.

Scalia's argument to the contrary is an extraordinary combination of naked political commentary, original-intent jurisprudence, and scathing criticism of the Supreme Court. In effect, he argues that direct, oral speech and conversation aimed at persuading women entering or leaving abortion clinics not to have abortions is *core political speech* on a festering issue of public importance and, for that reason, does fall under the *original intended content* of the First Amendment (though of course he doesn't say "intended content"). Because the Colorado law prohibits this speech, it is overbroad, and should (in part) be invalidated. The unusual form of speech—conversation and counseling outside medical facilities—doesn't deprive it of protection. On the contrary, because, in a string of what Scalia regarded to be wrongly decided cases, the Court removed the contentious issue of abortion from the give-and-take of normal democratic processes, he saw those decisions as leaving opponents few avenues for changing the legal situation imposed on them. To deny them even this venue to make their case to their fellow citizens would, he suggested, be to allow wrongly decided Fifth Amendment "due process" cases to weaken the free-speech guarantee of the First Amendment. This argument, though rooted in strong, originalist objections to earlier decisions, is not, I am afraid, very well directed to the Colorado statute. No matter—Scalia's rhetorical guns were aimed at winning future battles.

Originalist worries are also raised by his position in other cases in which he found deviations from content-neutrality to be unconstitutional, despite the fact that the particular form of communication or expressive conduct was hardly *core political speech*. In *Texas v. Johnson* Scalia joined the majority in ruling that burning the American flag was constitutionally protected.[17] In *R.A.V. v. City of Saint Paul* he invalidated a city ordinance prohibiting swastikas, burning crosses, and other symbols known to arouse "anger, alarm, or resentment . . . on the basis of race, color, creed, religion, or gender."[18] Writing for the Court, he ruled that although the prohibited symbolic conduct might be a species of unprotected "fighting words," and so not protected free speech, the government may *not* selectively ban some fighting words while permitting others.

The relation of these opinions to the original assertive content of the First Amendment and to its original intent of protecting core political speech is tenuous. For one thing, the regulated behavior was not speech but a special form of expressive conduct. For another, the political message it was intended to communicate—that the United States of America, in the first case, or African Americans, in the second, are hateful and not deserving of respect—would have been constitutionally protected had it been stated in words, without the air of menace and attempt to incite or provoke carried by the conduct. For these reasons, it is doubtful that the conduct determinately falls under the original assertive content of the First Amendment.

Some may argue that the conduct doesn't fall determinately inside *or* determinately outside the original asserted content, in which case an originalist judge must appeal to original intent to precisify the content to reach verdicts. Even then it is not obvious that one could reach Scalia's results. Was it central to what the framers and ratifiers of the First Amendment were trying to achieve that the symbolic conduct exhibited in these two cases be unregulated? Although democratic self-government does require that citizens be free to place items on the public agenda by stating propositions they believe to be true, no matter what the ideological content of those propositions, it does not require and is not advanced by intimidating and provocative expressive behavior that inhibits rational discussion. Thus, I doubt that Scalia's decisions in these cases can be justified by his originalist philosophy of interpretation.

His opinion in *Brown v. Entertainment Merchants Association* extended his exquisite sensitivity to apparent violations of content-neutrality to another form of expressive content.[19] The issue in *Brown* concerned an attempt by the state of California to restrict violent video games for minors. Writing for the majority, Scalia extends to video games the status of protected speech on the same grounds that apply to books, plays, and movies. He does so despite the fact that, like unprotected obscene pornography and regulated, sexually explicit public activity (which he believed could be restricted), violent video games don't contribute propositions to rational discussions of public and political issues. In justifying this extension, he maintains that the country has no tradition of restricting children's access to depictions of violence. Why is that relevant? Perhaps because if there is no tradition of such restrictions, then there were no such restrictions at the founding, in which case to add one would be to *abridge* a freedom enjoyed then. But that argument is weak, since no similar form of expressive or symbolic conduct existed then. In addition, the propositional content of the games, to the extent they have such coherent content, falls well outside the original intent to protect core political speech. Thus, this free-speech decision, like those in *Texas v. Johnson* and *R.A.V. v. City of Saint Paul*, isn't strictly originalist.

Deferentialist Originalism

Three changes are needed to extract a defensible originalist philosophy of interpretation from Scalia's theory and practice. First, the legal content of a statute or constitutional provision must not be identified with the original linguistic meaning of the text used to adopt it; it should be identified with what lawmakers or ratifiers originally used it to assert or stipulate. That content is what a reasonable person who understood the linguistic meanings of the words in the text, the publicly available facts, the history of the lawmaking context, and the background of existing law into which the law is expected to fit would take to have been asserted in adopting the text. This change departs very little from Scalia's own thinking. Although it conflicts with his official formulations in "Common-Law Courts in a Civil-Law System," it fits the examples used there to support his theory and some of his own judicial practice.

Second, cases in which it is necessary to judicially rectify original content must be recognized. The initial duty of a judge is to ascertain the original asserted content and to reach the verdict it determines. But when the content is vague, no definite verdict may be determined; when it is inconsistent with surrounding law plus facts presented in a case, inconsistent verdicts may be determined. In these cases, the judge must modify existing legal content by deferring to the original intent of the lawmakers, as Scalia himself implicitly did in *Citizens United* and *Hill*.

Third, when rectifying original content, the task is to make a minimal change in existing content that maximizes original intent. This intent is not, as Scalia observed, a sum of private understandings of individual lawmakers, or of the factors motivating them. It is rationally derived from viewing the original asserted content in light of the publicly offered and understood reasons for it. Although this use of intent is a clear emendation of Scalia's explicit textualism, it is one that reflects not only an aspect of his practice but also that of virtually every other jurist.

Defending Deferential Originalism

The question of whether this deferentialist version of originalism is correct can be taken in two ways. One queries whether it accurately describes the legal duties of judges in the United States today. The other asks whether it is *normatively* superior to other conceptions of what the legal duties of those judges *ought to be*. The questions are independent. Since I have sketched my answers elsewhere, I won't repeat them here.[20] I will, however, relate them to Scalia.

What the legal duties of judges are is, at bottom, a question of what the body politic recognizes to be the basis of their legal authority. Since the written Constitution is still that basis, most prominent Supreme Court decisions have been clothed in originalist rhetoric and reasoning.[21] This, more than anything else, provided the fuel that fired Scalia's powerful and influential rhetoric. Yes, there have been a number of prominent, widely accepted, nonoriginalist results. But many remain vulnerable to Scalia-style attacks because the originalist understanding of the role of the judiciary remains embedded in the American psyche. No one knew this better than Scalia.

It should also be noted that respect for precedent is itself originalist. Because of the constitutional authority of the Supreme Court, all precedents are law, and so deserve a degree of deference, even though the bad ones can be overturned, limited, or isolated by revisiting the Constitution itself. Scalia knew that, like any workable theory, originalism doesn't demand perfection.[22]

One's normative evaluation of the role of the judiciary is tied to one's conception of the American project. During his life, Scalia witnessed the consolidation of government power, the expansion of the administrative state, the decline of federalism, the hardening of our class structure, and the rise of a credentialed, self-perpetuating, cognitive elite whose claim to expertise, real or imagined, separated them from ordinary citizens and provided them with privilege and influence. He saw these changes as threats to our representative government. The man behind the passionate opinions felt in his bones that, when it comes to the big decisions about our individual and collective lives, there is no such thing as expertise possessed by an elite governing class. There are only choices to be made derived from our deepest values using all the information we can gather. These are, he insisted, best made by the people and their elected representatives, not unelected justices or bureaucrats. In short, he believed what was once axiomatic, that in America the people rule. In this, as in so much, it is hard not to agree with him.

3

Power

VICTORIA NOURSE

That is what this suit is about. Power.
ANTONIN SCALIA

Power. It is a single word in a singular dissent in a singular case involving the fate of presidential power, *Morrison v. Olson*.[1] Other justices are known for pithy remarks, but single words are far from routine practice in Supreme Court rhetoric, the norm being multiword sentences. Justice Holmes never punctuated "social statics" with a silent exclamation point. Justice Scalia had no aversion to single-word sentences.

I take this rhetorical habit as a symbol of Justice Scalia's most important legacy: the theory of interpretation known as textualism. Textualism, like its rhetorical sister, the single-word sentence, startled a sleeping judiciary into attention to one of the most important judicial tasks: interpretation. As a scholar of statutory and constitutional interpretation, I am entirely grateful. The *Olson* dissent is a prescient opinion in many respects, but this is not because its textualism amounts to what Justice Scalia, at his best and most eloquent, defended as the rule of law. Quite the opposite. The *Olson* dissent reveals the ways in which textualism can amount to a power play, a means by which the interpreter can increase the interpreter's *power* over text.

In this chapter, I show how the practice of isolating single words led Justice Scalia to add meaning to the Constitution, small words perhaps, but words that the *Olson* dissent transformed from "the executive power" into "all executive power" under the Constitution. A small word, *all*, one likely to bring joy to presidential ears, but one not found in the Constitution. How is it that a theory of the rule of law becomes something quite different? My analysis reveals three stages of textual power: the first, *isolation* of text (focusing on the word *executive*); the second, *reduction* of text (taking the word out of context from larger constitutional text); and the third, *addition* to the constitutional text by pragmatic enrichment (adding meaning to the text). In service of this analysis, I invoke the work of linguists, philosophers of language, and behavioral economists. Textualist isolation, I will attempt to show, is a self-fulfilling prophecy. By isolating a word or two, the interpreter creates a new context.[2] That new context allows the interpreter to create a new meaning; it even invites the interpreter to *add* meaning to the Constitution, such as "all" executive power.[3]

Olson's Power

After Watergate, Congress created the independent-counsel law, authorizing a special prosecutor in cases involving executive branch misconduct. To prevent the president from firing his own prosecutor, as President Nixon had done, the statute made the prosecutor "independent." The prosecutor could not be fired by the president. In the same statute, however, Congress increased its own power to prompt investigations of the president's men. All that a congressional committee had to do was request an investigation—for example, for lying to Congress, a potential crime. The attorney general could reject an investigation only if he found "no reasonable grounds" to believe that a crime may have been committed.[4] When Congress and the president disagreed, disgruntled committee members requested a special counsel to determine if their political opponents were lying; not surprisingly, the attorney general found few reasons to resist, and investigations proliferated from the 1970s through the 1990s.

The Supreme Court's decision in *Olson* upholding the independent-counsel law ignores much of this real power play in favor of a heavy dose of doctrinal distinctions surrounding what is known as the "removal question" in constitutional law. The Constitution explicitly provides for how the president's men will be appointed,[5] but does not specify how they will be removed. This has been a subject of scandalous importance to more than one president, from Andrew Johnson, who was impeached over the issue, to Franklin Roosevelt, who pressed his own advantage in the Supreme Court.[6] The technical issue in *Olson* was whether the independent prosecutor was an "inferior" or "superior" officer. The Constitution prescribes that "inferior" officers may be appointed by the president, heads of departments, or a superior officer.[7] In *Olson*, the Supreme Court found that the independent counsel was an inferior officer and held that Congress could vest removal power in the attorney general rather than the president.

Olson cannot be understood without considering a seemingly grander struggle about the administrative state. For some time, conservatives had been arguing for a "unitary executive," by which they meant a president who had power to remove executive officials for whatever reason, even an arbitrary one, such as their hair color or political party. *Olson* symbolized this struggle because the special prosecutor was an "independent" agency—the prosecutor could not be removed by the president and only for "good cause." If the unitary executivists (and Justice Scalia was their patron saint) were to have their way, the Court should have ruled that Congress had no power to limit the president's removal power. If the Supreme Court were to hold that the president could remove the special prosecutor, so, too, the president could remove the heads of independent agencies like the Federal Trade Commission or the Nuclear Regulatory Agency for any reason at all.

In retrospect, unitary executivists exaggerated fears of a fourth branch. No ruling in *Olson* was going to put a dent in the administrative state; all it would do was change the rules about how the head of an independent agency could be removed. If the president won, he could fire the head of the Federal Trade Commission because of her hair color or the head of the Nuclear Regulatory Agency because of his political party, but the agencies would still exist. Independent agencies would become executive agencies, the only difference being the question of removing the agency's chief. Put in other words, the removal question is whether Congress may require that the president have a "good reason" to dismiss the head of an independent agency. Presidents typically can find a "good reason" to fire their subordinates. Political incentive, not law, prevents presidents from doing silly things like firing the head of the Securities and Exchange Commission because of her latest parking ticket.[8]

Although *Olson* was a kitten to the administrative state, it was a sleeping tiger to Congress's power to impeach executive officers, including the president. The independent-counsel law did more than guarantee the counsel's independence. It created strong incentives for Congress to transform political disputes into criminal charges. Given limited resources, a prosecutor can weigh all sorts of factors about whether to prosecute or even investigate an offense. But the independent-counsel statute created a situation that gave the attorney general almost no discretion *not to name a special counsel.* There are always plenty of political incentives for the president's opponents in Congress to try to characterize their opponents as criminals. Over time, the law's incentives were powerful enough to prompt impeachment of a president. Long after the *Olson* decision, independent counsel Kenneth Starr's Whitewater investigation would morph into claims of presidential perjury about a sexual affair, leading Republican opponents to issue articles of impeachment against a sitting president for the first time in over a hundred years.

The Rhetorical Virtues of Isolation

Power. The single-word sentence was meant to startle, to attract attention. It was emblematic of a larger linguistic strategy, one characteristic of Justice Scalia's textualism. Let us call this strategy "semantic isolation," the deliberate isolation of words from longer constitutional or statutory texts. Isolation creates emphasis. We are drawn to the word *power* because it is stark, alone. Its isolation makes us think. Unfortunately, its virtues also lead to vices. Isolation creates so much emphasis it can lead us astray. Watching the shiny word twist in apparent purity can blind us, creating a "focusing illusion." Precisely because focus narrows the information economy, it invites enrichment, by means of conventional norms and the interpreter's preferences.

There are virtues to isolation as a rhetorical strategy. Isolation disrupts the mindless flow of legal doctrine. Justice Scalia was absolutely correct that power was at issue in *Olson*. But whose power? The power of the president to remove officers? The power of the independent counsel, free from virtually any electoral accountability, to indict an executive official? The power of the Congress to leverage its authority to criminalize its political disputes, or to bootstrap impeachment? Justice Rehnquist's majority opinion pays little attention to any of these questions, focusing instead on questions about the pigeonhole in which to place the counsel. Writing for the majority, Chief Justice Rehnquist wove a compact web of precedent and doctrine that convinced everyone else on the Court that the independent-counsel law was constitutional—except Justice Scalia.

Power. Like a sword, it punctured doctrine's edifice and focused the mind on what Justice Scalia passionately believed to sit at the case's core: The president's power to control members of the executive branch. For Justice Scalia, what was at stake was the status of independent agencies, the great symbol of the administrative state's overreach. Justice Rehnquist, himself a conservative, was more of a pragmatist; he feared that a ruling against the counsel would mean that independent agencies from the Federal Trade Commission to the Nuclear Regulatory Agency were unconstitutional. Justice Scalia was entirely prepared to accept that eventuality, and he was prepared to do it, not based on the doctrine but the text of the Constitution—namely, Article II, Section 1, which provides executive power to the president. Justice Scalia wrote that the president had to have "all" power to dismiss independent agents like the independent counsel: "To repeat, Article II, § 1, cl. 1, of the Constitution provides: 'The executive Power shall be vested in a President of the United States.' As I described at the outset of this opinion, this does not mean *some of* the executive power, but *all of* the executive power."[9]

Justice Scalia was correct that power was at play in *Olson*. In fact, he was quite prescient about the dangers of willy-nilly allowing the prosecution of executive branch officials at Congress's whim. But both he and the majority failed to understand that this was no ordinary case of an "independent agency." The standard independent agency case (one where the head of the agency cannot be removed by the president because she is protected by a "good-faith" removal clause) presents no serious constitutional impediment to presidential removal.[10] The independent counsel was different. The counsel law was a unique statute raising questions about power—not simply about the perennial question of the president's "removal" power but, more importantly, about Congress's power to punish its political enemies by criminal sanction. History would later confirm the dangers of such a law: the statute led to the impeachment of President Clinton based on Kenneth Starr's wide-ranging independent-counsel investigation, an affair spelling the statute's death as power improvidently granted.[11]

The Rhetorical Vices of Isolation

Isolation, when applied to interpretation, can yield what I have called "petty textualism."[12] We can see this most easily in cases involving statutory interpretation, but the same occurs, with much larger consequences, in constitutional law. Let us start with a simple example. A statute provides for "attorney's fees as part of the costs." In a leading statutory case, *West Virginia University Hospitals, Inc. v. Casey*, Justice Scalia wrote for the majority an opinion that isolated the term *attorney's fees*, and concluded that witness fees were excluded.[13] An "attorney" is not a witness; ergo, no witness fees. Notice what happens if, like Justice Stevens in dissent, we switch our attention and focus on the term *costs*. If we focus on "costs," it seems to follow that the costs of witnesses are covered because they are costs of the lawsuit. Focus on the term *attorney's fees*, and the claimants fail; focus on the term *costs* and the claimants win.

The isolationist method predetermines who wins and who loses the case because the isolationist method has the capacity to *exclude text* and, because of that exclusion, to invite *added meaning* to the statute. First, let us see how isolation excludes text. Focusing on the term *attorney's fees* or the term *costs* eliminates text concerning the relationship between fees and costs. The statute says "fees *as part of* the costs." In other words, the full, nonisolated text tells us that "costs" is a larger category than "fees," suggesting that focusing on "attorney's fees" alone is not a proper reading of the statute. Second, let us see how isolation invites additions to text. Justice Scalia read the statute as if it said "only" attorney's fees, even if the statute says no such thing. The statute does not say it covers "only" attorneys' fees; in fact, it says quite the opposite, that "attorney's fees" are not exclusive; they are only one element of a larger category known as "costs."

From this humble statutory example, three analytic stages of textualism emerge: isolation, reduction, and addition. Apply this three-part analysis to Justice Scalia's dissenting opinion in *Olson*. First, *isolation*: Justice Scalia isolates the term *executive power* in the Constitution. As I noted earlier, there is a good argument that the real problem with the independent-counsel law was Congress's power: by focusing on executive power, we lose sight of such issues. Second, *reduction*: Justice Scalia focuses on a single clause of the Constitution, without regard to other clauses in the Constitution and, even further, pulls from that clause three words, "the executive power."[14] From that phrase, he extracts the doctrinal question in the case—whether the independent counsel is exercising executive power. Notice, however, that this focus eliminates by fiat, rather than reason, any concern about other parts of the Constitution that might apply, such as whether the counsel is an "inferior" or "superior" officer under the appointments clause. That clause specifies two different relationships between officers and the president, but the isolation method ignores this by focusing the interpreter solely on the terms "the executive power." Third, *addition*. Once the information economy is reduced to nothing more than a word or two, the interpreter adds something of his own, and the addition solidifies the isolationist focus. Justice Scalia reads Article II, Section 1 as giving the president not only "the executive power" but also "*all* executive power." Thankfully, the term *all* is not in the Constitution; it has been added by Justice Scalia. The three steps have been completed: isolation, reduction, and addition.

ISOLATION AND THE FOCUSING ILLUSION

Behavioral economists have known for some time that "focusing" has the power to obscure. There are many familiar aspects of this critique, but one that is not well known, though it should be, is the concept of "bounded awareness." Our minds are subject to limitations, and one such limitation is focalism—the tendency to focus on one thing to the exclusion of others. This literature tees off a well-known, well-replicated study in which individuals are asked to watch basketball players pass a ball back and forth. Viewers are asked to count the number of times the basketball passes from one player to another. Focused on counting, many viewers miss a woman in a gorilla suit who stops, beats her chest, and walks through the game. The study won the

Ig-Nobel, a prize for work that illuminates an important idea (the "gorilla in the room") with humor.[15]

A real Nobelist, Daniel Kahneman, pioneered this idea, calling it the "focusing illusion." He first developed this insight by asking rather basic questions about whether people believed that they would be happier if they lived in California. He concluded that isolating factors led to inaccurate judgments about relative well-being. More recently, Kahneman has argued that the focusing illusion reflects the dangers of "fast-thinking": we make snap judgments based on available information, but these judgments are often wrong because they are based on too little information. The fast-thinking system is automatic, preferring to jump to quick conclusions. It indulges in "focusing." By contrast, the "slow-thinking" system is capable of rational reflection, but it is lazy. It can search out other information, but it requires prompting and structures demanding further reflection.[16]

Textualist isolation has all the attributes of the focusing illusion, or what Kahneman calls "What you see is all there is." No linguist argues that one can determine the meaning of a sentence by excluding context. That is precisely, however, what textualist isolation performs. "What you see is all there is" is the textual mantra in both constitutional and statutory law. Of course, if one is not looking for the gorilla, one will not find it. So, too, if one is ripping words from context, it will be hard to pay attention to the context that the interpreter brings to the project, or even other words at all. For all the virtues of forcing lawyers to read text, Justice Scalia's textualism, in practice, has been full of the vices of the focusing illusion, as we will see below.

REDUCTION AND BLIND SPOTS

If the Nobelists and the Ig-Nobelists are correct, then the focusing illusion risks systematic overconfidence in inadequate information. Focusing failures can lead to very serious decision errors. The *Challenger* space mission killed seven astronauts. The scientists knew that the launch was planned for a day with very low temperatures. They also knew that one risk involved O-ring failure. They searched for launches with O-ring failure at low temperatures; the lack of a clear pattern inspired launch approval. Focus was the problem. If mission control had run a regression analysis without O-ring failures on the prior seventeen launches, that would have led to an unambiguous conclusion that the *Challenger* had a 99 percent chance of malfunction under then-existing conditions. The information was accessible but ignored.[17]

The ubiquity of this problem can be seen with the following riddle. A boy and his father are in a car crash. The father dies. The boy is rushed to the hospital. When the boy's face is revealed, the surgeon says, "I cannot operate; this is my son." Readers struggle to solve the riddle by considering whether the surgeon could be a stepfather or an adopted father. Even those who should know better fail to consider a simpler explanation: that the surgeon is a mother, not a father. Women as well as men puzzle over this claimed riddle because of the focusing effects of the dramatic severance of the parental relationship and concern for the child's life. Our fast thinking leads us to conclude, without reflection, that the prototype of a surgeon is male.[18]

There is a reason Kahneman won a Nobel Prize: his conclusions apply to all reasoning, not only riddles or failed space shots. Professor Max Bazerman of Harvard Business School studies the focusing illusion in complex negotiation settings. He and his colleagues, Avishalom Tor and Dolly Chugh, argue that people tend to focus on the information they know and systematically fail to the make the effort to understand the other party's knowledge and incentives. They began this research based on a noted problem in decision theory: the Monty Hall game. The problem is modeled after a TV game show in which Monty Hall shows the contestants three doors and the contestant must choose one. "Years after the show went off the air, statisticians, economists, and journalists noted that contestants tended to make a systematic mistake."[19] The contestant would pick a door, and if it did not reveal a prize, Monty would ask the contestant whether she wanted to switch doors. As a simple matter of probability, contestants should always switch doors, but they didn't. Bazerman and his colleagues showed that this was more than a simple probability mistake.[20] They changed the game: Monty points to another door, and the contestant is told Monty is mean, suggesting Monty wants to prevent the contestant from winning the game. In that case, the contestants should not switch, but in fact they do. The cognitive failure here is a failure to understand Monty's incentives and decision rules, the key to a winning strategy.

The cognitive blind spot has an interpretive analogue. Isolating text is not necessarily a bad thing. Unlike the realist attack on statutory interpretation as a hopeless substitute for policy positions or what the judge "ate for breakfast," the focusing illusion suggests that we can improve our statutory reasoning, but we must understand our biases as well as our blind spots. Even the most well-intentioned and fair judges must fear error, but if they slow down their thinking, there may be some hope. That hope lies in exercising mental effort to "disconfirm" the interpreter's original conception, either by opening the contextual frame to other text or by looking at other information. Just as the space shuttle's engineers had to open their analysis beyond O-ring failure, and just as the contestants in Monty Hall had to think like Monty, interpreters cannot interpret single words in a vacuum, lest they invite irrational thinking. Slow thinking requires that interpreters look to other information to reveal their own assumptions.

ADDITION AND PRAGMATIC INFERENCE

The focusing illusion not only occludes other important information — potentially missing the gorilla in the room — it invites the interpreter to add new information because the text has been artificially decontextualized, and the information economy has been reduced. When adding meaning, the interpreter is unlikely to see that this is "new" information, just as the viewers of the gorilla video did not see the gorilla, or the NASA engineers lost their way. None of them saw, at the time, that they were using other information, background context they brought to the task, to interpret the situation. More importantly, the information they brought to the problem was not seen as something *they brought* because it was not seen at all.

So too, in statutory and constitutional interpretation, once the information economy is reduced to a word or two, the interpreter may end up adding information to interpret the situation, precisely because the information economy is so sparse. Enter the linguistic concept of pragmatic inference. I will use the term *pragmatic enrichment* to mean the kind of addition to meaning that philosophers of language describe when they talk about interpretation. Pragmatic enrichment can go by many different names, including *implicature, impliciture, explicature, presupposition,* and others. In my terms, *enriched meaning* refers to the addition of apparent meaning to a literal text. So, for example, if I write "fifth," and the interpreter reads this as "the Fifth Amendment to the Constitution," she has used her context (the legal one) to pragmatically enrich the word *fifth*.

Almost all communication requires some form of pragmatically enriched meaning. These meanings can be true, false, and cancelable. Let us consider the kind of examples used by the famous linguistic philosopher Paul Grice, who introduced the notion of the linguistic implicature. The idea was that listeners would add unstated context to make sense of limited communications.[21] So, for example, in the case of a recommendation letter that said, "she attended all classes," the reader, given the conventions of recommendation letters (the unstated context), is likely to interpret the statement "she attended all classes," as "she was not a very good student." From Grice's example, we can glean an important feature of meaning: the power of unstated background context. In the example, normal conventions of writing recommendation letters govern its meaning. Notice that the meaning comes, as well, from *what is absent from the text, what is omitted.* The interpreter "fills in the blanks" with stereotypical, conventional background meanings to ascribe meaning, to add and enrich compact expression.

Pragmatic enrichment may be a well-established concept, but Grice's work has been controversial. He is well known for positing four types of conversational maxims—manner, quantity, relevance, and quality.[22] One need not engage in the great maxim debate, however, to accept the principle that pragmatic inferences can enrich the meaning of text. The idea of enrichment follows from the basic idea that speech is *economical:*[23] it communicates more than the words themselves do. "Some of the students did well," says in six words what a pragmatically enriched meaning, once spelled out, says in twelve words, "Some of the students did well and most did not do well." Pragmatic enrichment is essential to communication because communication depends upon an information economy in which meaning is conveyed by fewer words than would be required without enrichment.

There are good reasons to believe that these principles apply to ordinary communication as well as more formalized communications like statutes and constitutions. If ordinary citizens typically enrich meaning with apparent context, it follows that similar interpretive principles apply to statutes and constitutions.[24] There is little doubt that statutes and constitutions are intended to communicate. Legislators aim to solve general problems—end discrimination, stop hunger, freeze the debt—and without communication, those efforts would be futile. Constitutional drafters must be even briefer if they are to create a workable framework for the ages. However lengthy, every statute and every constitution is economical in the sense that it might have been longer—if one sought, for example, to negate all possible implications.[25]

When interpreters add meaning to statutes and to the Constitution, they rarely note that they are adding meaning to the text. The additions are often small but, at the same time, decisive. They are decisive because they seem to add *hard edges* to the doctrine to create a "rule-like" appearance.[26] So, in our "attorney's fees" example, the isolation of the term *attorney's fees* eliminates other contextual information from the sentence ("as part of"). It also leads Justice Scalia to make a pragmatic inference from the isolation of the term. Let us see the progression: isolation from context, pragmatic inference from isolation. If this seems to be a self-fulfilling prophecy, it is. Justice Scalia interprets "attorney's fees" as "only attorney's fees"; of course, "only" does not exist in the statute; its meaning has been added. Notice, however, that the inference of exclusivity depends upon isolation: it is only because the term *attorney's fees* is isolated that it yields such an inference. If the term *attorney's fees* were not isolated—that is, if it were read in the context of the term *costs*—then one could not make an inference of exclusivity. The statutory phrase "as part of the costs" leads to an antiexclusivity implication that the term *costs* includes more than "attorney's fees." In short, the isolation of the term *attorney's fees* creates the possibility of pragmatic enrichment, which leads to the interpretive conclusion against witness fees. In short, the method employed—the isolation—leads to the interpretive conclusion.

Let us return to *Olson* and power. We have already seen the first two steps of the analysis: isolation and reduction. Now, it is important to add the third step: addition. One of the most important passages in *Olson* reveals how Justice Scalia concludes his analysis by adding words to the Constitution that do not exist in the Constitution. Like his short sentences, the addition is small, but apparently decisive. I quote the passage in full to show the subtle moves in his own words: "To repeat, Article II, § 1, cl. 1, of the Constitution provides: 'The executive Power shall be vested in a President of the United States.' As I described at the outset of this opinion, this does not mean *some of* the executive power, but *all of* the executive power."[27] Of course, Justice Scalia may not have meant that the president had "all" executive power. He may simply have meant that the president had all executive power to remove his agents. That is not what Justice Scalia wrote, however. Having limited the information economy to a single word, he added his own meaning. No founding father, who fought against a powerful king, would have subscribed to the view that the president has "all" executive power. This is not the rule of law; indeed, it is precisely contrary to the rule of law. To use Justice Scalia's word, it is power.

Conclusion

As a disruptive force, rhetorical isolation can make one think. But disruption has its costs. Isolation can take text out of context. It can deny the power of the relationship between texts. Taken to an extreme, it can create a "ransom note" Constitution, in which pieces of text are pulled out and rearranged in ways that have no relationship to the original document, and in which the Constitution's most central relationships are destroyed. Lest this seem exaggerated, one need only consider the claim, made by the academy's premier textualist, John Manning, that the separation of powers is a principle that textualists should avoid because it is not explicitly recognized in the Constitution's text.[28] Because the Constitution does not literally say "the separation of powers," there is no such principle. That is like saying, "because there is no statement on the dashboard of your car that says "this car moves" the car does not move. Textualism of this kind remakes the Constitution in the interpreter's eyes.

References

Allott, Nicholas, and Ben Shaer. 2017. "Inference and Intention in Legal Interpretation." In *The Pragmatic Turn: Inference and Interpretation*, edited by J. Giltrow and D. Stein. Berlin: De Gruyter Mouton, 83–118.

Calabresi, Steven G., and Christopher S. Yoo. 2008. *The Unitary Executive: Presidential Power from Washington to Bush*. New Haven, CT: Yale University Press.

Chabris, Christopher F., and Daniel J. Simons. 2009. *The Invisible Gorilla: How Our Intuitions Deceive Us*. New York: Crown.

Chugh, Dolly, and Max H. Bazerman. 2007. "Bounded Awareness: What You Fail to See Can Hurt You," *Mind and Society* 6, no. 1, 1–18.

Endicott, Timothy Andrew Orville. 2000. *Vagueness in Law*. New York: Oxford University Press.

Gormley, Ken. 2001. "Monica Lewinsky, Impeachment, and the Death of the Independent Counsel Law: What Congress Can Salvage from the Wreckage—a Minimalist View." *Maryland Law Review* 60, no. 1, 97–148.

Grice, H. Paul. 1975. "Logic and Conversation." In *Syntax and Semantics*, vol. 3, *Speech Acts*, edited by Peter Cole and Jerry L. Morgans, 41–58. New York: Academic Press.

Hofstadter, Douglas, and Emmanuel Sander. 2013. *Surfaces and Essences: Analogy as the Fuel and Fire of Thinking*. New York: Basic Books.

Kahneman, Daniel. 2011. *Thinking, Fast and Slow*. New York: Farrar, Straus and Giroux.

Manning, John F. 2011. "Separation of Powers as Ordinary Interpretation." *Harvard Law Review* 124 (June): 1939–2040.

Mertz, Elizabeth. 2007. *The Language of Law School: Learning to "Think Like a Lawyer."* New York: Oxford University Press.

Mikhail, John. 2015. "The Constitution and the Philosophy of Language: Entailment, Implicature, and Implied Powers." *University of Virginia Law Review* 101 (June): 1063–1103.

Nourse, Victoria. 2016. *Misreading Law, Misreading Democracy*. Cambridge, MA: Harvard University Press.

———. 2017. "Picking and Choosing Text: Lessons for Statutory Interpretation from the Philosophy of Language." *Florida Law Review* 69 (November): 1409–37.

———. 2018. "Reclaiming the Constitutional Text from Originalism: The Case of Executive Power." *California Law Review* 106 (February): 1–49.

O'Sullivan, Julie R. 1996. "The Independent Counsel Statute: Bad Law, Bad Policy." *American Criminal Law Review* 33 (Spring): 463–509.

Tor, Avishalom, and Max H. Bazerman. 2003. "Focusing Failures in Competitive Environments: Explaining Decision Errors in the Monty Hall Game, the Acquiring a Company Problem, and Multiparty Ultimatums." *Journal of Behavioral Decision Making* 16, no. 5, 353–74.

Wilson, Deirdre, and Dan Sperber. 2012. *Meaning and Relevance*. Cambridge: Cambridge University Press.

PART 2

The Rhetoric of Statutory Textualism

4

No Vehicles on Mars

BRIAN G. SLOCUM

When assessing Justice Scalia through the lens of rhetoric, which, unlike logic or dialectic, seeks effectiveness rather than truth or completeness, his impact is manifest. One definition of rhetoric is that it is involves "the creation of discourse which changes reality through the mediation of thought and action" (Tindale 2004, 19). Undoubtedly, Justice Scalia altered reality, and it was his rhetorical skill in expounding a particular conception of the rule of law and a corresponding methodology of interpretation that helped him do so. He is widely regarded as one of the most influential Supreme Court justices of the last several decades due in large part to his effective advocacy of textualism in statutory interpretation and originalism in constitutional interpretation. It may be true, as some critics claim, that Justice Scalia's direct influence on the Supreme Court's rulings was relatively modest, as he was unable to influence the voting of his colleagues in various important cases (Greene 2016). The influence of Justice Scalia's theory of legal interpretation, though, is an entirely different matter. Justice Scalia's influence on the rhetoric and methodology of legal interpretation can be measured in various ways, such as the increase in the Supreme Court's citation of dictionaries (a practice strongly advocated by Justice Scalia) after Justice Scalia's appointment to the Court in 1986. Justice Scalia's advocacy of his theory of interpretation, textualism (which he may not have created, though he was its most famous advocate), was thus undoubtedly effective in various ways.

Notwithstanding his enduring legacy, Justice Scalia's need to define the rule of law and interpretation in dichotomous terms ultimately undermined his project and, ironically for someone who fetishized language, revealed a poor understanding of language itself. This chapter briefly describes Justice Scalia's view of the rule of law and his argument that only textualism is consistent with its requirements. The chapter also critiques Justice Scalia's attempts to create "communion" with his critics by emphasizing the contextual nature of language and the necessity of judicial "judgment" when engaging in interpretation. The chapter argues that Justice Scalia's attempts to show that his "fair-reading" approach would narrow the range of acceptable judicial decision-making and acceptable argumentation fail, as does his demonstration of a textualist approach to H. L. A. Hart's famous no-vehicles-in-the-park hypothetical. The chapter concludes that Justice Scalia's arguments rest on fictional notions of language that, unlike other fictions and constructs, are unnecessary and undermine the goal of ingenuous legal interpretation.

The Rule of Law and Textualism

Justice Scalia's view of the basic requirements of the rule of law was contestable but certainly mainstream. The traditional idea of the rule of law requires that particular cases be decided on the basis of rules that are prior to, and more general than, the particular cases (Radin 1989). The governing rules should also provide advance notice that allows people to plan their affairs with reasonable confidence that they can know in advance the legal consequences of various actions (Fallon 1997). Justice Scalia similarly advocated that the rule of law requires predictability and, as a consequence, clear rules (Scalia 1989). He further advocated a mainstream, positive-law theory of the rule of law, maintaining that it requires that judges base decisions on the law rather than unwritten or personal notions of justice (Scalia and Garner 2012, 243).

If the above principles of the rule of law are accepted, a very general notion of proper judicial interpretation emerges, along with modest requirements about the determinacy of language. If notice is a necessary aspect of the rule of law, it would follow that any methodology that purports to systematically disregard the text of the law would fail to comply with rule-of-law principles. Avoiding a resulting "rule-of-men" standard depends on the "intellectual integrity of interpretation" (Scalia and Garner, 2012, xxix). Judges have a part in creating law, in the sense that they must adapt legal doctrines to new situations, thereby giving laws new content (5). Nevertheless, courts should act as "faithful agents" of the legislature (4). Such a notion, though, is incoherent unless one accepts that "words convey discernible meanings" (xxix).

Based on the requirements outlined above, it would seem that a range of interpretive methodologies would be consistent with the rule of law. Justice Scalia, though, framed the debate dichotomously and posited that one interpretive methodology follows ineluctably from the rule-of-law requirements. According to Justice Scalia, the choice is between a purely discretionary style of judging (i.e., any nontextualist methodology, but typically intentionalism) and one that contains limits on judicial discretion (i.e., textualism). One framework requires "broadly applicable general principles" of law (Scalia 1989, 1185), and the other allows for a seemingly unbounded "personal discretion to do justice" (1176). Unlike other interpretive methodologies (such as intentionalism), textualism requires broadly applicable general principles, because it provides that judges should "ask how a reasonable person, conversant with the relevant social and linguistic conventions, would read the text in context" and that they should apply the resultant "public meaning" even when harsh results obtain or a review of the legislative history of the statute indicates that the situation before the court was unanticipated by the legislature (Manning 2003, 2392–93). Textualism is thus the only interpretive methodology consistent with the rule of law, because it "does not invite the judge to apply his own willful predilections, whereas every other philosophy . . . invites the judge to do what he thinks is good, what he thinks is right" (Lat 2012, 2).

The Dangers of Communion

Convincing readers that such an extreme, dichotomous position (i.e., that textualism is the only methodology consistent with rule-of-law requirements) is nevertheless correct requires the rhetor, in this case Justice Scalia, to adapt to audience demands. Doing so includes creating "communion" between the rhetor and the audience, which involves determining the subgroups that comprise the audience and taking "into account the beliefs and attitudes of the participants" (Tindale 2004, 16–17, 33). Certainly, the main subgroup to which Justice Scalia attempted to appeal consisted of judicial conservatives (e.g., Federalist Society members and others) predisposed to agree with his jurisprudential program. Another subgroup, though, consisted of critics of textualism, who have long argued that textualism focuses too much on the semantic meaning of legal provisions and fails to account for the contribution that context makes to meaning. The two groups, while perhaps containing some overlap, have differing philosophies and agendas that are in some ways irreconcilable. The conservative subgroup is interested in such things as describing and criticizing judicial activism and promoting judicial restraint in legal interpretation, while the critics of textualism are interested in demonstrating the indeterminate nature of semantic meaning and the necessity of judicial inferences from context (including from legislative history) about legislative purpose.

In Justice Scalia's 2012 book (his last sustained defense of his interpretive philosophy), his rhetoric attempted to satisfy the concerns of both subgroups, as though he were playing a *den-den daiko* (a Japanese pellet drum), which sounds when it is turned on its axis from side to side, causing the beads hanging on threads on either side of the body of the drum to strike it. Thus, in appealing to critics, Justice Scalia was careful to frame his version of textualism as though it approached language in a sophisticated way. In particular, the importance of context is emphasized at various points in the book. For instance, Justice Scalia emphasized the importance of the "full context" when interpreting language (Scalia and Garner 2012, 16), later emphasized that "[o]f course, words are given meaning by their context" (56), argued that judges should discern "literal meaning in context" (40), and asserted that courts should "assume the contextually appropriate ordinary meaning" (70). Justice Scalia similarly acknowledged the reality of linguistic indeterminacy, indicating that "language [is] notoriously slippery" (xxix), conceding that "many words have more than one ordinary meaning" and that more common words have more possible meanings (70), and reasoning that "there will and must be cases near the borderline [of a concept] which are not obviously on either one side or the other" (56). Justice Scalia also seemed to recognize the discretionary nature of some of the principles of interpretation, such as the canon of constitutional avoidance, indicating that its trigger (doubts about the constitutionality of an interpretation) cannot be defined "precisely in the abstract" and is the cause of many judicial disagreements (250). He thus indicated the importance of judicial "judgment" when engaging in interpretation (33).

Conversely, hitting the other side of the pellet drum (and appealing to judicial conservatives), Justice Scalia portrayed language as determinate and argued that judges should be constrained by the linguistic meaning of the text. He thus argued that "most interpretive questions have a right answer" and "variability in interpretation is a distemper" (Scalia and Garner 2012, 6). If most interpretive questions have a right answer, and judges should be limited by the linguistic meaning of the text, it follows (for Justice Scalia) that the choice of interpretive methodology should be framed in dichotomous terms. Thus, to reject textualism is to embrace "the notion that words can have no definite meaning" (6), a position which is motivated by a "desire for freedom from the text." Even worse, the rule of law is threatened by "nontextual means of interpretation, which erode society's confidence in a rule of law that evidently has no agreed-on meaning" (xxviii). The solution, of course, is that the "legal system must regain a mooring that it has lost: a generally agreed-on approach to the interpretation of legal texts" (xxvii). Due to the "breakdown in the transmission of this heritage to successive generations" there has been "uncertainty and confusion in our systems of private ordering and public lawmaking" and "distortion of our system of democratic government" (xxviii). Instead, a commitment to "textualism will provide greater certainty in the law, and hence greater predictability and greater respect for the rule of law" (xxix).

One danger of attempting to create communion with both allies and critics is that the speaker may have to resort to vacuousness or high levels of generality in order to appease both sides and obscure irreconcilable conflicts. The cost, of course, is that the effort fails to meaningfully advance understanding of the issues involved. Justice Scalia's "pellet drum" attempts to accommodate critics and conservatives may not have advanced understanding of interpretive issues, but they did, inadvertently, raise fundamentally important issues of language and interpretation. If language is "notoriously slippery" and can only be given meaning by considering the "full context," making judicial "judgment" crucial to interpretation, how can it be that "most interpretive questions have a right answer?" Is it that all judges, if they are intellectually honest, will consider the contextual evidence in the same way, as though the human language faculty is designed to assess contextual evidence in a certain manner? Or, somewhat differently, is it that contextual clues are easy to assess and typically select a certain, determinate meaning? Furthermore, the interpretive process is complicated by the existence of judicially created principles of interpretation. Justice Scalia concedes that the trigger for certain principles of interpretation, such as the canon of constitutional avoidance, cannot be defined "precisely in the abstract" and are the cause of many judicial disagreements. This problem would seem endemic to interpretation, but Justice Scalia does not attempt to address the difficulties (inadvertently) illustrated by his rhetoric.

Interpretive Dissensus

Ignoring the tension between contextual complexity and interpretive consensus enabled Justice Scalia to claim that his "fair-reading" approach would "narrow the range of acceptable judicial decision-making and acceptable argumentation" (xxviii). A partial justification for this claim is Justice Scalia's assertion (an aspect of his dichotomous view of interpretation) that alternatives to textualism posit that the judge's role is "to do what he thinks is good, what he thinks is right." Justice Scalia was, of course, constructing a paper tiger argument. No mainstream methodology of interpretation frames the constituent question of interpretation as involving a search for the judge's conception of what is "good" or "right." Rather, some version of legislative intent (often objectified) or purpose is sought, and the relevant provision is interpreted in light of that intent or purpose. Once the paper tiger argument is dissolved, though, the desirability of a narrow range of acceptable judicial decision-making is uncertain.

One difficulty with Justice Scalia's claim about narrowing the range of judicial decision-making and acceptable argumentation is that it is unclear whether the quotation is directed to the constituent question of interpretation (i.e., its goal, such as determining the public meaning of the language) or the allowable determinants of meaning (i.e., the evidence that determines the public meaning). Most (if not all) methodologies of interpretation will have a single presumptive goal of interpretation (e.g., interpreting the provision consistent with its public meaning or, conversely, with legislative intent), and in that sense all provide for a narrow range of acceptable judicial decision-making. Similarly, all methodologies recognize multiple determinants of meaning (e.g., dictionary definitions, rules of grammar). Presumably, it is Justice Scalia's argument that his "fair-reading" methodology allows for a narrower range of determinants of meaning (excluding, for example, legislative history), which will result in greater interpretive consensus and, thus, greater adherence to the rule of law. The accuracy of this position (in reality, an empirical claim) is, however, far from certain and may well be false.

In fact, Justice Scalia's 2012 book itself suggests that judicial dissensus may not be a particularly acute problem after all. In his introduction to that book, Judge Frank Easterbrook (a committed textualist) notes that the Supreme Court, which primarily handles hard cases, decides almost half of those cases unanimously and many of the others by lopsided votes (Scalia and Garner 2012, xxiii). Judge Easterbrook also notes that the "amount of real disagreement has not increased in the last 70 years" (xxiii). One should assume that lower federal courts (which do not have the discretion to accept only "hard cases") are even less riven by interpretive disputes that can be attributed to differences in interpretive methodology. Perhaps judges do assess context in roughly similar ways, but note that such a presumption would undermine the exigency Justice Scalia identified in advocating for recognition of a causal relationship between implementation of textualism and judicial consensus (and adherence to the rule of law). If interpretive outcomes already reveal widespread agreement among judges, there is no compelling reason to offer broad and fundamental critiques of the current interpretive practices of judges. Instead, it may be that the methodologies of interpretation currently employed by judges do not significantly differ in either the constituent question asked in interpretive cases or the allowable determinants of meaning.

Other reasons also undermine Justice Scalia's claims about the range of judicial decision-making and consensus. Consider a methodology of interpre-

tation with only one explicitly allowable determinate of meaning (a truly narrow range which even Justice Scalia does not advocate), say "ordinary meaning." Under this methodology, a judge must determine the legal meaning of
a provision solely on the basis of the ordinary meaning of its language. Even
under such a limited methodology, there would be significant disagreements
regarding the "correct" meaning of any given provision because its ordinary
meaning would be disputed (Slocum 2015). Furthermore, even if there were
agreement regarding the provision's ordinary meaning, the ordinary meaning of the language may be general, vague, or ambiguous, rendering impossible sole judicial reliance on the ordinary meaning. Also, such an approach
would guarantee an incorrect result in some (perhaps many) cases, because
legislators sometimes desire that language carry some specialized technical
or legal meaning. Still, such a system would undoubtedly narrow the range
of acceptable argumentation (even though it may not increase judicial consensus), considering that, ostensibly, the parties would only debate ordinary
meaning. Considering that various cases would be undecidable on the basis
of ordinary meaning because of the generality, vagueness, or ambiguity of
the language, and with no other articulable determinate of meaning, it is not
intuitive that this methodology would narrow the range of acceptable judicial
decision-making (or lessen judicial dissensus) compared to the existing system of interpretation practiced by judges.

A narrow range of acceptable argumentation is thus not obviously co-
extensive with a narrow range of decision-making. Narrowing the range of
acceptable argumentation would, by itself, not foreclose judicial discretion
(and, thus, the possibility for judicial dissensus). Naturally, limiting acceptable judicial grounds of decision-making to ordinary meaning would constitute a narrower allowable range of determinants (excluding many current
principles of interpretation). The "fair-reading method," though, does not rely
solely on ordinary meaning, as the dozens of approved canons and interpretive principles in Scalia's book illustrate. Adding complexity and choice to the
"ordinary meaning" scenario described above is unlikely to increase judicial
consensus. Instead of one determinate of meaning (namely, ordinary meaning), the "fair-reading" judge must balance various determinants of meaning,
decide which combination of determinants is appropriate under the circumstances and the persuasive weight to give each determinate, and if there are
conflicting determinates, decide which determinates should prevail. Justice
Scalia did not offer any system for addressing such issues and was thus not in
a position to declare that universal adoption of his methodology would result
in greater judicial consensus.

The No-Vehicles-in-the-Park Hypothetical

Justice Scalia did not rely solely on "high theory" in making his arguments, also engaging in his 2012 book in the low-theory task of demonstrating the validity of his claims about his high theory of interpretation. If "variability in interpretation is a distemper," as Justice Scalia claimed, it should be possible to take a basic interpretive hypothetical and demonstrate how all should agree on its resolution. If done well, such a demonstration would also fulfill the rhetorical argumentation goal of inviting the audience to come to conclusions through its own experiencing of the evidence, rather than through the speaker's imposition of certain views on the audience (Tindale 2004, 24). To be effective, argumentation should build on the consensus it establishes with its audience, taking into account features of that audience, and should invoke the experiential element and invite collaboration (66, 81). Justice Scalia attempted to build this consensus through a step-by-step examination of H. L. A. Hart's famous no-vehicles-in-the-park scenario. While it may be debatable whether Justice Scalia invited the audience to come to conclusions through its own experiencing of the evidence, his use of the hypothetical served to illustrate the opposite of what he intended.

Hart's no-vehicles-in-the-park scenario poses the following questions: "A legal rule forbids you to take a vehicle into the public park. Plainly this forbids an automobile, but what about bicycles, roller skates, toy automobiles? What about airplanes? Are these, as we say, to be called "vehicles" for the purpose of the rule or not?" (Hart 1958, 607). It is odd that Justice Scalia would choose this famous hypothetical to demonstrate the determinacy of language (and, correlatively, the desirability of textualism). Hart created the hypothetical in part to illustrate the challenges caused by the difficulties of categorizing objects and defining words (such as *vehicle*) and the consequent fuzziness associated with such attempts. Hart indicated that while a general word must have a "core of settled meaning," "there will be, as well, a penumbra of debatable cases in which words are neither obviously applicable not obviously ruled out" (607).

Language study since the creation of the hypothetical has only confirmed Hart's analysis. Psychologists and linguists are not troubled that some objects (e.g., "car") are more representative of a category (e.g., "vehicle") than others (e.g., "motorcycle") because they recognize degrees of category membership. The referential parameters of a word may be fuzzy because the term cannot be defined in terms of necessary and sufficient conditions, even though some things may clearly fall within the scope of the term (Slocum 2015). The problem (and part of the reason why the no-vehicles-in-the-park hypothetical is so intriguing) is that while the fuzziness associated with natural language concepts, such as "vehicle," does not undermine most day-to-day verbal interactions, where a high degree of precision is not necessary to successful communication, the requirements of the legal system are different. Interpretive questions (e.g., does a certain object fall within the scope of the "vehicle" concept) need definite yes or no answers, and frequently the dispute will involve some object at the margins of the relevant concept (e.g., is a car without an engine a "vehicle"?).

Despite the purpose, and the continuing salience, of the no-vehicles-in-the-park hypothetical, Justice Scalia indicates that his analysis of it can serve as a "useful illustration of the fair-reading method" (Scalia and Garner 2012, 36). In addition to the items listed by Hart, Scalia adds the following items for consideration:

ambulances	rollerblades
baby strollers	scooters
gliders	Segways
golf carts	skateboards
Heeleys roller shoes	tricycles
mopeds	unicycles
motorcycles	unmotorized wheelchairs
motorized wheelchairs	

Scalia asserts that although decisions regarding the application of the hypothetical statute will "induce some critical thinking," "judges who use the fair-reading method will arrive at fairly consistent answers" because the "relevant line of inquiry is pretty straightforward" (36).

Note that even at the start of the analysis, Scalia hedges his claim. The claim is not that the fair-reading method will produce "consistent answers" but, rather, "*fairly* consistent answers" (emphasis added). *Fairly* is a vague term that is classified as a "downtoner" (Zhang 2011, 574). Similar to terms such as *sort of, a bit*, and *somewhat, fairly* softens an expression so that it appears less assertive and less open to challenge or refutation. Thus, how much consistency must be present in order to declare that answers are "fairly" consistent? Furthermore, what is the scope of the questions asked that may produce the fairly consistent answers? If the questions involve objects such as picnic baskets, balloons, footballs, and jeans (along with an infinite number of other objects never referred to as "vehicles"), consistent answers among judges should be expected. Of course, one does not need any particular interpretive methodology to answer such easy questions. If, instead, the questions involve objects that might be the subjects of litigation (such as the items listed by Hart as well as Scalia), Justice Scalia does not establish that the "fair-reading method" would produce greater unanimity than would other interpretive approaches, such as intentionalism.

The rest of Scalia's analysis is similarly unpersuasive, if his goal is to demonstrate how the determinacy of language should produce uniformity in judicial interpretations. Scalia indicates that interpreters should "consult (without apology) what the lexicographers say" because "they have studied dozens if not hundreds of instances of actual English usage to arrive at the core meaning of *vehicle*" (Scalia and Garner 2012, 36–37). Yet Justice Scalia rejects the definitions offered by the lexicographers. He rejects a broad dictionary definition that describes a vehicle as "a means of carrying or transporting something," along with another that defines the term as follows: "[a] means of conveyance, usu. with wheels, for transporting people, goods, etc.; a car, cart, truck, carriage, sledge, etc." or "[a]ny means of carriage or transport; a receptacle in which something is placed in order to be moved." Scalia concedes that "[a]nything that is ever called a vehicle (in the relevant sense) would fall within these definitions (37)." He claims, however, that it is "common usage" that is relevant and not every "means of conveyance with wheels" or every "receptacle in which something is placed in order to be moved" is commonly referred to as a vehicle (37). He also rejects another dictionary meaning that describes a vehicle as "[a] self-propelled conveyance that runs on tires; a motor vehicle (37)." Justice Scalia rejects this definition as being too broad because it would include a "remote-controlled, miniature model car (37)."

So, does Justice Scalia find another lexicographer who might provide a narrower definition than the ones rejected above? Apparently not. Instead, Justice Scalia creates his own definition: "The proper colloquial meaning in our view (not all of them are to be found in dictionaries) is simply a sizable wheeled conveyance (as opposed to one of any size that is motorized)." It would seem, then, that the lexicographers were not particularly helpful after all. In defense of his "colloquial" definition, Justice Scalia quotes Justice Holmes's famous reasoning in *McBoyle v. United States* that "it is possible to use the word [vehicle] to signify a conveyance working on land, water or air," but "in everyday speech 'vehicle' calls up the picture of a thing moving on land" (Scalia and Garner 2012, 38).[1] Scalia agrees with this conclusion (*not seeming to realize that airplanes would therefore be permitted into the park!*), but it is not clear how it follows from his definition of *vehicle*.[2] Certainly, an airplane is a "sizable wheeled conveyance." Is an additional, necessary feature of a "vehicle" being applied? Scalia does not provide an answer.

Armed with his self-created definition, Scalia reasons that "remote-controlled model cars, baby carriages, [and] tricycles" would not fall under it (Scalia and Garner 2012, 37–38). But how does one decide whether an object is "sizable" enough to qualify as a vehicle? If the definition of *vehicle* sets forth necessary and sufficient conditions that would include anything that is (1) sizable, (2) wheeled, and (3) a conveyance, there must be some size threshold for the category. Thus, is there some standard (unmentioned by Scalia) for evaluation? If so, its nature is not clear. Notwithstanding his goal of demonstrating an interpretive methodology that will produce consistent answers across judges, Scalia indicates uncertainty concerning the application of his definition to "bicycles," indicating that they are "perhaps" not vehicles (albeit confirming later that they are not vehicles), and "Segways," indicating that they are "perhaps" vehicles (38). Why the distinction between the two (similarly sized) objects? Justice Scalia does not offer an explanation, nor does he explain the basis for his uncertainty. Furthermore, apparently a "scooter" is not a vehicle (and neither is a "motorized wheelchair"), but a "moped" is (38).

Justice Scalia's failure to provide some criterion for judgments about the "sizable" threshold undoubtedly benefits his analysis, considering that any attempt to precisify *sizable* would reveal the arbitrary and discretionary nature of a cutoff that is based on language alone. Certainly, what is "sizable" depends on context, as does the meaning of any gradable adjective (e.g., *tall, fast*; see Raffman 2014). The relevant context most importantly includes the object that the adjective *sizable* modifies. A "sizable building" is different from a "sizable human." What, though, is a "sizable conveyance"? Does any car qualify, even though they vary dramatically in size? Considering that Justice Scalia does not list cars as objects to be considered under the statute, it would appear he would assert that any sort of car (only if designed for travel on public roads or to transport humans?) would qualify as a vehicle. The context relevant to any criterion must in some sense account for the purpose of the provision. The determination of purpose relevant to such a specific question, though, is based on world knowledge, not knowledge of semantics (which Justice Scalia does not seem willing to concede). Would Justice Scalia recast his definition, dropping the "sizable" requirement (or reinterpreting it), for a vehicular manslaughter criminal provision that the prosecution seeks to apply to a bicycle rider who killed an elderly woman?[3]

Like most terms, *vehicle* cannot be defined (whether by linguists or nonlinguists) in terms of determinate necessary and sufficient conditions of category membership that would result in consensus regarding its application to any object. By failing to acknowledge this linguistic reality, Justice Scalia unwittingly illustrated the enduring appeal of the no-vehicles-in-the-park hypothetical. The hypothetical is enticing and instructive because it does not admit of easy or noncontestable solutions, even though the scenario presented is straightforward and commonplace. Justice Scalia's demonstration of how the "fair-reading method" would be applied to the scenario merely reinforces the instructive nature of the hypothetical and the inability of textualism to overcome inherent indeterminacies in language. It is true that Justice Scalia's analysis relied on a limited number of determinants of meaning (illustrating his narrow range of acceptable judicial decision-making arguments), but the analysis failed to demonstrate that his "fair-reading method" would result in increased judicial consensus (and note even his own uncertainty regarding some of the examples).

Context and Fictions

What is clear from the no-vehicles-in-the-park hypothetical is the inelimin-able influence of extratextual considerations on legal interpretations. As with language generally, the meaning of Scalia's definition of *vehicle* depends on context. Justice Scalia declares that only a "sizable wheeled conveyance" is a vehicle, but is this phrase a general assertion of the "ordinary meaning" of *vehicle*, or is it a definition selected on the basis of the context of the statute? If the latter (which seems more likely, although Scalia glosses over such issues and purports to give a general definition for *vehicle*), by what process does Justice Scalia determine the appropriate context for the statute? Justice Scalia insists that legislative purpose must be derived from the text of a statute, but words, even when their meaning is undisputed, do not contain some intrinsic purpose (even when combined into sentences and paragraphs). Instead, pur-pose is discerned from other sources, such as inferences about the speaker's intent (or what a "reasonable" speaker would intend). The flaw in Justice Scalia's logic is the proposition that inferences about the speaker's purposes can be avoided if the interpreter refrains from explicitly considering those purposes. Thus, in the no-vehicles-in-the-park example, Justice Scalia is un-doubtedly making inferences about what a typical legislature would intend, given the situation (consider his definition of a vehicle as "sizable" in order to exclude toy cars), even as he explicitly disclaims any interest in what the actual legislature intended.

Justice Scalia's consideration of context convinced him to reject the defi-nitions of the linguistic experts (whose assistance he had earlier touted as valuable) and create his own definition of *vehicle*. Considering his claim that, by limiting the determinants of meaning to semantic meaning, inter-preters should reach "fairly consistent answers," Justice Scalia's position is, at its essence, a claim that all speakers of English understand the language in precisely the same way he does (making his comment about the importance of linguistics experts rather odd and unnecessary). Justice Scalia could not, of course, explicitly offer his views as the standard of language meaning. Instead, like other judges, he employed something analogous to the classic "appeal to authority" argumentation strategy. Even outside the law, rhetors often appeal to third-party objective standards for support for their positions (Tindale 2004, 121). This is done through different constructions of *audience* (Tindale 2013). For instance, the Universal Audience (UA), comprised of "all those who are competent and reasonable" (i.e., not any actual audience of the rhetor), tests the validity of claims about what is universally acceptable (Sigler 2015, 328). The UA is conceived in order to evaluate topics such as philosophical discourse, which seeks to transcend the beliefs of a particular group and appeals instead to reason (336).

For legal interpretation, an objective standard is the default, along with the corresponding presumption that the words in legal texts are to carry their ordinary meanings. Certainly, many judges allow the perceived intent or purpose of the statute to guide their interpretations, and thereby sometimes deviate from the interpretation that would have been chosen without consideration of intent or purpose. For a textualist like Justice Scalia, though, an objective standard should determine the selected interpretation. Hence, Justice Scalia would seek not "subjective intent" but what, considering the "full context," the words mean to "reasonable people at the time they were written" (Scalia and Garner 2012, 16). The "reasonable person" is, naturally, a construct, yet its fictional nature is not something Justice Scalia would want emphasized. In a 1990 law review article, he stated that it would be impossible to operate a legal system without legal fictions but lamented that he "never thought" the "legal realists did us a favor by pointing out that all these legal fictions were fictions: Those judges wise enough to be trusted with the secret already knew it" (Scalia 1990, 589).

Objective, yet fictional, standards are often appropriate devices to evaluate the reasonableness or validity of arguments. To argue for the elimination of such standards in legal interpretation would be to misunderstand the nature of the interpretive enterprise, where actual intent is often, and some would say never, available or sufficient to resolve the interpretive dispute. Furthermore, an objective standard cannot extinguish the subjectivity inherent in the evaluative enterprise. Even the characterization of the UA will depend on the creator's own culture and worldview (Sigler 2015, 328). Yet an understanding of the imperfect nature of any objective standard of evaluation should not immunize the rhetor from criticism of the constructed standard. Sometimes, characterization of the standard will be transparently flawed. For instance, outside of the law, when making arguments about how some event or issue should be understood, speakers will sometimes claim that even a Martian would agree with the speaker's point (Tindale 2004, 118). The Martian represents the "reasonable" position, according to a human standard, but the standard has no substantive content and is thus not accessible to critique. Instead, the Martian standard "stands as a subjective first-person perspective masquerading as an objective third-person one" (121).

In contrast, sometimes the fault lies not with the characterization of the objective standard but with a misunderstanding of its determinants. The objective, reasonable-person standard must be distinguishable from the judge's own position, but, at the same time, there is no empirical method of comparing overall interpretations against the standard. Still, as with rhetoric, the intersubjective agreement of a community is a necessary and fundamental feature of the standard. The objective reasonable-person standard itself may be constructed and fictional, but its determinants should, to the extent possible, be based on accurate understandings of language. The central fiction that Justice Scalia would want secreted is, thus, not the reasonable-person standard but his position regarding the determinacy of language (and thus interpretation), which is necessary to his efforts to establish a nexus between rule-of-law requirements and textualism. If Justice Scalia's views about the determinacy of language are incorrect, yet drive interpretations, his version of the objective, reasonable-person standard is no more sophisticated than a Martian standard.

Conclusion

Justice Scalia's rhetoric regarding the primacy of the language in legal texts had the salutary effect of causing even his critics to consider language more carefully. Still, his views on language undermined his rule-of-law project. Interpretive methodologies are necessarily based on certain fictions, if one defines fiction in this context as a principle or presumption that is based on a generalized notion of reality rather than an inference from the specific facts of the case before the court. Although sometimes necessary, fictions can be pernicious when, instead of serving as at least generally accurate, presumption-based shortcuts for determining realities, they rest on presumptions that are erroneous. Such fictions are especially pernicious when they undermine or obscure any effort to create legal structures that are rooted in reality. Justice Scalia's rule-of-law claims could have been underscored by a very general notion of proper judicial interpretation, along with modest claims about the determinacy of language.

Instead Justice Scalia offered an extreme, dichotomous view of interpretive methodologies. If his views about the determinacy of language and the consequent possibility of uniformity of interpretive results, are erroneous, his attempts to prove a nexus between textualism and the rule of law fail. There undoubtedly is a method of prioritizing the language in legal texts while recognizing its underdetermined nature, and it is unfortunate that a rhetor as talented and influential as Justice Scalia was not interested in seriously developing such a theory.

References

Fallon, Richard H. 1997. "'The Rule of Law' as a Concept in Constitutional Discourse." *Columbia Law Review* 97:1–56.

Greene, Jamal. 2016. "The Age of Scalia." *Harvard Law Review* 130:144–84.

Hart, H. L. A. 1958. "Positivism and the Separation of Law and Morals." *Harvard Law Review* 71:593–629.

Lat, David. 2012. "The Benchslap Dispatches: Justice Scalia on Judge Posner's 'Hatchet Job.'" Bloomberg Law. Online at https://abovethelaw.com/2012/09/the-benchslap-dispatches-justice-scalia-on-judge-posners-hatchet-job/.

Manning, John F. 2003. "The Absurdity Doctrine." *Harvard Law Review* 116:2388–486.

Radin, Margaret Jane. 1989. "Reconsidering the Rule of Law." *Boston University Law Review* 69: 781–819.

Raffman, Diana. 2014. *Unruly Words: A Study of Vague Language*. Oxford: Oxford University Press.

Scalia, Antonin. 1989. "The Rule of Law as a Law of Rules." *University of Chicago Law Review* 56:1175–88.

———. 1990. "Assorted Canards of Contemporary Legal Analysis." *Case Western Reserve Law Review* 40:581–97.

———, and Brian Garner. 2012. *Reading Law: The Interpretation of Legal Texts*. St. Paul, MN: Thomson/West.

Sigler, J. E. 2015. "The New Rhetoric's Concept of Universal Audience, Misconceived." *Argumentation* 29:325–49.

Slocum, Brian. 2015. Ordinary Meaning: A Theory of the Most Fundamental Principle of Legal Interpretation. Chicago: University of Chicago Press.

Tindale, Chistopher W. 2004. Rhetorical Argumentation: Principles of Theory and Practice. London: SAGE.

———. 2013. "Rhetorical Argumentation and the Nature of Audience: Toward an Understanding of Audience—Issues in Argumentation." *Philosophy and Rhetoric* 46, no. 4, 508–32.

Zhang, Grace. 2011. "Elasticity of Vague Language." *Intercultural Pragmatics* 8, no. 4, 571–99.

5

The Two Justice Scalias

LAWRENCE M. SOLAN

In the tradition of Justice Oliver Wendell Holmes and Judge Learned Hand, Justice Antonin Scalia committed himself to developing and promoting an objective approach to legal analysis. Scalia focused on the interpretation of statutes and the Constitution, whereas Hand is best known for his contributions to common-law subjects, even though, like Scalia, Hand was a federal judge. Holmes did both.[1] Law students today still learn the "Hand Formula" in tort law and still learn the primacy of objective historical evidence over testimony about the parties' recollections of their earlier states of mind in disputes over contract formation. As for tort law, liability was to be based on negligence, and negligence can be determined by applying a calculus in which liability would be imposed only when the harm times the probability of its occurring exceeds the burden of taking the precautions that would have prevented it from occurring.[2] To a large extent, liability still is based on the Hand Formula (see Stein 2017 for recent critical discussion).

Even more relevant to the current discussion, consider the objective theory of contract norm. Still quoted is Learned Hand's famous summary:

A contract has, strictly speaking, nothing to do with the personal, or individual, intent of the parties. A contract is an obligation attached by the mere force of law to certain acts of the parties, usually words, which ordinarily accompany and represent a known intent. If, however, it were proved by twenty bishops that either party when he used the words intended something else than the usual meaning which the law imposes on them, he would still be held, unless there were mutual mistake or something else of the sort.[3]

This account, however, leaves a gnawing question. Do we really not care what people mean when they speak, as Hand put it, or do we care, but regard objective, contemporaneous evidence of communicative intent more probative of what that intent actually was? A consequentialist approach would say no, we do not care. People must be held responsible for their own actions, including acts of speech, regardless of what they intended. Alternatively, one may argue that by objectifying the interpretive enterprise, one is more likely to uncover what the parties meant and how they were understood than by asking them as witnesses to provide their accounts at trial. In both instances, the objective approach permits us to concern ourselves more with how the speaker (legislature in statutory interpretation, putative promisor in contract-formation cases) was likely to have been understood.

Judge Easterbrook has stated the issue colorfully, taking the evidentiary, objective intentionalist approach over the consequentialist one: "Under the prevailing will theory of contract, parties, like Humpty Dumpty, may use words as they please. If they wish the symbols "one Caterpillar D9G tractor" to mean "500 railroad cars full of watermelons," that's fine—provided parties share this weird meaning. A meaning held by one party only may not be invoked to change the ordinary denotation of a word, however. Intent must be mutual to be effective."[4] Justice Scalia, at different times, espoused each of these approaches to the interpretation of statutes. The common goal was to devise a set of procedures, to be applied with relative uniformity, that would simulate the likely intended meaning of the legislature in enacting a law whose application is in dispute, without engaging in individual inquiry into the thought processes of the legislators.[5] Yet Scalia's justificatory rhetoric varied. At times it was the procedure itself that that he espoused and defended for its own sake. At other times he argued that his methodology was most likely to simulate the intent of the legislature, making him a more faithful agent. This article describes these two quite different rhetorical strategies in support of the textualist approach that Scalia articulated in his opinions and his extrajudicial writings. To some extent they are mutually reinforcing, and to some extent they are in tension with each other.

The heart of Scalia's philosophy was that in the realm of legal construction, language reigns. The Constitution empowers the legislature to enact laws—not intentions. Because of the power of language, interpretive theory should respect what was said and rein in the discretion of those who construe the law. But language does not always provide the legal system with a clear answer of whether or how a law should be applied in novel situations. Scalia was surely sophisticated enough to recognize this, and dealt with it somewhat differently from time to time.

Creating a Science of Statutory Interpretation:
The Irrelevance of Legislative Intent

Consider these excerpts from Scalia's "Common-Law Courts in a Civil-Law System: The Role of United States Federal Courts in Interpreting the Constitution and Laws," the opening essay in his 1998 volume, *A Matter of Interpretation: Federal Courts and the Law*:

> You will find it frequently said in judicial opinions of my court and others that the judge's objective in interpreting a statute is to give effect to "the intent of the legislature." . . . Unfortunately, it does not square with some of the (few) generally accepted concrete rules of statutory construction. One is the rule that when the text of a statute is clear, that is the end of the matter. Why should that be so, if what the legislature intended, rather than what it said, is the object of our inquiry? In selecting the words of the statute, the legislature might have misspoken. Why not permit that to be demonstrated from the floor debates? Or indeed, why not accept, as proper material for the court to consider, later explanations by the legislators—a sworn affidavit signed by the majority each house, for example, as to what they *really* meant?[6]

Instead, Scalia opted for "objectified intent," which he defined as "the intent that a reasonable person would gather from the text of the law, placed alongside the remainder of the *corpus juris*." He considered this approach to be most in tune with there being a "science of statutory interpretation," a project he admired. This position is very much akin to that of the "new originalists" in constitutional law, who seek what they call "original public meaning" rather than the actual communicative intent of the framers (see, e.g., Solum 2015). To the new originalists, we should understand the Constitution as would an idealized, educated individual of the founding era who decided whether to vote in favor of adoption on the basis of how he understood the language presented to him.

Scalia's search for objectified intent was frequently embodied in his invocation of the "ordinary meaning" canon. This approach to statutory interpretation promotes both respect for the legislative process and respect for a rule of law that is accessible to those whom the law governs (see Scalia 1998; Eskridge 2016; Slocum 2015 for discussion). By not permitting the approach to be defeasible in light of contrary evidence, however, Scalia's approach risked undermining those goals by declaring evidence of communicative intent off limits. As noted earlier, the position was part of a commitment to reestablish the notion of a science of statutory interpretation.

The philosophy was repeated in his decisions. Below, for example, is an excerpt from his concurring opinion in *Green v. Bock Laundry Machine Co., Inc.*[7] It is an ugly story. A prisoner had his arm torn off by a laundry machine that he was operating while on work release. He sued the company that manufactured the machine. At trial, the machine company succeeded in introducing evidence of Green having been convicted of burglary. The legal issue in the case—which the laundry machine company won—was the interpretation of Rule 609 of the Federal Rules of Evidence, which at the time read as follows:

> For the purpose of attacking the credibility of a witness, evidence that the witness has been convicted of a crime shall be admitted if elicited from the witness or established by public record during cross-examination but only if the crime (1) was punishable by death or imprisonment in excess of one year under the law under which the witness was convicted, and the court determines that the probative value of admitting this evidence outweighs its prejudicial effect to the defendant, or (2) involved dishonesty or false statement, regardless of the punishment.

Green was the plaintiff in the case, so, reading the rule at face value, there was no call for an evaluation of whether the probative value of the admitting the evidence of his crime outweighed its prejudicial effect to the defendant. After all, it was the defendant offering the evidence in an effort to prejudice the jury against the plaintiff. Thus, the trial court admitted the evidence and Green lost his tort case (in addition to losing his arm).

At the Supreme Court, the justices all agreed that the rule could not mean what it says—that in a civil case, the defendant has the right to this balancing, but the plaintiff does not. This left open two possible outcomes. The word *defendant* could be understood to refer only to criminal defendants, or the word *defendant* could be understood to refer to parties in general, at least in civil cases. A majority of the Court took the first option. Scalia concurred:

> The meaning of terms on the statute books ought to be determined, not on the basis of which meaning can be shown to have been understood by a larger handful of the Members of Congress; but rather on the basis of which meaning is (1) most in accord with context and ordinary usage, and thus most likely to have been understood by the whole Congress which voted on the words of the statute (not to mention the citizens subject to it), and (2) most compatible with the surrounding body of law into which the provision must be integrated—a compatibility which, by a benign fiction, we assume Congress always has in mind. I would not permit any of the historical and legislative material discussed by the Court, or all of it combined, to lead me to a result different from the one that these factors suggest.[8]

But there was another way of rescuing Rule 609—the one that the dissenting judges chose and later was chosen as the actual replacement for the poorly drafted original rule. Instead of limiting the benefit of an inquiry into the prejudicial effect of introducing a prior criminal conviction to criminal defendants, the Court could have opened up that opportunity to all parties by substituting the word *party* for *defendant* in the rule. It is hard to see how making that change does more damage to the language of the original rule than does adding the word *criminal* before *defendant*, as the majority did. The rule was obviously drafted with a serious error. As for trying to preserve as much meaning in the original rule as possible, both sides recognized the need to amend the rule judicially, since it would cause great havoc to strike it down and leave a gap in the rules of evidence until a new one was enacted.

Well known in this same vein of reasoning is Justice Scalia's dissent in *Smith v. United States*,[9] in which a majority of six justices held that a person who had attempted to trade an unloaded machine gun for cocaine had "used a firearm" during and in relation to a drug trafficking crime. The mandatory sentence for that crime was thirty years in prison. The majority looked up the word *use* in a host of dictionaries, virtually all of which defined it tautologically, given how broad and amorphous the verb is. Scalia objected to the majority's entire enterprise, which, incidentally, itself had avoided any reference to the internal history of the law's enactment, likely in deference to him. He remarked,

> In the search for statutory meaning, we give nontechnical words and phrases their ordinary meaning. . . . To use an instrumentality ordinarily means to use it for its intended purpose. When someone asks, "Do you use a cane?," he is not inquiring whether you have your grandfather's silver-handled walking stick on display in the hall; he wants to know whether you walk with a cane. Similarly, to speak of "using a firearm" is to speak of using it for its distinctive purpose, i. e., as a weapon. To be sure, "one can use a firearm in a number of ways," including as an article of exchange, just as one can "use" a cane as a hall decoration—but that is not the ordinary meaning of "using" the one or the other. The Court does not appear to grasp the distinction between how a word can be used and how it ordinarily is used. It would, indeed, be "both reasonable and normal to say that petitioner 'used' his MAC-10 in his drug trafficking offense by trading it for cocaine." It would also be reasonable and normal to say that he "used" it to scratch his head.[10]

Perceptively, Scalia has identified the "pet fish problem," discussed by philosophers of language (see Kamp and Partee 1995; Fodor and Lepore 1996). The prototypical (or "ordinary") meaning of a phrase is not equivalent to the sum of the ordinary meanings of its constituents. The prototypical pet (at least in U.S. culture) is a dog about the size of an Irish setter. The prototypical fish is one that resembles a salmon or bass in both shape and size. But the prototypical pet fish is a goldfish or guppy. By the same token, looking up the word *use* in a dictionary and then substituting the definition for the word itself in the phrase, "use a firearm" creates a pet fish problem. (For further discussion of this issue in legal contexts, see Eskridge 2016; Solan and Louk, forthcoming.)

Yet there are gaps in Scalia's dissenting rhetoric, and how one evaluates its legitimacy as a theory of legal interpretation depends upon how one fills in the gaps. For one thing, it is not clear what Scalia meant (or what current legal theorists mean) by "ordinary meaning." Scalia was entirely right that one typically thinks of using a gun as using the gun as a weapon. This observation exposes an important indeterminacy in the application of the ordinary meaning approach to legal interpretation. Should we distinguish between ordinary usage that results from the state of the world on the one hand, and ordinary usage that results from the level of comfort in how we describe things, on the other? As Scalia notes, we largely think of using a gun as a weapon, but are comfortable speaking about using guns for other purposes, consistent with the majority position in *Smith*.

Compare that case to *Church of the Holy Trinity v. United States*,[11] the 1892 case that Scalia (1998) derides, both for its reliance on legislative history and for its rhetoric that adduces the "spirit" of the statute. Yet, at least to my mind, the decision in *Holy Trinity Church* shares much with Scalia's dissent in *Smith*. The issue in the earlier case was whether a Manhattan church that paid to bring its new rector from London to New York had violated a law that made it a crime to "prepay the transportation . . . of any . . . foreigner or foreigners, into the United States, . . . under contract or agreement, . . . made previous to the importation or migration of such . . . foreigner or foreigners, to perform labor or service of any kind in the United States."[12]

The Supreme Court said no in a unanimous decision written by Justice Brewer. Recognizing that a perfectly reasonable reading of the statute would include the church's conduct, the Court nonetheless ruled purposefully: "[W]e cannot think Congress intended to denounce with penalties a transaction like that in the present case. It is a familiar rule, that a thing may be within the letter of the statute and yet not within the statute, because not within its spirit, nor within the intention of its makers."[13] But the Court also relied heavily on the ordinary understanding of the word *labor*, which appears in the law's title, as well as its body (*service* took a back seat in the analysis, a fair ground for criticizing it):

No one reading such a title would suppose that Congress had in its mind any purpose of staying the coming into this country of ministers of the gospel, or, indeed, of any class whose toil is that of the brain. The common understanding of the terms labor and laborers does not include preaching and preachers; and it is to be assumed that words and phrases are used in their ordinary meaning. So whatever of light is thrown upon the statute by the language of the title indicates an exclusion from its penal provisions of all contracts for the employment of ministers, rectors and pastors.[14]

The fact that Brewer relied on "common understanding," whereas Scalia relied on "ordinary meaning," really should make no difference. If anything, Brewer's ordinary-meaning argument is stronger than Scalia's because it is both linguistically awkward and uncommon to speak of a member of the clergy performing labor, where it is linguistically natural, although unusual in fact, to describe a person trading a gun for drugs to have used a gun in that transaction.

This is not to say that the two justices shared a judicial philosophy in any broader sense. Brewer really was trying to ascertain the intent of the legislature, both from the ordinary meaning of the terms used in the law and from circumstances surrounding the law's passage. Scalia, in contrast, although dissenting from the left, applied what he considered to be a standard methodology in the science of statutory interpretation, largely for its own sake.

Yet Scalia took a risk in eschewing so much extrinsic evidence of legislative intent in favor of a much narrower concept of relevant evidence. What would happen if the extrinsic evidence really did suggest that the better reading of the statute was one in which some meaning other than the ordinary one appeared to reflect the legislators' goal? The answer to this question is that Scalia generally stuck to his guns and advocated the result that his brand of formalism found.

Consider *Chisom v. Roemer*,[15] a 1991 case in which Justice Scalia dissented. Section 2 of the Voting Rights Act of 1965 outlawed voting schemes that led to the systematic inability to elect minority candidates even in voting districts in which a minority population predominated. The Act bars voting schemes in which minority voters "have less opportunity than other members of the electorate to participate in the process *and* to elect *representatives* of their choice." The word *representatives* was added as part of a 1982 amendment that expanded the Act by eliminating the requirement that a violation required an intention to disadvantage minority voters.

The original language of Section 2 read as follows: "No voting qualification or prerequisite to voting, or standard, practice, or procedure shall be imposed or applied by any State or political subdivision *to deny or abridge* the right of any citizen of the United States to vote on account of race or color." The amendment expanded the statute by changing *to results in.* "No voting qualification or prerequisite to voting or standard, practice, or procedure shall be imposed or applied by any State or political subdivision *in a manner which results in a denial or abridgement* of the right of any citizen of the United States to vote on account of race or color."[16] The original statute required proof of discriminatory intent, whereas the amended version did not. The amendment was triggered by congressional disapproval of the Supreme Court's narrow interpretation of the Act in earlier decisions.

Chisom concerned the Louisiana system for electing state supreme court justices. The case made its way to the Supreme Court, where the issue was whether the Voting Rights Act applied to judicial elections, because justices are typically not considered to be "representatives." A majority in the U.S. Supreme Court held that the Voting Rights Act must be applied to judicial elections as well as to legislative elections. Its application in that realm had been uncontroversial prior to the 1982 amendment to the Act. The majority reasoned that it would make little sense to infer that Congress intended to narrow the reach of the Act in such a way as to create a safe harbor for racist schemes in judicial elections as part of a statutory amendment that expanded the reach of the Voting Rights Act to include districting that was not intended to disadvantage minority candidates.

Moreover, the introduction of "representatives" into the amendment was a paraphrase of two statements by Justice White in *White v. Regester,*[17] in which White wrote of the election of "legislators." It is not easy to explain why Congress would replace "legislators" with "representatives" unless it intended to convey a more expansive set of elected officials to whom the Voting Rights Act would apply. In addition, the majority concluded, the broader interpretation of the statute is far more consistent with the law's purpose than would be a narrow one that exempted the election of judges.

Justice Scalia pushed back hard in his dissenting opinion, written on behalf of himself and two other justices. He focused on the ordinary meaning of the words in the statute: "I thought we had adopted a regular method for interpreting the meaning of language in a statute: first, find the ordinary meaning of the language in its textual context; and second, using established canons of construction, ask whether there is any clear indication that some permissible meaning other than the ordinary one applies. If not—and especially if a good reason for the ordinary meaning appears plain—we apply that ordinary meaning."[18] Scalia continued:

Today, however, the Court adopts a method quite out of accord with that usual practice. It begins not with what the statute says, but with an expectation about what the statute must mean absent particular phenomena ("we are convinced that, if Congress had . . . an intent [to exclude judges], Congress would have made it explicit in the statute, or at least some of the Members would have identified or mentioned it at some point in the unusually extensive legislative history," ante at 501 U. S. 396 [emphasis added]); and the Court then interprets the words of the statute to fulfill its expectation. . . . Our job begins with a text that Congress has passed and the President has signed. We are to read the words of that text as any ordinary Member of Congress would have read them, and apply the meaning so determined. In my view, that reading reveals that § 2 extends to vote dilution claims for the elections of representatives only, and judges are not representatives.[19]

Much has been written about Scalia's hostility toward introducing legislative history as evidence of legislative intent (e.g., Eskridge 1990; Nourse 2012; Siegel 2000). His position in *Chisom*, however, goes further. The problem is not just a matter of legislative history, but extends to all kinds of individualized inquiry into the context in which the law was enacted, all of which undermine the enterprise of objectifying statutory interpretation.

Ordinary Meaning as a Window into Legislative Intent

A second rhetorical strategy in Justice Scalia's body of work was that legislative intent is indeed relevant, but that the ordinary sense of the words used in a statute, combined with a limited number of interpretive rules of thumb, constitute the only evidence needed to determine that intent. This approach is consistent with research from the linguistic, psychological, and philosophical communities (Slocum 2015; Solan 2010; Winter 2003) in that it is likely to reflect the ways in which people conceptualize. For one thing, it is consistent with prototype theory in the realm of lexical semantics. Beginning with the important work of Berkeley psychologist Eleanor Rosch (1975), theorists have recognized that people not only know the conditions under which a concept obtains, but they also have a sense of how good a fit there is between a concept and a thing or event in the world. The more prototypical, the better the fit. The precise status of prototypes in our psychology remains a matter of significant debate. Are prototypes a matter of central tendency, or a matter of having the strongest constellation of essential features?[20] Do we use prototypes in determining category membership or merely in making goodness-of-fit judgments? By the same token, the ordinary-meaning approach to statutory interpretation is consistent with Grice's (1975) cooperative principle. People communicate with the goal of having others understand them. While there is room for debate in the legislative context about how well that assumption holds, it seems fair enough, at least as a default, to assume that it applies, at least to some extent.

Similarly, legal analysts are not in accord about what makes ordinary meaning ordinary (see Lee and Mouritsen 2018), but they are in accord that ordinary meaning plays an important role in how well our experiences fit into the conceptual frameworks that we have already committed to and that are reflected in the words we use. For this reason, it makes sense to project a relationship between ordinary meaning and legislative intent.

As for Scalia's espousing this perspective, consider *Morales v. TWA*,[21] a 1992 case in which Scalia wrote the opinion for a unanimous court. The issue there was whether the Airline Deregulation Act preempted state consumer protection law concerning deceptive advertising by airlines. Scalia introduced the issue in the case: "The question, at bottom, is one of statutory intent, and we accordingly "begin with the language employed by Congress and the assumption that the ordinary meaning of that language accurately expresses the legislative purpose." The law preempted states from "enact[ing] or enforc-[ing] any law, rule, regulation, standard, or other provision having the force and effect of law relating to rates, routes, or services of any air carrier."[22] The issue was whether a state (Texas) prohibition against deceptive advertising in airline fares should count as "relating to" the various categories of covered activities. The Supreme Court answered affirmatively in its unanimous decision.

I raise this case here because it reflects a somewhat different rhetoric by Justice Scalia. In this (and many other cases, as well as in his later scholarly writings), he puts legislative intent and, in some instances, legislative purpose front and center, while continuing to limit evidence of the legislative state of mind largely to the language of the statute itself (see, e.g., Scalia and Garner 2012).

Over time, Scalia wrote many opinions in which he referred to the actual intent of the enacting legislature as evidenced by the language it used. This is a very natural inference to draw. Psychologists have shown that we develop theories of the minds of those with whom we interact from a very young age (see, e.g., Bloom 2000). Scalia did not always speak of "intent" in his opinions. Yet he used many state-of-mind verbs that are used to express various notions of communicative intent. Below are some examples:

> When, *Chevron* said, Congress leaves an ambiguity in a statute that is to be administered by an executive agency, it is presumed that Congress meant to give

the agency discretion, within the limits of reasonable interpretation, of how the ambiguity is to be resolved.[23]

Given the language here, I find it much more plausible that Congress meant to reach—as it said—the carjacker who intended to kill.[24]

Absent a clear statutory requirement to the contrary, we must assume the validity of this state-law regulatory background and take due account of its effect. "The existence and force and function of established institutions of local government are always in the consciousness of lawmakers and, while their weight may vary, they may never be completely overlooked in the task of interpretation."[25]

These are not statements of an anti-intentionalist, whether or not Scalia regarded himself as such. Rather, they are statements of a theorist who regards intent as central to interpretation but believes that evidentiary rules should restrict the means by which the legal system infers intent. This is quite different from the formalist stand in which intent and purpose are regarded as being at odds with the actual legislative process.

Finally, while I have pitted Scalia's support of formalism for its own sake against his efforts to find the best evidence of legislative intent, he sometimes resorted to both arguments in the same case. Perhaps the most dramatic example is his dissenting opinion in *King v. Burwell*,[26] the Obamacare case decided in 2015, only about six months before Scalia's death. The Affordable Care Act required people to purchase health insurance, but also provided subsidies for those who could not afford insurance without spending too large a proportion of their annual income. In one provision of the statute, these subsidies are to be made available to those who purchase insurance over an exchange "established by a State." However, not all of the states established such exchanges. For those that did not, the law provided for the federal government to establish an exchange on behalf of that state. Mr. King, a citizen of Virginia, would not have met the income threshold for having to purchase insurance, absent the subsidy. Virginia did not establish its own exchange, relying instead on the federal government to establish an exchange in Virginia. King argued that he was not entitled to the subsidy, and would therefore not have to purchase the insurance.

I will not detail the argument that Chief Justice Roberts set forth on behalf of a majority of six. However, its main force was that, in a long and complicated statute, the structure of the law made it clear that Congress intended the subsidies to be available both to people living in states that established their own exchanges and in states in which the federal government set up an exchange on the state's behalf.

Scalia dissented on two different grounds. First, there are principles of statutory interpretation, and the majority disobeyed them:

> Words no longer have meaning if an Exchange that is not established by a State is "established by the State." It is hard to come up with a clearer way to limit tax credits to state Exchanges than to use the words "established by the State." And it is hard to come up with a reason to include the words "by the State" other than the purpose of limiting credits to state Exchanges. "[T]he plain, obvious, and rational meaning of a statute is always to be preferred to any curious, narrow, hidden sense that nothing but the exigency of a hard case and the ingenuity and study of an acute and powerful intellect would discover." [citation omitted]. Under all the usual rules of interpretation, in short, the Government should lose this case. But normal rules of interpretation seem always to yield to the overriding principle of the present Court: The Affordable Care Act must be saved.[27]

But Scalia did not stop there. He also argued that the actual intent of the lawmakers was inconsistent with the majority's opinion: "Any effort to understand rather than to rewrite a law must accept and apply the presumption that lawmakers use words in 'their natural and ordinary signification.'"[28] The difficult question is how defeasible this presumption is. To Scalia, not very. To others, it is easier to override the presumption based on specific evidence of actual intent. Scalia, instead, regarded the defeasibility as requiring a high burden when the proposed meaning strays too far from the prototype: "Ordinary connotation does not always prevail, but the more unnatural the proposed interpretation of a law, the more compelling the contextual evidence must be to show that it is correct." I have not found precedent for this sliding scale approach to the interpretation of statutes.

Conflicting Rhetoric about Coherence

Ordinary meaning was not the only means for construing statutes, according to Scalia. A second important consideration was coherence. Many legal scholars, including those at odds with Scalia's textualist approach, have also taken the position that coherence is one of the hallmarks of the rule of law (Dworkin 1986; Eskridge 2016; Shapiro 2014).

Scalia also gave two reasons for wanting to construe laws as being internally coherent, and even consistent with remote parts of the code (sometimes called the whole-act rule and whole-code rule, respectively). The first is that the rule of law will operate better if judges construe laws so as to make them fit together well. It has nothing to do with legislative intent, as Scalia made clear in *West Virginia University Hospitals, Inc. v. Casey*, a 1991 U.S. Supreme Court case. Justice Scalia, writing for the majority: "Where a statutory term presented to us for the first time is ambiguous, we construe it to contain that permissible meaning which fits most logically and comfortably into the body of both previously and subsequently enacted law. We do so not because that precise accommodative meaning is what the lawmakers must have had in mind (how could an earlier Congress know what a later Congress would enact?), but because it is our role to make sense rather than nonsense out of the *corpus juris*."[29] The issue in that case was whether a civil rights statute that permitted successful litigants against a state to recover "a reasonable attorney's fee" in addition to other damages should be construed to permit plaintiffs to recoup fees paid for expert witness services as part of those fees, or whether expert fees were a separate matter. Having scoured the United States Code for helpful analogies, Scalia found a number of fee-shifting laws that mentioned both attorney's fees and expert costs. He reasoned that if Congress had wanted the cost of experts to be reimbursable, it would have said so.

Yet the quotation above suggests that Scalia was less concerned about inferring legislative intent with respect to expert fees than he was concerned with making the law operate as sensibly as it could be made to do so. It is a basic rule-of-law value that like situations should be treated alike, and when a statute leaves doubt, judges will be advancing the rule of law if they operate according to that value when the language permits. Such a perspective sounds more like Ronald Dworkin than like Antonin Scalia.

Without question, the language gave the court leeway to do so in this instance. "Attorney's fee" can be used to convey the money the attorney has earned by providing services, or the amount reflected in the lawyer's bill, which may include all kinds of disbursements in addition to charging for the attorney's own work. Scalia, on behalf of the majority, resolved this indeterminacy in favor of a narrower reading in order to make the statute cohere with a reasonable inference that Congress itself had divided the law into those that include the reimbursement of expert fees and those that do not by the way it worded the two types of statute.

But the situation was a little more difficult than that. The law that the Court was interpreting had recently been enacted by Congress to override a Supreme Court decision that had barred the awarding of attorney's fees generally in civil rights cases because the statute did not specify that such fees were recoverable. Moreover, prior to that earlier decision, as the dissenting opinion of Justice Stevens recounted, courts had been awarding attorney's fees in civil rights cases under what they had believed to be their equitable power to do so. Let us assume that both sides were right in what they said: Congress frequently (but not always) refers specifically to expert fees when it intends for them to be reimbursable but did not do so here; and at the same time, Congress probably had no intention of reducing the recovery that could be realized by successful civil rights litigants when it enacted the fee-shifting provision. Congress itself resolved this issue; very soon after *West Virginia University Hospitals* was decided, Congress amended the statute to override this decision as well, clarifying that expert fees were to be recoverable.

In some instances, Scalia engaged an intentionalist defense of coherence. Let us return to his concurring opinion in *Green v. Bock Laundry Machine Co., Inc.* There, he deemed the presumption that Congress "always has in mind" coherence to be a "benign fiction."

The analysis invites inquiry: Just how benign is the fiction that Congress always has in mind the meaning "most compatible with the surrounding body of law into which the provision must be integrated?"[30] It is benign if it turns out to be true—and not a fiction at all. It is also relatively benign if members of Congress do not have this compatibility in mind, but if you asked them, they would agree that they should, and in some other way aspire to simulate the results of such a state of mind. But it is not benign—rather it is perni-cious—if the legislators not only do not have this in mind, but their minds are at least in some cases in a state inconsistent with this fiction. That would be the case if the complexities of the legislative process prevent legislators from considering such things even if they might think it a good value to have in principle.

Work by scholars such as Gluck and Bressman (2013), Nourse (2011) and Nourse and Schachter (2002) has shown through empirical studies that infer-ences that courts make about congressional intent based on various canons of construction do not always match the actual mindset of the statutory draft-ers. Assumptions about how people use language—legislators in particular—undergird many of these principles of interpretation. Yet this recent empirical work has shown a gap between the judicial assumptions about linguistic prin-ciples that legislators have in mind and the reality of what they have in mind.

Conclusion

Justice Scalia's rhetoric reveals that he was not of a single mind when it came to the interpretation of statutes. A purely formalist thread and an evidence-restricted intentionalist thread both run through his body of work. I am per-sonally more comfortable with the latter. Whatever one's personal philosophy, my goal has been to show that Justice Scalia wrote with a somewhat more complex set of legal values and linguistic presumptions than is often recognized.

References

Armstrong, Sharon L., Lilia R. Gleitman, and Henry Gleitman. 1983. "What Some Concepts Might Not Be." *Cognition* 13:263–308.

Bloom, Paul. 2000. *How Children Learn the Meanings of Words*. Cambridge, MA: MIT Press.

Dworkin, Ronald. 1986. *Law's Empire*. Cambridge, MA: Harvard University Press.

Eskridge, William N. 1990. "The New Textualism." *UCLA Law Review* 37:621–91.

———. 2016. *Interpreting Law: A Primer on How to Read Statutes and the Constitution*. St. Paul, MN: West Academic.

Fodor, Jerry, and Ernest Lepore. 1996. "The Red Herring and the Pet Fish: Why Concepts Still Can't Be Prototypes." *Cognition* 58:253–70.

Gluck, Abbe R., and Lisa Schultz Bressman. 2013. "Statutory Interpretation from the Inside—an Empirical Study of Congressional Drafting, Delegation, and the Canons: Part I." *Stanford Law Review* 65:901–1025.

Grice, H. P. 1975. "Logic and Conversation." In *Syntax and Semantics*, vol. 3, *Speech Acts*, edited by Peter Cole and Jerry L. Morgan, 41–58. New York: Academic Press.

Holmes, Oliver Wendell. 1899. "The Theory of Legal Interpretation." *Harvard Law Review* 12: 417–20.

Kamp, Hans, and Barbara Partee. 1995. "Prototype Theory and Compositionality." *Cognition* 57: 129–91.

Lee, Thomas R., and Stephen C. Mouritsen. 2018. "Judging Ordinary Meaning." *Yale Law Journal* 127:788–879.

Lynch, Elizabeth B., John D. Coley, and Douglas L. Medin. 2000. "Tall Is Typical: Central Tendency, Ideal Dimensions, and Graded Category Structure among Tree Experts and Novices." *Memory and Cognition* 28:41–50.

Nourse, Victoria. 2011. "Misunderstanding Congress: Statutory Interpretation, the Supermajoritarian Difficulty, and the Separation of Powers." *Georgetown Law Journal* 99:1119–77.

———. 2012. "A Decision Theory of Statutory Interpretation: Legislative History by the Rules." *Yale Law Journal* 122:70–152.

———, and Jane Schachter. 2002. "The Politics of Legislative Drafting: A Congressional Case Study." *New York University Law Review* 77:575–624.

Prinz, Jesse. 2004. Furnishing the Mind: Concepts and Their Perceptual Basis. Cambridge, MA: MIT Press.

Rosch, Eleanor. 1975. "Cognitive Representations of Semantic Categories." *Journal of Experimental Psychology: General* 104, no. 3, 192–233.

Scalia, Antonin. 1998. *A Matter of Interpretation*. Princeton, NJ: Princeton University Press.

———, and Bryan Garner. 2012. *Reading Law: The Interpretation of Legal Texts*. St. Paul, MN: Thomson/West.

Shapiro, Scott. 2014. *Legality*. Cambridge, MA: Harvard University Press.

Siegel, Jonathan R. 2000. "The Use of Legislative History in a System of Separated Powers." *Vanderbilt Law Review* 53:1457–1538.

Slocum, Brian G. 2015. Ordinary Meaning: A Theory of the Most Fundamental Principle of Legal
    Interpretation. Chicago: University of Chicago Press.
Solan, Lawrence M. 2010. The Language of Statutes. Chicago: University of Chicago Press.
———, and David Louk. Forthcoming. "The Pet Fish Problem in Legal Interpretation."
Solum, Lawrence. 2015. "The Fixation Thesis: The Role of Historical Fact in Original Meaning."
    Notre Dame Law Review 91:1–78.
Stein, Alexander. 2017. "The Domain of Torts." Columbia Law Review 117:535–611.
Winter, Steven L. 2003. A Clearing in the Forest: Life, Law, Mind. Chicago: University of Chi-
    cago Press.

6

Textualism without Formalism:
Justice Scalia's Statutory Interpretation Legacy

ABBE R. GLUCK

Of all the criticisms leveled against textualism, the most mindless is that it is "formalistic." The answer to that is, of course it's formalistic! The rule of law is about form. . . .
Long live formalism.

ANTONIN SCALIA

Justice Scalia's most enduring legacy is likely to be the method of statutory
interpretation—"textualism"—that he brought to the U.S. Supreme Court
and to all of the courts below it. With his three decades' worth of relentless
insistence on text-focused interpretation of statutes, Justice Scalia changed
the way judges of all interpretive stripes approach that task, the process in-
graining in the minds of many, for better or for worse, the notion that a pur-
pose- or pragmatism-driven approach to statutory cases was not consistent
with the judicial role. Underpinning this approach from the start was Justice
Scalia's proclaimed faith in formalism and that statutory interpretation was
amenable to it.

But in the end, Justice Scalia was no interpretive formalist. The rules of
statutory interpretation that he advanced are not predictable, or even fully
listable. The doctrines of the field that he entrenched are not treated as precedent—they do not control from case to case—or, really, as any kind of "law."
The result is that they have not created a stable law of methodology to bind
future litigants and courts (Gluck 2010). The doctrines do not even have a
clearly defined jurisprudential source, such that those who wish to add or
delete any rules know what legitimates them or who has the power to change
them (Gluck 2011). Even as Justice Scalia, more than anyone else, emphasized
the importance of formalism in statutory interpretation, he either never really
wanted it to succeed or did not fully appreciate its implications. What would it
take to make statutory interpretation truly formalist? Why did Justice Scalia's
vision fall short?

Justice Scalia Created a Field, but
That Does Not Make It Formalist

First things first. No one had a more important impact on the modern theory and practice of statutory interpretation than did Justice Scalia. He, more than any other, made legislation/statutory interpretation a field. A big part of that contribution stems from Justice Scalia's stated belief in the applicability of legal formalism to that project. He foresaw the rising, now completely dominant, number of statutory cases on the federal docket. He thought that serious legal doctrines could, and should, be applied to those cases. And he elevated, entrenched—and in many cases, even created—those legal doctrines themselves.

The magnitude of Justice Scalia's contribution is captured beautifully in a 1992 article by the late Philip Frickey, another giant in the field and one who did not share Justice Scalia's interpretive philosophy. The article, titled "From the Big Sleep to the Big Heat: The Revival of Theory in Statutory Interpretation" (1992), details how, as late as the early 1980s, even as lawyers were flooded with statutory cases in litigation, they had little help from theorists, judges, or academics on how to frame arguments and what principles to apply. Statutory interpretation was not a field viewed as intellectually vibrant; doctrines were not centralized or easily accessible in a single place; it was not taught in law schools.

Justice Scalia, as Professor Frickey put it, brought the heat. Recognizing also the foundational roles of other esteemed law professors–turned–jurists like Frank Easterbrook and Richard Posner, who brought the Chicago School's public-choice theory to bear on the field and "provided much of the initial intellectual agenda for the revival of theory in statutory interpretation," Justice Scalia "contributed most of the fireworks." Frickey wrote, "[I]n Scalia, the so-called 'new textualism' found the right person—brilliant, bold, and nothing if not persistent—at the right place (the Supreme Court), at the right time" (Frickey 1992, 254–55).

What Justice Scalia did was much more than merely diminish the credibility of legislative history and focus everyone on statutory text (and he certainly did both of those things). He brought *doctrine* to the field. It is not the case that judges were not looking at text or not thinking about the rule of lenity and such in statutory cases before Justice Scalia, but it is the case that Justice Scalia recast all of those varied interpretive presumptions into the collected rules of the field—doctrines that every good lawyer must now brief and cite in litigation. These presumptions, the so-called "canons of construction" are now taught in most American law schools—many of them in the Holy Grail of legal education: the mandatory first-year curriculum.

Justice Scalia transformed these presumptions into the field's doctrines by hammering them home in case after case. He realized—after naively first introducing textualism in an essay that actually rejected the policy-based interpretive presumptions (Scalia 1997)—that even textualist judges need somewhere to turn when text provides no single answer. Justice Scalia rigorously insisted that the canons—both those based on language (e.g., the presumption that Congress does not use redundant language) and those based on policy (e.g., the presumption against preemption of state law)—were more legitimate rules of decision than legislative history, statutory purpose, or other materials. Several of the most important canons were actually created on his watch, including the federalism canon; the "no elephants in mouse holes" rule (presume Congress does not bury major policy changes); the major questions rule (presume Congress does not delegate major questions to agencies); and the modern-day version of the presumption against extraterritorial application of statutes—indeed, the latter three were Scalia's own creations.[1] His last book, a treatise written with Professor Bryan Garner (Scalia and Garner 2012), catalogs some seventy canons and advocates for more than fifty of them.

These presumptions frame the debate in every modern case, and are used today by all judges—liberal, conservative, purposivist, textualist, and pragmatic alike. Indeed, Justice Elena Kagan—who graduated law school in 1986, during textualism's early ascendance—recently announced that Justice Scalia "changed the way everybody does statutory interpretation" (Kagan 2016 at 20: 14) and that "we are all textualists now" (Kagan 2015, at 8:28).

This is a contribution that cannot be overstated. In defining a new battlefield and establishing the possible array of weapons from among which to choose, Justice Scalia did establish a new way of practicing statutory interpretation. That is field creation to be sure, and it certainly made statutory interpretation more predictable in a number of ways, in particular by establishing a common language for lawyers and judges to use. But it does not make the field *formalist*.

And yet the core of Justice Scalia's textualism, as he himself presented it, was supposed to be formalism. Justice Scalia's aim was to bring rules, objectivity, and a disciplined approach to statutory cases. He famously proclaimed in his seminal piece that introduced textualism: "*[O]f course it's formalistic! The rule of law is about form. . . . Long live formalism*" (Scalia 1997, 25). One of his most famous essays, "The Rule of Law as a Law of Rules," emphasized that "[p]redictability, or as Llewellyn put it, 'reckonability,' is a needful characteristic of any law worthy of the name. There are times when even a bad rule is better than no rule at all" (Scalia 1989, 1179).

But formalism's fate would not have been any different even if Justice

Scalia had lived another twenty years. The reason? As the rest of this chapter illustrates, the justice himself was never completely committed to interpretive formalism for statutes in the first place.

Consider this challenge: think of any other field of law in which we do not know what the rules are, what legitimates them, where they come from, and who has the power to change them. Think of any other field of law in which federal judges insist that *no one*—not Congress, not the Court—can control the doctrines that apply (Gluck 2011). Think of any other field of law that occupies the majority of the federal docket yet whose fundamental mission remains so unclear. Justice Scalia woke the field from slumber but did not fully theorize its path. Formalism could not possibly succeed without addressing these issues. And this is the project for the post-Scalia era, formalist or not.

Why Statutory Interpretation Is Not Formalist

Even as practiced by Justice Scalia himself, statutory interpretation has never been fully formalist. By advocating consistent interpretive rules, formalism seeks to realize "rule-of-law values" such as transparency, predictability, and objectivity in the law. We have not gotten there in statutory interpretation, and we likely never will. Quite simply, as my previous work details, federal judges do not seem to actually desire the consequences that follow from a truly doctrinalized statutory interpretation regime (Gluck 2011; Gluck and Posner 2018).[2]

Consider the consequences that judges find distasteful. A landscape of defined and binding rules for statutory interpretation would reduce decision-making flexibility. Understanding the field's doctrines as ordinary legal rules ("common law") also would open the door to superior judges or—worse, in the eyes of many judges—other branches of government controlling a judge's interpretive approach. That is because Congress can legislate to override common law, and superior judges also can bind lower judges with respect to it.

Such a rule-based regime would also demand some jurisprudential clarity. It would either require federal judges to admit they are creating federal common law when they create interpretive rules—an admission formalists abjure because most formalists discourage any kind of judicial lawmaking as activist—or else it would force them to identify the canons as coming from some nonjudicial source, most likely Congress, which most judges do not want to do either, because they do not want to give Congress control. Even accounting for any judges who would adopt a formalist interpretive approach if the Supreme Court adopted one—a number my recent research suggests is not as high as one might assume—the justices themselves may be the most averse of all to formalism's consequences. The Supreme Court has never treated the rules of interpretation as precedential, subject to congressional control, or even admitted that the Court itself has created many of them.

THERE ARE TOO MANY RULES, AND WE DO NOT AGREE ON WHAT THEY ARE

First, there are too many available rules for statutory interpretation to be formalist. There are more than *one hundred* interpretive presumptions. It is worth noting here that Justice Scalia's interest in formalism was in part motivated by his distaste of "totality of the circumstances" inquiries, or multifactor balancing tests. He argued that such inquiries confer too much discretion on judges, destroying predictability and uniformity, and encouraging arbitrary decision-making. His most important statutory interpretation article, "Common-Law Courts in a Civil-Law System," likewise called the many presumptions of interpretation "a lot of trouble," because "it is virtually impossible to expect uniformity and objectivity when there is added, on one or the other side of the balance, a thumb of indeterminate weight" (Scalia 1997, 28).

Nevertheless, statutory interpretation, as Scalia himself developed it, now more closely resembles a multifactor test than a formalist regime. A field with more than one hundred potentially applicable doctrines, with no order ranking those doctrines and no clear rule about when individual doctrines are triggered and in what order they are triggered, effectuates an intense methodological pluralism. It is not for nostalgic reasons that Karl remains, even post-Scalia, one of the most common citations in the field for his infamous exposition that for every canon there is another applicable canon to counteract it (Llewellyn 1950, 401–6).

That there is no ranking or ordering among the canons is well-established. When two textual canons compete head-to-head, for instance, there is no hierarchy to solve an impasse. It remains unanswered whether a policy canon is still relevant if legislative history alone would clarify statutory language.[3] There is still no agreement about whether even very strong policy rules, like lenity, are opening presumptions to overcome or, rather, tiebreakers at the end after all sources are considered.[4]

The triggers for the rules themselves also are unclear. Does one need ambiguity to invoke a canon of interpretation? Over his last two terms on the bench, Justice Scalia wrote several opinions protesting the Court's answers to that question.[5] Even when we do understand ambiguity to be a doctrinal trigger in statutory interpretation, we have no cabined, objective, or predictable definition of ambiguity in the first place—a point recently made by

Judge Brett Kavanaugh, the most well-known conservative jurist on the Federal Courts of Appeals (Kavanaugh 2014). This absence of precision makes the inquiry decidedly nonformalist, and even discretion-enabling.

The point is not to pose a critique of the state of affairs. Rather, the point is simply to illustrate not only that formalism has not succeeded in statutory interpretation, but also that, in fact, Justice Scalia never really tried to achieve it. Understanding these shortcomings is essential because textualists, as did Justice Scalia, lean heavily on textualism's purported formalism to argue for textualism's normative superiority compared to other interpretive methodologies. They also cling to formalism as the justification for why it is acceptable to forgo an interpretive approach that is more tethered to the way Congress actually operates and drafts. The justification is that congressional reality is impossible to decipher, and so we trade off the value of that democratic connection to Congress in exchange for the "rule-of-law" values and the benefits that a formalist regime brings (Scalia 1997). Justice Scalia's textualism has brought benefits, but not those benefits. We need to recognize this fact to move past these kinds of arguments.

JUDGES DO NOT TREAT INTERPRETIVE RULES AS REAL LAW

The second type of evidence of the absence of complete formalism in statutory interpretation is the enduring and mystifying ambiguity of the legal status of its methodology. The doctrines of the field—the presumptions and other tools that are applied as methodological decision-making rules—do not receive stare decisis effect. In other words, the use of the federalism canon, or the rule against superfluities, or a piece of legislative history in one case does not require it to be used in the next case, even where the same statute is being construed. So, too, a vote of 8-to-1 by the Court about the utility or lack thereof of an interpretive tool does not bind the Court in any subsequent case. Nor do the federal courts even view interpretive methodology as a "rule of decision" subject to the famous *Erie* doctrine—which requires federal courts to apply state "law" to state legal questions—and so they do not seek out state interpretive rules even in circumstances when they apply all other types of state law (Gluck 2011).

No other field's decision-making doctrines share these characteristics. Analogous interpretive rules, whether rules of contract interpretation, burden shifting, or other decision-making rules, all have a clear legal status. These other kinds of methodological rules are precedential and viewed as law. The absence of precedential effect alone might be fatal to a successful formalism, but even if it is not, some understanding of what the legal status of a field's rules are in the first place seems essential.

Nevertheless, statutory interpretation canons are actual decision rules. If there is any doubt, one need only scan the recent Supreme Court docket. Seemingly "common sense" or "intuitive" grammar canons, like the "last antecedent rule," have decided major cases involving personal liberty and Social Security rights over the past decade.[6] Policy canons have decided cases ranging from the reach of chemical weapons conventions to the extraterritorial application of the securities laws.[7] To say that these canons do not function as decision rules is to say that the entire way in which judges express the bases for their decisions in statutory cases is fraudulent cover for something else. Of course, the "real" process of judicial decision-making—what makes judges actually decide cases the way they do—is difficult to know, but the question of how much doctrine drives actual decision-making permeates every area of law, and that does not stop us from viewing the decision-making rules of other fields as legal doctrines. Why have formalists given statutory interpretation doctrines a pass?

As further evidence that Justice Scalia did not fully think through these implications, his treatise with Professor Garner styles many of his approved interpretive rules as applicable to "all legal texts" including contracts, wills, and statutes (Scalia and Garner 2012). But Justice Scalia, like everyone else, thought that contract interpretation rules were precedential. He also thought they were common-law rules, such that they could be decided by legislatures, whose views would overrule those of courts (just consider the Uniform Commercial Code if there is any doubt). And yet, when asked this question about statutory interpretation, he protested the idea of methodological stare decisis for statutory interpretation doctrine and explicitly posited that legislative mandating of statutory interpretation rules might be unconstitutional (Scalia and Garner 2012).

These are significant oversights. How to explain them? An important answer lies in the question of the stakes of, and also of the federal courts' interest in, safeguarding judicial power. The stakes for judges of being bound to a particular interpretive methodology in statutory cases are awfully high. Statutory cases generally implicate many more kinds of players—the public, Congress, agencies, states, and so forth—than contract cases. The courts may see themselves as having different kinds of roles in different kinds of statutory cases. A precedential interpretive approach that would command for all cases the same kind of methodology, the same emphasis on one particular kind of tool over another, may not fit with a judicial conception of role that differs across cases.

More concretely, the stakes for judicial power also seem too high for many judges. As noted, a formalist regime would mean the Supreme Court could (and should) dictate rules of interpretation to lower courts. That would make these rules common law. But, as noted, common-law rules also can be legislated by Congress. Case law, empirical work, and judicial writing all confirm that most judges (like Justice Scalia) have a visceral, highly negative reaction to such a proposition about congressional power (and even Supreme Court power) over statutory interpretation.

Federal judges in this context seem to have a unique, constitutional-law-level intuition that is not replicated elsewhere. Namely, they seem to believe that the choice of interpretive method is so inherent in each individual judge's power to adjudicate that it cannot be controlled by anything or anyone else. This view of statutory interpretation doctrine as inherently personal is not compatible with formalism. It also is an exceptional perspective on the Article III power that conceives of that power as individually held, rather than held as a unit by Article III judges all acting under the supervisory power of the Court and, sometimes, Congress.

This is not something we see in any other power derived from Article III. Even constitutional interpretation is regulated by doctrines. Lower courts do not dispute the Court's power to announce decision-making regimes, such as the tiers of scrutiny or the various First Amendment tests to bind the inferior federal courts. To be clear, the relevant comparison here is not to originalism or to a different, overarching constitutional theory. My point is not that formalism or the Constitution requires that textualism, purposivism, or any other overarching theory of interpretation should receive stare decisis effect or a firm legal status. My point is that the individual decision-making rules within all of these regimes—and indeed shared by all of these regimes—have a concrete legal status across all other areas of law, but not in statutory interpretation (Gluck 2011). Justice Scalia was never willing to engage with this puzzle.

FORMALISM REQUIRES A SOVEREIGN SOURCE OF LAW

Where do canons and presumptions come from? No one needs to be reminded that most federal judges generally do not believe they have free-floating federal lawmaking power, and interpretive formalists certainly also ascribe to that position. Justice Scalia himself took a very stingy view of the federal courts' federal lawmaking power. He, like most formalists, believed that law must be linked to a sovereign source. That is one key holding of the famous *Erie* case.

It seems incontrovertible, however, that many of the canons come from judges. Virtually every policy or constitutionally inspired canon was created in the federal courts. The notions that judges should look to dictionaries, or legislative history, or agency deference as tools of interpretation were also originated by federal judges. The grammar/Latin canons are more complex. Some of these canons, including *ejusdem generis* (construe general term in list consistent with more specific terms that precede it) and *inclusio unius* (presume inclusion/exclusion of one term means intentional exclusion/inclusion of others), appear to have been used since late sixteenth- or early seventeenth-century England, and they make their first appearances in federal court opinions in the early nineteenth century.

But even if Latin canons preexisted our federal courts, it was our federal courts that adopted them and put them into service in everyday statutory cases. That act of adoption is itself an act of federal common lawmaking, just as it is when federal courts adopt state statutes of limitations or other jurisdictions' rules as rules of decision in the federal courts. Just because rules have an old pedigree does not make them "general," omnipresent, or intangible law (which the Supreme Court regardless held in *Erie* was no longer a legitimate source of law). Once they are adopted by the federal courts for use in federal cases, these rules are federal common law, like anything else, and so they require a federal sovereign source.

That formalists generally do insist outside of this context that every legal doctrine has an ascertainable, legitimate source is clear in recent debates in the international-law arena, in which scholars have debated whether certain international-law norms are illegitimate if they do not have a source in U.S. law. Judge Kavanaugh considered this debate in a high-profile 2010 case, concurring to note the potential conflict between *Erie* and the use of such external policy norms in statutory interpretation: "[I]n the post-*Erie* era, the canon does not permit courts to alter their interpretation of federal statutes based on international-law norms that have not been incorporated into domestic U.S. law. . . . *Erie* means that, in our constitutional system of separated powers, federal courts may not enforce law that lacks a domestic sovereign source."[8] The opinion goes on to argue that it is Congress, and not the courts, that must serve as the "domestic sovereign source" of legal principles, including those that would incorporate such external norms into domestic law.

Justice Scalia was never willing to engage this question when it comes to statutory interpretation doctrines, and no other federal judges have publicly engaged with it either, outside of this international-law norm-context. In fact, when it comes to statutory interpretation, most judges think the opposite: namely, that legislatures cannot control interpretive methodology.

Justice Scalia once proclaimed that the question of whether Congress has the power to legislate interpretive rules was "academic" (Scalia and Garner 2012, 345). In fact, Congress has legislated thousands of interpretive rules across the U.S. Code, from definitions of statutory terms to presumptions of interpretation, like ERISA's famous preemption/savings clause.[9] The bigger question is whether, if Congress can do this—if Congress can create as law these presumptions of federal statutory interpretation—why can't the courts? Why can't the courts admit what they are doing? But either way—and this is really the point for purposes of this chapter—a developed, formalist theory of statutory interpretation would have grappled with these questions one way or the other.

This may be one explanation for a conspicuous omission in the Scalia/Garner treatise: the complete omission from the book of the dozens of policy and subject-matter presumptions that the Court routinely applies. Among these canons are well-known presumptions, including the presumption in favor of arbitration, the presumption against extraterritoriality, the presumption that exemptions to the tax code are narrowly construed, the presumption in favor of Native American rights, the presumption that ambiguities in bankruptcy law favor the debtor, the presumption against retroactivity, the presumption in favor of the common law, and dozens more.[10] These presumptions can be extremely powerful, and are often decisive in statutory cases. That Justice Scalia could author a treatise on the "approved canons" and not even mention these canons—presumptions that his own Court used often and, in many cases, he himself applied and in several cases even created[11]—is odd indeed. As noted, Justice Scalia's most important writing on statutory interpretation expressed discomfort with the policy canons. He called them "thumb on the scales" and "dice-loading" rules (Scalia 1997, 28). He was willing to use them nonetheless—because he had to, because text cannot answer every question. But he never appeared to develop a satisfactory theory of why, and that may explain why he did not address their validity in the treatise.

ACTIVISM IN THE RULES

Formalism requires rules that are defined and predictably applied, but it does not necessarily require the rules to be normatively neutral (if such a concept is even possible). A rule that says, "Whenever the outcome is in doubt, the government loses," would be formalist, even if embracing an obvious value preference.

This point is relevant here because Justice Scalia often insisted, as part of his formalist defense of textualism, that textualism's rules are value-neutral.

This is not accurate. Putting aside the policy canons, which are unquestionably normative in that they favor values like federalism, Native American rights, bankrupt debtors, arbitrators, and so on, textualism's linguistic and grammar canons also are based on inherent value judgments.

Justice Scalia pilloried purposivism and pragmatism for being "activist," for doing things to statutes that Congress did not, and for helping Congress when Congress's own drafting fell short. But textualism's text-based canons assume and impose a perfection and omniscience on Congress—consistency, lack of redundancy, fully inclusive lists, and so on—that empirical work shows Congress cannot come close to achieving and in many cases affirmatively does not even wish to achieve (Gluck and Bressman 2013). Making statutes consistent where Congress did not, or removing redundancies where Congress inserted them on purpose, is just as activist a judicial shaping of statutes outside of the legislative process as is imposing a pragmatist view.

There are good reasons why courts might legitimately take this approach—reasons traditionally favored by the legal system, including the value of public notice—but that does not make it a passive endeavor. Textualism muscles the U.S. Code in ways Congress did not, just as Justice Breyer shapes the Code with recourse to purpose, or Judge Posner shaped the code to advance pragmatic values. One can say, "Judges shall always consult purpose first," and that might be just as formalist, and have the same level of neutrality, as saying "Judges shall always read text to be consistent." The values are just different.

Two Illustrative Opinions and Justice Scalia's Legacy:
King and *Lockhart*

By way of conclusion, it is illustrative to consider two of the last statutory interpretation cases with Justice Scalia's imprint: *King v. Burwell*,[12] the 2015 statutory interpretation challenge to the Affordable Care Act (ACA), President Obama's health reform statute, and *Lockhart v. United States*,[13] a case about penalty enhancements in the Child Criminal Pornography Act. These cases offer some concrete examples both of Justice Scalia' remarkable legacy and also the gaps in his formalist vision.

KING: TEXTUALISM'S BIGGEST TEST

The specific question in *King* concerned the phrase "Exchange established by the State," in a provision about the calculation of health care subsidies essential to the ACA's ability to function. Read literally, that provision appeared to award those subsidies only to states that operated their own health insurance marketplaces ("exchanges") and not to the other half of the states, which had opted, as the ACA allowed, for the federal government to operate the exchanges for them. A literal reading of the text, virtually everyone agreed, would destroy the insurance markets in the federal-exchange states and take the ACA down.

The case was set up to be a text-and-canon battle of epic proportions: How would the Court's textualism handle four poorly drafted words in the two-thousand-page ACA that could not possibly carry their literal meaning without destroying the entire scheme? The briefing was a testament to Justice Scalia's impact. This was a case about a potential drafting error—four words that could not possibly mean what they said, in light of what the ACA was trying to do. But none of the briefing was willing to go to purpose, or legislative history (of which there was very little), or even to mention the realistic proposition that there may have been a drafting mistake. All of the briefing was textualist.

At the same time, however, *King* was a dangerous case for textualism. It was a self-conscious attempt by the ACA's opponents to use the Court's preference for this text-and-canon approach, with its associated reluctance to delve into legislative complexity, to make the Court a pawn in a game of rough politics. The case's architects sought, as they put it, to "exploit" the four isolated words to pull the statute apart by concentrating on "bits and pieces of the law," the instantiation of what Professor Thomas Merrill wrote in 1994 was the greatest risk to the then newly ascendant theory of textualism: converting the Court's role to answering a clever puzzle, masking in neutral-sounding interpretive presumptions a deeply unforgiving view of Congress (Gluck 2015).

Returning to Professor Frickey's article about textualism mentioned at the outset of this chapter, Frickey also highlighted one case as the tipping point that opened the door to textualism. That case was *United Steelworkers of America v. Weber*, in which the Court relied on an approach heavily driven by purpose and legislative history to interpret Title VII of the Civil Rights Act to permit affirmative action. For the many lawyers and judges who felt the Court went too far in *Weber*, textualism offered a course correction. When *King* was briefed, it seemed that *King* could be textualism's *Weber*, a case that showed the dangers of textualism without moderation, one that could embarrass its proponents and the Court, and possibly incite a change of methodology going forward.

But the Court did not take the bait. Instead, writing for the majority, Chief Justice Roberts delivered an opinion that was indeed "textualist" in the sense of eschewing purpose and focusing only on the words of the statute. But it also differed significantly from Justice Scalia's textualism, in its surprising lack of reliance on canons, in its insistence that the words must be read in the broader statutory context, not microscopically, and in its realistic approach to Congress's limitations.

King was a victory for Justice Scalia in an important sense, because the Court was conspicuous in its determination not to even whisper about "purpose" or legislative history. Chief Justice Roberts instead chose the concept of a "legislative plan"—the *written* words, as a whole, on the page—as the relevant context in which the four words had to be interpreted. When he wanted to produce proof of Congress's aims, he cited the enacted text—the statutory findings—rather than legislative history. It was a rational, forgiving reading of the statute, but it used many textualist tools.

But *King* also revealed textualism's weaknesses in several important ways, not least of which was the fact that the briefing was a Llewellynian nightmare of warring canons that proves the central thesis of this chapter: that textualism, as Justice Scalia advanced it, provides no more of a predictable or formalist way of deciding cases than does relying on other legislative materials. The fact that the Court did not rely on canons to decide the case seems related to this weakness; the Court was perhaps concerned that deciding such a big question by picking one of many available and conflicting canons might have appeared to be a cop-out, or even illegitimate.

The case also underscored like no other the dangers of textualism's vastly oversimplified vision of Congress. The Chief Justice's response to those dangers instead pushed aside textualism's assumption that Congress drafts perfectly and omnisciently, detailed the messiness of ACA's enactment, but nevertheless assumed that Congress drafts rationally, and concluded the Court must "do [its] best."[14]

LOCKHART: A VICTORY FOR TEXTUALISM AND ITS "ABSENCE OF METHOD"

After *King*, the future of Justice Scalia's textualism seemed unclear. Was *King* a special case for a special statute, or did it signal that a portion of the Court was interested in moving away, at least to some extent, from textualism's vision?

Lockhart dispelled those questions. That case, with dueling opinions written by Justices Sotomayor and Kagan—by no means the Court's staunchest textualists—was Justice Scalia all the way through, The case concerned penalty enhancements in the Child Pornography Prevention Act of 1995 that were applicable to those with a prior state conviction "relating to aggravated sexual abuse, sexual abuse, or abusive sexual conduct involving a minor or ward." The question was whether the limitation "involving a minor or ward" applied only to the last item on the list or to all of the items.

The Court decided a man's criminal sentence based on two grammatical canons that it is virtually assured Congress never considered when drafting. It was "Scalia and Garner 101." The majority, per Justice Sotomayor, applied what she called a "timeworn textual canon," the so-called "last antecedent rule," which presumes that a modifier at the end of a series only applies to the last antecedent.[15] The dissent, per Justice Kagan, would have had the case turn on the "series-qualifier canon," a rarely applied presumption that "a modifier at the end of the list 'normally applies to the entire series.'"[16] Each justice cited the Scalia/Garner treatise's "approved canons" to justify her respective choice. Justice Scalia died shortly before the case was decided, but he was active in oral argument. His position is clearly expressed in Justice Kagan's dissent, and his method is just as clearly present in Justice Sotomayor's majority.

As a matter of legitimacy, even for textualist-formalists, why would those two grammar canons be the methodologies that framed the debate in the case? Neither canon is normatively superior to the other, nor is there any way to predict which one would have applied. There exists no hierarchy or decision rule to choose between them (something Justice Scalia himself acknowledged at oral argument, and so suggested a third canon—lenity—as tiebreaker). Judge Easterbrook likewise identifies *Lockhart* as an example of how textualism suffers from what he calls an "absence of method" (Easterbrook 2017, 81, 85). As the first case decided after Justice Scalia's death, *Lockhart* evinces the justice's enormous and enduring influence across the entire federal bench. Indeed, then-Judge Gorsuch praised *Lockhart* and stated that "it would be hard to imagine a more fitting tribute" to Justice Scalia than these "dueling textualist opinions" (Gorsuch 2016, 907–8).

Textualism, as Scalia practiced it, endures. The question is what comes next.

Conclusion

Justice Scalia created the field of modern statutory interpretation, but he, like the textualism he entrenched across the U.S. courts, was not ever really formalist. There are too many rules; the rules lack predictable means of application; they lack a clear legal status or even a defined source; and they are as activist as pragmatism and purposivism, albeit in a different way. Many of these gaps, at least for Justice Scalia, seem left by design, or at least in an effort to avoid the difficult questions of lawmaking power of the federal courts in the modern statutory era.

But make no mistake: Justice Scalia deserves the credit for ushering in the law of that era, indeed for insisting there should be a law for our statutory age. For that, he will always be a giant in the field. But it is now time to clarify exactly what this field is about and what jurisprudential theory and source of law legitimates it. Formalists would expect no less.

References

Easterbrook, Frank H. 2017. "The Absence of Method in Statutory Interpretation." *University of Chicago Law Review* 84:81–97.

Frickey, Philip P. 1992. "From the Big Sleep to the Big Heat: The Revival of Theory in Statutory Interpretation." *Minnesota Law Review* 77:241–67.

Gluck, Abbe R. 2010. "The States as Laboratories of Statutory Interpretation: Methodological Consensus and the New Modified Textualism." *Yale Law Journal* 119:1750–1863.

———. 2011. "Intersystemic Statutory Interpretation: Methodology as 'Law' and the Erie Doctrine." *Yale Law Journal* 120:1898–1998.

———. 2015. "Imperfect Statutes, Imperfect Courts: Understanding Congress's Plan in the Era of Unorthodox Lawmaking." *Harvard Law Review* 129:62–111.

———, and Lisa Schultz Bressman. 2013. "Statutory Interpretation from the Inside—An Empirical Study of Congressional Drafting, Delegation, and the Canons: Part I." *Stanford Law Review* 65:901–1026.

———, and Richard A. Posner. 2018. "Statutory Interpretation on the Bench: A Survey of Forty-Two Judges on the Federal Courts of Appeals." *Harvard Law Review* 131:1298–1373.

Gorsuch, Neil M. 2015. "Of Lions and Bears, Judges and Legislators, and the Legacy of Justice Scalia." *Case Western Law Review* 66:907–8.

Kagan, Elena. 2016. "Justice Elena Kagan on Supreme Court and Constitutional Law: McCormick Lecture at the University of Arizona Rogers College of Law." C-SPAN (Aug. 31, 2016), online at https://www.c-span.org/video/?414445-1/justice-elena-kagan-supreme-court-con stitutional-law.

———. 2015. "The Scalia Lecture: A Dialogue with Justice Elena Kagan on the Reading of Statutes." *Harvard Law Today*. Online video at https://today.law.harvard.edu/in-scalia-lecture -kagan-discusses-statutory-interpretation/.

Kavanaugh, Brett M. 2014. "Fixing Statutory Interpretation." *Harvard Law Review* 129:2135–44.

Llewellyn, Karl N. 1950. "Remarks on the Theory of Appellate Decision and the Rules or Canons about How Statutes Are to Be Construed." *Vanderbilt Law Review* 3:395–406.

Scalia, Antonin 1997. "Common Law Courts in a Civil Law System." In *A Matter of Interpretation: Federal Courts and the Law*. Princeton, NJ: Princeton University Press.

———. 1989. "The Rule of Law as a Law of Rules." *University of Chicago Law Review* 56:1175–88.

———, and Brian Garner. 2012. *Reading Law: The Interpretation of Legal Texts*. St. Paul, MN: Thomson/West.

Party Like It's 1989:
Justice Scalia's Rhetoric of Certainty

FRANCIS J. MOOTZ III

There would appear to be little connection between Associate Justice Antonin Scalia and musical superstar Prince, other than the fact that both died within weeks of each other. Nevertheless, I find that one of Prince's signature anthems provides insight into the rhetorical frames used by Justice Scalia. During the 1980s, Prince released his bestselling song "1999," urging us to "party like it's 1999" in the face of the threat posed by the impending new millennium. He exhorted his audience to go out strong, rather than acquiescing in a catastrophic fate:

> 'Cuz they say two thousand zero zero, party over,
> Oops out of time
> So tonight I'm gonna party like it's 1999.[1]

In this chapter, I contend that Justice Scalia was motivated by a similar sentiment during his career. In 1989—his third year on the Court—Justice Scalia published two jurisprudential lectures and authored a number of opinions (particularly, dissents) that established the rhetorical structure that he employed during the next three decades. Rebelling against the nightmare of unconstrained courts creating law rather than applying it in a ministerial manner, Justice Scalia celebrated the relative certainty delivered by his originalist methodology. Justice Scalia became more strident as his vision failed to become reality in succeeding years. He refused to accept defeat, undoubtedly frustrated that the Court was disregarding his clear articulation in 1989 of the way to avoid judicial activism. Justice Scalia ultimately recognized that the jurisprudential apocalypse had occurred around him, and his angry (often embarrassing)[2] opinions in his later years obscured the promise of his 1989 vision.

Justice Scalia's Quest for Certainty:
Originalism and the Rule of Law

As a former law professor, Justice Scalia had faith in the potential for legal scholarship to shape practice by providing a coherent method to guide argument and decision-making. In 1989 he published two lectures that adumbrate his jurisprudential approach in measured terms. Drawing from his practice career in government, his academic career as a law professor, and his judicial experience from four years on the Court of Appeals and three years on the Supreme Court, Justice Scalia espoused a well-rounded and informed theory of decision-making.

In "The Rule of Law as a Law of Rules," Justice Scalia argues that justice requires an evenhanded application of determinate rules across numerous situations, rather than asking judges to exercise case-by-case decision-making by balancing incommensurable factors. The latter approach is the legacy of common-law adjudication, in which the law purportedly works itself pure through countless individual judgments reflecting the nuance of the circumstances of each case. Whatever the merits of permitting private state law to develop through judicial elaboration, the advantage of case-by-case adjustment to nuanced factors is offset by the danger of uncertainty and fragmentation in a constitutional system in which the Supreme Court "can review only an insignificant proportion of the decided cases" (Scalia 1989b, 1178). Justly weighing the circumstances of each case is not a methodology that can constrain the decision-maker or future judges, because "it is no more possible to demonstrate the inconsistency of two opinions based upon a 'totality of circumstances' test than it is to demonstrate the inconsistency of two jury verdicts. Only by announcing rules do we hedge ourselves in" (Scalia 1989b, 1180).

What does Justice Scalia mean by a rule? Taking the Sherman Act prohibition of contracts in restraint of trade as an example, he argues that permitting a court to examine the attendant circumstances to determine if a particular vertical restraint is lawful confers too much discretion, whereas a judicial "rule" that all vertical restraints are legal establishes a rule of law to which judges can be held accountable (Scalia 1989b, 1177). He admits that the court, by announcing and following a blanket rule, will fail to advance the congressional policy in some individual cases, "but such phenomena would be so rare that the benefit of a rule prohibiting divisions of territory far exceeds the harm caused by overshooting slightly the precise congressional goal" (Scalia 1989b, 1183). A rule, then, is defined as a method that delivers a determinate result.

It is immediately apparent that Justice Scalia is faced with a dilemma. If

judges often must provide the rule that follows from general legislative provisions, as is the case with the Sherman Act, then how can this judicial activity itself be subject to rules without encountering an infinite regress? Justice
Scalia argues that his commitment to adhere to the ordinary textual meaning
that the statute held at the time of enactment provides an invariant, empirical
foundation upon which binding rules may be established, thereby eliminating
wide swaths of discretion that judges might otherwise exercise (Scalia 1989b,
1184–85). In the end, though, Justice Scalia makes a relatively modest claim:

> Lest the observations in this essay be used against me unfairly in the future,
> let me call attention to what I have *not* said. I have not said that legal deter-
> minations that do not reflect a general rule can be entirely avoided. We will
> have totality of the circumstances tests and balancing modes of analysis with
> us forever—and for my sins, I will probably write some of the opinions that
> use them. All I urge is that those modes of analysis be avoided where pos-
> sible; that the *Rule* of Law, the law of *rules*, be extended as far as the nature of
> the question allows; and that, to foster a correct attitude toward the matter,
> we appellate judges bear in mind that when we have finally reached the point
> where we can do no more than consult the totality of the circumstances, we
> are acting more as fact-finders than as expositors of the law. I have not even
> tried to address the hardest question, which is: When is such a mode of analy-
> sis avoidable and when not? To what extent do the values of the Rule of Law,
> which I have described, justify the imprecision that it necessarily introduces?
> At what point *must* the Rule of Law leave off and the rest be left to the facts?
> (Scalia 1989b, 1186–87)

Justice Scalia urges judges to adhere to the ordinary meaning of legal texts as
understood at the time of enactment in order to best serve the rule of law's
virtue of certainty, but he expressly acknowledges that no methodology is
capable of definitively resolving all legal cases.

In a later lecture, Justice Scalia continues his analysis of originalism as an
imperfect, but satisfactory, grounding for a jurisprudence of rules. As part of
a speaker series in honor of Chief Justice Taft at the University of Cincinnati
Law School, Justice Scalia gave a lecture entitled "Originalism: The Lesser
Evil" (Scalia 1989a). Lauding Taft for his originalist methodology in *Myers v.
United States*,[3] Justice Scalia champions the effort to understand the text and
structure of the Constitution against the backdrop of the founders' understandings of these provisions, even while admitting that this is not the only
possible method of interpretation (Scalia 1989a, 851–53). He acknowledges
that originalism is "not without its warts" (Scalia 1989a, 856) and concedes
that originalist exegesis confronts serious epistemic difficulties.

Properly done, the task requires the consideration of an enormous mass of material—in the case of the Constitution and its Amendments, for example, to mention only one element, the records of the ratifying debates in all the states. Even beyond that, it requires an evaluation of the reliability of that material—many of the reports of the ratifying debates, for example, are thought to be quite unreliable. And further still, it requires immersing oneself in the political and intellectual atmosphere of the time—somehow placing out of mind knowledge that we have which an earlier age did not, and putting on beliefs, attitudes, philosophies, prejudices and loyalties that are not those of our day. It is, in short, a task sometimes better suited to the historian than the lawyer. (Scalia 1989a, 856–57)

Indeed, Justice Scalia criticizes Chief Justice Taft's opinion for its (inevitable) gaps in analysis, revealed in part only by subsequent historical research, and he admits that the current Supreme Court justices, working under much more compressed time constraints, are not the ideal source for accurate historical analysis (Scalia 1989a, 857–61).

Justice Scalia acknowledges that originalism suffers from another, more serious, problem: it is difficult for judges to hew to the methodology in the face of difficult cases. In the unlikely event that a state were to reinstate public lashing as a punishment, Justice Scalia acknowledges that a "faint-hearted originalist" might not have the fortitude to uphold the law under the public understanding of the Eighth Amendment in 1791 (Scalia 1989a, 861–62).[4] However, he emphasizes that this defect is the result of human frailty and is not peculiar to originalist methodology. In difficult cases, the non-originalists likely will moderate their approach as well, "which accounts for the fact that the sharp divergence between the two philosophies does not produce an equivalently sharp divergence in judicial opinions" (Scalia 1989a, 864). Justice Scalia prefers originalism because it is grounded in the certainty of applying rules according to historical meanings that can in principle, be recovered. Yet, he fully understands that epistemic difficulties or exceptions by faint-hearted originalists who seek to do justice in a particular case will tend to result in occasional accommodations to contemporary values that amount to a kind of "compromise" between competing constitutional theories of interpretation (Scalia 1989a, 864).

In his 1989 lectures Justice Scalia presents a measured and reasonable defense of adhering to the value of certainty to the extent possible, even while acknowledging the epistemic and volitional obstacles to achieving complete adherence. Justice Scalia puts his faith in a "pure" jurisprudence of rules, grounded in the fixed, original understanding of the governing text, but he is astute enough to recognize that we necessarily will fall short in our good-faith effort to follow this rigorous path. Justice Scalia embraces originalism because he believes that the non-originalists cannot offer a coherent account of how we can constrain judges, nor can they explain how non-originalist methodology comports with our constitutional tradition of the rule of law. In his view, non-originalists invite a wholesale failure of the judicial function, whereas faint-hearted originalists suffer occasional concessions to reality while generally holding firm to rule-of-law values.

Putting the Promise of 1989 into Action:
Justice Scalia's Rhetoric of Certainty

As he was delivering his jurisprudential lectures during the 1987 and 1988 Supreme Court terms, Justice Scalia was putting his theory into practice in his court opinions. He sounds a consistent theme, particularly when dissenting. Fighting against the lure of equities that arise in hard cases and tempt judges to engage in common-law reasoning, Justice Scalia stood firmly on the side of rules, regardless of the injustices that might follow in individual cases. Moreover, although far less expressly in his early years on the Court, he sought to ground the governing rules objectively, by connecting them with an original understanding of the relevant legal text. Before Justice Scalia devolved into a frustrated firebrand in his later years, his opinions carefully deployed his jurisprudential philosophy in concrete cases. In the remainder of this chapter I explore how Justice Scalia's seemingly simple and facially persuasive rhetorical claims encountered difficulties and complexities that prevented them from receiving the Court's endorsement.

CLEAR RULES YIELD CERTAIN RESULTS.

I begin with Justice Scalia's core value: enforcing clear rules yields consistency and predictability. Consider a simple, typical case. In *Houston v. Lack*,[5] a federal prisoner acting *pro se* filed a notice of appeal from a decision denying his habeas petition. His notice was received and filed by the Clerk thirty-one days after the decision, which was one day late under the statute, even though the prisoner delivered his notice to prison authorities 27 days after the judgment. The Court acknowledged that, under *Fallen v. U.S.*, an imprisoned *pro se* defendant is not held to strict filing requirements for appealing a criminal conviction, because he has no control over the filing once it is delivered to prison officials.[6] The majority in *Fallen* had concluded that that the purpose of the filing rule and the ends of justice were undermined by strict adherence to the filing deadline, whereas the concurring justices had argued that the "filing" itself occurred when the appeal was delivered to the proper prison authority. In *Houston*, the Supreme Court began by deciding that the *Fallen* exception to the filing rule does not apply in a civil appeal. This holding would appear to resolve the appeal definitively; because the prisoner's habeas appeal was untimely, the court lacked jurisdiction to hear the appeal.

However, the *Houston* court held that a *pro se* prisoner "files" his habeas civil appeal when the papers are delivered to the appropriate prison official. After acknowledging the many cases holding that the word "filing" in civil jurisdictional statutes means "received by the Clerk of Court," the Court nevertheless held that "filing" has a different meaning for a *pro se* habeas appeal by a prisoner.[7] One can only imagine the depth of Justice Scalia's scorn for this doctrinal move. After the *Fallen* court had expressly carved out an exception in the criminal context to the clear rule requiring "filing," the *Houston* court achieves essentially the same result in a civil context by changing the meaning of "filing" to an interpretation that had been expressly rejected by the *Fallen* majority. Deciding that the word *filing* means something different because of a particular context openly subjects the determination of the meaning of the rule to equitable impulses. In dissent, Justice Scalia argues that the "decision obliterates the line between textual construction and textual enactment."[8] The word *filing* means to accomplish certain behavior, and Justice Scalia emphasizes that the Court has no authority to carve out exceptions under the guise of defining *filing* more broadly to do justice in a particular case.

Justice Scalia emphasizes that the Court's obligation is to adhere to a rule and to refuse to succumb to a discretion-granting standard. "It would be within the realm of normal judicial creativity (though in my view wrong) to interpret the phrase 'filed with the clerk' to mean 'mailed to the clerk,' or even 'mailed to the clerk or given to a person bearing an obligation to mail to the clerk.'"[9] However, the *Houston* court does not even pretend to uphold a unitary definition of *filed* that could serve as a determinant rule for all cases. Justice Scalia reads the phrase "filing with the Clerk" in its ordinary sense within the larger statutory context, arguing that referring to congressional intent, purpose, or equity in the discernment of meaning invites uncertainty. He concludes that it "may turn out that we will not often agree that equity requires anything other than 'received by the clerk,' but parties will often argue it, and the lower courts will sometimes hold it. Thus wasteful litigation in our appellate courts is multiplied."[10]

When one looks more closely at the case, however, Justice Scalia's simple story fractures along several lines. The majority agrees with the need to adhere to rules that generate certain results, and for this very reason it rejects a general "mailbox rule." The detailed and careful record-keeping by prisons ensures that the *Houston* ruling will not engender any uncertainty in its application.[11] Justice Scalia's slippery slope critique misses the mark because the majority has expressly endorsed the shared goals of clarity and certainty.

Of course, Justice Scalia is not concerned solely with certainty. He insists that the Court should only create a rule when the statute fails to do so. Justice Scalia finds that the ordinary meaning of "filing with the Clerk" is clear: the Clerk must actually receive the notice. Even if the *Houston* rule can provide certain results, it is a rule that contravenes the rule expressed by the statutory language. However, the precedents clearly establish that a civil notice of appeal is "filed" when it is received by the Clerk, and not when the Clerk formally "files" the notice by stamping it and entering it in the case file.[12] Justice Scalia provides no linguistic explanation of why "filing with the Clerk" means "received by the Clerk's office" rather than formally filed in the case. Of course, it would be manifestly unjust to hold a litigant responsible for delay by the Clerk, but the majority in *Houston* is simply insisting that the injustice is even greater when the appellant is incarcerated and proceeding *pro se*.[13]

One final, but important, dimension of the case is Justice Scalia's baseline assumption that the rules for criminal appeals should be enforced differently than those for civil appeals. Justice Scalia does not challenge using the "mailbox rule" as an exception for incarcerated *pro se* appellants in a criminal case. He emphasizes that a civil appeal is fundamentally different because the appeal statute is jurisdictional.[14] This is a perplexing assumption, given the original understanding of the Great Writ of habeas corpus and the unique role it has played, and continues to play, in preserving the fundamental interest in liberty.[15] Not all criminal appeals seek the release of a prisoner held by the government, but every habeas petition seeks precisely that relief. Glibly comparing a habeas petitioner to a tort defendant seeking to overturn a judgment that orders it to pay money flies in the face of the historical context and understanding of this constitutionally protected writ.

What appears to be a simple case involving a clear rule turns out to reveal the complexities in recovering historical meaning and underscores the inescapable need to argue persuasively for an interpretation in shifting contexts. Justice Scalia proclaims that there is a singular and simple answer that the wooly-headed and soft-hearted majority ignores in the interest of seeking an equitable result, but declaration is not demonstration. Posturing as the steely adherent to the rule at hand, Justice Scalia ignores the many dimensions of that rule that are the product of ongoing hermeneutical discernment and rhetorical elaboration by courts.

DEVIATING FROM CLEAR RULES INTRODUCES
NEEDLESS AND WASTEFUL CONFUSION.

Justice Scalia repeatedly argues in his jurisprudential writings that adherence to rules is the only means of avoiding confusion and uncertainty that will clog the courts. He repeats this theme in his opinions as well, characterizing the Court's tendency to balance equities as a relinquishment of clarity and certainty. This theme formed part of his rationale in *Houston*, but he makes this claim independently in other opinions. Justice Scalia's concurring opinion in a case decided at the same time as *Houston* provides a good example. The Court affirmed the dismissal of one of sixteen plaintiffs in an employment discrimination case who was not listed on the notice of appeal.[16] The majority held that the Court lacked jurisdiction over the appeal with regard to the omitted plaintiff, despite acknowledging (with a citation to *Houston*) that it was bound to read the rules liberally and to seek to avoid having mere technicalities preclude a hearing on the merits of the appeal. Justice Scalia agreed that if the caption on the notice of appeal had utilized "et al." it might have been an example of a situation where the Court would permit a liberal reading of the rule against an apparent technical defect, but he stresses that the majority opinion improperly softened the result by endorsing unhelpful generalities.

> The principle that "mere technicalities" should not stand in the way of deciding a case on the merits is more a prescription for ignoring the Federal Rules than a useful guide to their construction and application. By definition all rules of procedure are technicalities; sanction for failure to comply with them always prevents the court from deciding where justice lies in the particular case, on the theory that securing a fair and orderly process enables more justice to be done in the totality of cases. It seems to me, moreover, that we should seek to interpret the rules neither liberally nor stingily, but only, as best we can, according to their apparent intent. Where that intent is to provide leeway, a permissive construction is the right one; where it is to be strict, a permissive construction is wrong.[17]

Undoubtedly, Justice Scalia meant to say "original public meaning" in place of "intent," but his meaning is clear. The rule itself suggests its scope, and this scope should not be determined by a judge weighing the equities of a liberal construction of the rule in a particular case. He chides the majority for citing *Houston* when the decision in *Torres* stands in "stark contrast" to the *Houston* court's overtly equitable decision.[18] By replacing the rule at hand with general platitudes, the rule of law as the law of rules becomes impossible.

This critique is also voiced in his many attacks on the use of legislative history to buttress decisions that are clearly decided on the text of the law.[19] Resort to legislative history is not a harmless rhetorical flourish in easy cases, he argues. Rather, it incentivizes bad legislative practice and creates a resource that can lead the courts astray in difficult cases.[20] The point is not that legislative history is irrelevant to a persuasive effort, but that the recourse to legislative history encourages strategic behavior that increases litigation and uncertainty in difficult cases.

This theme was prevalent in two cases involving the interpretation of the Freedom of Information Act. Justice Scalia insisted that the Court's tinkering with the clear rules to serve the ends of justice would introduce endless problems. In one case, Chief Justice Rehnquist permitted prisoners to obtain copies of their pre-sentence investigation reports, even though the rules of criminal procedure (enacted after FOIA) only permit a review in person.[21] Justice Scalia argues that the majority's opinion focuses on the prisoner's need for the report rather than on the carefully enumerated exceptions in the statute.

> I have no doubt . . . that today's decision will be a bombshell in the area of FOIA law. Contrary to settled precedent, the Court has adopted the principle that the individuating characteristics of the requester may be taken into account for purposes of one of the most important and frequently invoked exemptions, Exemption 5. To be sure, only a particular individuating characteristic, which the Court takes pains to narrow, is the subject of the present suit. But once we have adopted the principle, we have condemned the lower courts (and, I suppose, ourselves) to an appreciable increase in the volume of FOIA litigation, as one requester after another tests whether some statute, some principle of law, some court rule, justifies taking *his* particular characteristics into account. I respectfully dissent from this unfortunate holding.[22]

In another FOIA case decided that year, Justice Scalia rejected the majority's effort to protect documents from release by claiming that previously generated documents were "compiled for law enforcement purposes" when they were gathered as part of a later investigation. Justice Scalia argued that the exemptions in FOIA have consistently been interpreted narrowly, in line with the ordinary understanding of the statutory language, concluding that the documents should not be subject to exemption from release.

> I fear today's decision confuses more law than it clarifies. From the prior opinions of this Court, I had thought that at least this much about the Freedom of Information Act was clear: its exemptions were to be "narrowly construed." . . .
> Narrow construction of an exemption means, if anything, construing am-

biguous language of the exemption in such fashion that the exemption does not apply. The word "compiled" is ambiguous . . . because "compiled" does not always refer simply to the "process of gathering," or "the assembling," . . . but often has the connotation of a more creative activity.

. . . .

If used in this more generative sense, the phrase, "records or information compiled for law enforcement purposes" would mean material that the government has acquired or produced for those purposes—and not material acquired or produced for other reasons, which it later shuffles into a law enforcement file. The former meaning is not only entirely possible; several considerations suggest that it is the preferable one."

. . . .

But even if the meaning of "compiled" I suggest is not necessarily the preferable one, it is unquestionably a reasonable one; and that creates an ambiguity; and our doctrine of "narrowly construing" FOIA exemptions requires that ambiguity to be resolved in favor of disclosure.

. . . .

I find today's decision most impractical, because it leaves the lower courts to guess whether they must follow what we say (exemptions are to be "narrowly construed") or what we do (exemptions are to be construed to produce a "workable balance").[23]

The majority sought to determine law enforcement's legitimate need for privacy without hewing to the rule in FOIA and applicable criminal procedure statutes that clearly provide only for review of the documents in question.

We can summarize this line of argumentation by referring to Justice Scalia's dissent in a case that provided redress in Federal District Court for Medicare claims that were not seeking damages despite the general jurisdiction of the Court of Claims for Medicare claims. Justice Scalia vociferously protested the ad hoc approach to jurisdiction.

Nothing is more wasteful than litigation about where to litigate, particularly when the options are all courts within the same legal system that will apply the same law. Today's decision is a potential cornucopia of waste. Since its reasoning cannot possibly be followed where it leads, the jurisdiction of the Claims Court has been thrown into chaos. On the other hand, perhaps this is the opinion's greatest strength. Since it cannot possibly be followed where it leads, the lower courts may have the sense to conclude that it leads nowhere, and to limit it to the single type of suit before us. Even so, because I think there is no justification in law for treating this single type of suit differently, I dissent.[24]

Deviating from a clear rule is not just jurisprudentially wrong; it causes collateral damage by bollixing the judicial system.

Justice Scalia's concerns are certainly legitimate, but they are not so easily translated to doctrine. A court cannot place administrative convenience above justice, and it would make no sense to deny a claim simply because the decision might lead to a multitude of future claims seeking to define the scope of the emerging rule. A clear rule, such as "the plaintiff always wins," would certainly be subject to ongoing litigation if the rule were softened to provide that the "defendant wins if its case is superior," but these effects do not in and of themselves mean that the reading of the rule is wrong. The independent argument that a court ruling will spur litigation assumes that litigation over the rule is counterproductive rather than clarifying. It would appear that Justice Scalia's use of "clarity" as to the reach of a decision is not in itself a valid consideration without understanding the context in which the litigation might occur. For example, in his infamous *Heller* opinion, Justice Scalia notes that the right to own a firearm for self-defense is limited, and that the scope of the right "is the very product of an interest balancing by the people";[25] having earlier suggested that long-standing prohibitions on gun ownership might pass constitutional muster,[26] he concludes that "there will be time enough to expound upon the historical justifications for the exceptions we have mentioned if and when those exceptions come before us."[27] There is nothing surprising about this result, except that Justice Scalia has used this as an independent point of attack on opinions that seek a balancing of interests through future litigation no less than he does.

JUSTICE SCALIA COULD SKILLFULLY BALANCE EQUITIES AND DETERMINE RULES FROM PRECEDENTS WHEN HE DEEMED IT NECESSARY.

Justice Scalia acknowledged that "for his sins" he would undoubtedly write opinions in which he engaged in a "balancing of factors" analysis, and in his triumphant, originalist opinion in *Heller* he was forced to admit that the constitutional issues required balancing. (Scalia 1989b, 1186–87). In his early years on the Court he displayed great effectiveness when the case called for such an approach, and he was not overly apologetic when the doctrine required it. Consider a case in which a car dealer was convicted for mail fraud because he had mailed false odometer statements as part of transferring ownership.[28] Justice Scalia dissented, arguing that the odometer fraud conviction should not be subject to enhancement merely because the mails were used incidentally rather than directly in furtherance of the odometer tampering.[29] Concluding that the necessary relationship of the mailing and the underlying crime is not subject to mathematical precision, Justice Scalia analogized to the precedents that distinguished a mailing that permitted the fraud to continue, versus a mailing that was part of the fraud itself.[30] The lack of a firm rule provided all "the more reason to adhere as closely as possible to past cases. I think we have not done that today, and thus create problems for tomorrow."[31]

More famously and consequentially, Justice Scalia vigorously dissented in a case involving drug testing of certain federal employees. The Fourth Amendment prohibits "unreasonable search and seizures," and therefore calls for an assessment of the reasonableness of the government's seizure in the given context. In a companion case, Justice Scalia joined with the majority to uphold regulations that required blood and urine tests following specified train accidents or major incidents, and that authorized breathalyzer or urine tests of certain employees who violated specified safety rules.[32] In these circumstances he regarded the individualized suspicion necessary to support a warrant unnecessary. In the *von Raab* case, however, Justice Scalia dissented from the decision to permit blanket drug testing of employees seeking a position dealing directly with drug interdiction or that involved carrying a firearm.[33] In Justice Scalia's mind, these regulations required the Court to weigh the government interest in keeping these occupations free of drug users with the individual employee's interest in liberty from unreasonable intrusions into their privacy.

He begins by expressly accepting the need to balance competing interests to resolve the question. "While there are some absolutes in Fourth Amendment law, as soon as those have been left behind and the question comes down to whether a particular search has been 'reasonable,' the answer depends largely upon the social necessity that prompts the search."[34] He then attacks the majority's willingness to uphold the regulations without any evidence that there is a problem to be solved, or that drug testing will effectively address any such problem.

> In my view the Customs Service rules are a kind of immolation of privacy and human dignity in symbolic opposition to drug use.
>
>   . . . .
>
> The Court's opinion in the present case . . . will be searched in vain for real evidence of a real problem that will be solved by urine testing of Customs Service employees.
>
>   . . . .
>
> What is absent in the Government's justifications—notably absent, revealingly absent, and as far as I am concerned dispositively absent—is the recitation of *even a single instance* in which any of the speculated horribles actually occurred . . .
>
>   . . . .

What better way to show that the Government is serious about its "war on drugs" than to subject its employees on the front line of that war to this invasion of their privacy and affront to their dignity? To be sure, there is only a slight chance that it will prevent some serious public harm resulting from Service employee drug use, but it will show to the world that the Service is "clean," and—most important of all—will demonstrate the determination of the Government to eliminate this scourge of our society![35]

By according weight to the government's pretextual reasoning, the protections of the Fourth Amendment are severely undermined. If the government's generalizations suffice "to justify demeaning bodily searches, without particularized suspicion, to guard against the bribing or blackmailing of a law enforcement agent, or the careless use of a firearm, then the Fourth Amendment has become frail protection indeed."[36]

Justice Scalia's opinions in these cases demonstrate keen insight, nuanced balancing, and passion. When forced to engage in traditional judging practices by general constitutional language, Justice Scalia often impressed his opponents and supporters alike with his honest and transparent reasoning. Unfortunately, as the dream of 1989 began to evaporate, he refused to permit himself to engage in realistic judging. His strained and unpersuasive rhetorical efforts in the *Heller* majority opinion purporting to recover the historically fixed meaning of the Second Amendment are the results of his increasingly dogmatic approach to interpretation [37]

Conclusion

In 1989 Justice Scalia had articulated his approach to judicial decision-making and had demonstrated this approach in action. His voice on the Court had outsized influence, moving the Court to careful textual analysis in historical context as an important part of its practice. However, the majority of the Court regarded his strong claims for the possibility of adhering to clear and simple rules as unduly simplistic. Even with the qualifications he spelled out in his jurisprudential talks, he simply could not demonstrate that results in most cases follow inevitably to a single answer. In 1989, the theory of public-meaning originalism served as an anchor for his analysis of rules. However, as he encountered challenges to his assessment of how properly to determine and follow the rule at hand, originalist theory became more the focus. Ultimately, originalism became Justice Scalia's dogma, with the ironic result that there was greater uncertainty in the law in light of the epistemic and volitional difficulties of adhering to an originalist methodology. Justice Scalia became a caricature of himself in defending his dogma, writing in an angry and self-important tone that undermined his credibility and influence. Critics found it easy to dismiss Justice Scalia as an ideologue.

Elsewhere I have challenged the plausibility of Scalia's new originalism as a theory of judicial decision-making, but in this chapter I have attempted to grant him his due. At the beginning of his judicial career, Justice Scalia was an effective spokesperson and a skilled jurist who, by recognizing some of the practical limitations of his theoretical approach, made an effective case for what the Court should consider in its deliberations. His approach was not fully consistent, nor was it fully and faithfully implemented in his opinions. But this condition holds true for all justices and judges, simply because the art of judging is not reducible to empirical inquiry or technical precision. In 1989 he was engaged in dialogue and contesting decisions from his well-articulated perspective. Although not persuasive to me—and, more importantly, to a majority of the Court—as a complete account of judicial decision-making, Justice Scalia effectively challenged conventional accounts and patterns of decision-making. We would all do well to return to that moment periodically, and to party like it's 1989.

References

Berman, Mitchell N. 2017. "The Tragedy of Justice Scalia." *Michigan Law Review* 115:783–808.

Chemerinsky, Erwin. 2000. "The Jurisprudence of Justice Scalia: A Critical Appraisal." *University of Hawaii Law Review* 22:385–401.

Failinger, Marie A. 2003. "Not Mere Rhetoric: On Wasting or Claiming Your Legacy, Justice Scalia." *University of Toledo Law Review* 34:425–508.

Mootz, Francis J., III 2010. "Ugly American Hermeneutics." *Nevada Law Journal* 10:587–606.

———. 2017. "Getting Over the Originalist Fixation." In *The Nature of Legal Interpretation: What Jurists Can Learn about Legal Interpretation from Linguistics and Philosophy*, edited by Brian G. Slocum, 156–90. Chicago: University of Chicago Press.

Newman, Stephen A. 2006. "Political Advocacy on the Supreme Court: The Damaging Rhetoric of Antonin Scalia." *New York Law School Law Review* 51:907–26.

Prince. 1982. "1999" (vocal performance). Recorded on *1999*, Warner Bros. Records.

Scalia, Antonin. 1989a. "Originalism: The Lesser Evil." *University of Cincinnati Law Review* 57: 849–65.

———. 1989b. "The Rule of Law as a Law of Rules." *University of Chicago Law Review* 56:1175–88.

Shaman, Jeffrey M. 2012. "Justice Scalia and the Art of Rhetoric." *Constitutional Commentary* 28:287–92.

PART 3

Applied Rhetorical Theory

God's Justice, Scalia's Rhetoric, and Interpretive Politics

STEVEN MAILLOUX

Once again controversies over law and politics have accompanied the nomination of a justice to the U.S. Supreme Court. "Judge [Neil] Gorsuch may
act like a neutral, calm judge, but his record and his career clearly show that
he harbors a right-wing, pro-corporate special-interest agenda," said Senate
Minority Leader Charles E. Schumer prior to the confirmation of the latest
appointee to the Court.[1] The intersection of legal hermeneutics and ideological interpretation plays an especially significant role in these ongoing partisan debates, both within specialist academic discussions and in the popular imagination beyond the academy. For example, in the 2009 confirmation
hearings of Justice Sonia Sotomayor, we witnessed a lengthy public examination of how personal experience and political prejudices might impinge on
judicial impartiality. Republican Senator John Cornyn summarized his concerns, stating, "The test is really what kind of Justice will you be if confirmed
to the Supreme Court of the United States? Will you be one that adheres to
a written Constitution and written laws and respect the right of the people
to make their laws [through] their elected representatives, or will you pursue
some other agenda? Personal, political, ideological, that is something other
than enforcing the law?"[2]

In these earlier hearings, one authority cited in support of a Sotomayor
opinion on the Second Amendment was Judge Richard Posner of the Seventh
Circuit Court.[3] The mention of Judge Posner is somewhat ironic in these circumstances, for here we have a political conservative who published a book
the year before, *How Judges Think*, that argues for a legal pragmatism calling into question the very possibility of separating interpretation and politics (Posner 2008). The book includes a chapter called "The Supreme Court

Is a Political Court." The assertion of this title is not a criticism of the Court, but a descriptive claim about the unavoidability of politically influenced interpretive work in legal decisions. As Posner argues elsewhere, "Ideology, in the sense of moral and political values that transcend the merely personal or partisan, is not an illegitimate, but an inescapable, feature of legal judgment, especially in the case of appellate courts, above all the Supreme Court" (Posner 2003, 353). Political ideology necessarily comes into play in difficult cases in which there are "open areas," areas of hermeneutic indeterminacy because of inadequate guidelines from foundational texts and previously decided cases, and, Posner points out, it is precisely these difficult cases that make it to the Supreme Court (Posner 2008).

With this view of interpretive practice, Posner necessarily disagrees with Justice Antonin Scalia's originalist legalism, the latter's assertion that the rule of law is and should be a law of rules, a viewpoint that Scalia believes will ensure that he does not "indulge" his "political or policy preferences" in interpreting the law and judging cases (Scalia 1989, 1179). In the present essay I first discuss Justice Scalia's interpretive practice based on this theory of textual originalism and examine its rhetorical and ideological characteristics. Then I discuss the way that the formal aspects of his rhetoric often function as significant extensions of the legal substance of his arguments.

Scalia, Law, and Religion

The most influential rhetorician of the twentieth century, Kenneth Burke, argued that religion, especially theology, provides a thoroughgoing example of how rhetoric functions as persuasion. In *The Rhetoric of Religion* he argues his case by demonstrating, among other things, how language works within the interpretive exchange between politics and religion (Burke 1970). That is, he presents a rhetorical hermeneutics of political theology: a demonstration of how rhetoric functions interpretively to translate theological terms into political ones and to turn the political back into the theological.[4]

In "God's Justice and Ours," Justice Scalia provides a striking example of how politics and theology intertwine in relation to a rhetorical hermeneutics of the law. He begins his essay with the following disclaimer: "Before proceeding to discuss the morality of capital punishment, I want to make clear that my views on the subject have nothing to do with how I vote in capital cases that come before the Supreme Court. That statement would not be true if I subscribed to the conventional fallacy that the Constitution is a 'living document' — that is, a text that means from age to age whatever the society (or perhaps the Court) thinks it ought to mean" (Scalia 2002, 17). Scalia's rejection of the Constitution as a "living document" depends on his acceptance of the hermeneutic theory of originalism, which holds that the Constitution "means today not what current society (much less the Court) thinks it ought to mean, but what it meant when it was adopted" (Scalia 2002, 17). As an adherent of originalism, Scalia believes that the text means what it originally meant when ratified. For instance, he holds that at the time of its adoption, no one thought the Eighth Amendment abolished capital punishment, and therefore he rejects any attempt by a court today to impose a contemporary, abolitionist morality on the Constitution and ignore the amendment's original meaning.

But this is not the end of the matter for Scalia. He writes, "[W]hile my views on the morality of the death penalty have nothing to do with how I vote as a judge, they have a lot to do with whether I can or should be a judge at all. . . . [T]he choice for the judge who believes the death penalty to be immoral is resignation, rather than simply ignoring duly enacted, constitutional laws and sabotaging death penalty cases" (Scalia 2002, 17–18). That is, in Scalia's view, originalism forbids him from treating the Constitution as a living document and imposing his personal religious beliefs on the text, but those same religious beliefs would be directly relevant to a decision about whether he should continue as a judge who is legally bound to enforce capital punishment.

For Scalia, the relevant distinction here is between a hermeneutic legal question and a personal, ethical one. To address the latter, Scalia quotes Paul's letter to the Romans 13:1–5, which reads in part, "[T]he powers that be are ordained of God. . . . [A ruler] is the minister of God, a revenger to execute wrath upon him that doeth evil." Scalia interprets the "*core* of [Paul's] message" to be "that government—however you want to limit that concept— derives its moral authority from God. It is the 'minister of God' with powers to 'revenge,' to 'execute wrath,' including even wrath by the sword (which is unmistakably a reference to the death penalty)" (Scalia 2002, 19). Thus, Scalia uses Paul to answer his ethical question about capital punishment, but this question, he argues, is completely irrelevant to the hermeneutic issue of how a judge should interpret the Constitution in the first place.

But is it really? At the very least we must note how interpretive work, both legal and scriptural, permeates both Scalia's theoretical prologue and his ethical and ultimately theological deliberation. In the theoretical prologue, he argues for originalism in general and then applies it specifically to the Eighth Amendment (holding that capital punishment is constitutional). Scalia separates this hermeneutic theory and interpretive application from his personal ethics and religious beliefs. Only then does he quote and interpret Paul, which leads him to say that the judge should respect established law and support capital punishment: God has ordained that his governmental ministers be followed even in the execution of "wrath by the sword," which Scalia interprets as "unmistakably a reference to the death penalty."

But this also isn't the end of the matter. For further ethical guidance, Scalia again turns to his religious beliefs, specifically the teachings of the Roman Catholic Church. Here he runs into a problem: a recent church encyclical, *Evangelium Vitae*, and the latest version of the new Catholic catechism declare, under Scalia's interpretation, that "the death penalty can only be imposed to protect rather than avenge, and that since it is (in most modern societies) not necessary for the former purpose, it is wrong" (Scalia 2002, 20).[5] Thus, it would appear that, if Justice Scalia is to follow church authorities, he should resign from the Supreme Court. Instead, he turns his interpretive focus more intensely on the religious documents that contradict his moral belief in capital punishment.

He notes that traditional Catholic dogma does not support the church's new teaching. "Unlike such other hard Catholic doctrines as the prohibition of birth control and of abortion, this is not a moral position that the Church has always—or indeed *ever before*—maintained. . . . The current predominance of opposition to the death penalty is the legacy of Napoleon, Hegel, and Freud rather than St. Paul and St. Augustine." Then Scalia turns to the new teaching itself and the issue of its binding authority. He reports: "I am . . . happy to learn from the canonical experts I have consulted that the position set forth in *Evangelium Vitae* and in the latest version of the Catholic catechism does not purport to be binding teaching—that is, it need not be accepted by practicing Catholics, though they must give it thoughtful and respectful consideration. . . . So I have given this new position thoughtful and careful consideration—and I disagree. That is not to say I favor the death penalty (I am judicially and judiciously neutral on that point); it is only to say that I do not find the death penalty immoral." Scalia adds, "I am happy to have reached that conclusion, because I like my job, and would rather not resign" (Scalia 2002, 20–21).

If, as Judge Posner suggests, an ideology is "a general political orientation, . . . a body of more or less coherent bedrock beliefs about social, economic, and political questions" (Posner 2008, 94), can we not say that Justice Scalia's interpretation of these legal and religious texts is ideological? He has the "bedrock belief" in the morality of capital punishment, and his interpretations of both legal and religious texts are ideological extensions of that belief, at least in those places where others might reasonably see some ambiguity or indeterminacy, a rhetorical "open area" that could be filled by alternative interpretive arguments.

In his *New York Times* blog, Stanley Fish commented on the interpretive politics of Justice Scalia's jurisprudence. Fish initially agrees with certain aspects of Scalia's hermeneutics of originalism, in particular its equation of current textual meaning with original meaning. "Only if the Constitution is assumed to send a message that does not change over time can the claim of an interpretation to be right or an assertion that it is wrong be intelligible. In order to be right or wrong about something, that something must precede, and be independent of, your efforts to figure out what is. What a document is at the beginning—when it is drafted—will always be what it is." Thus, Scalia is correct, according to Fish, in rejecting the theoretical characterization of the U.S. Constitution as a "living organism."[6]

But Fish distinguishes his own intentionalist version of originalism from Scalia's textualist version. Scalia declares, "What I look for in the Constitution is precisely what I look for in a statute: the original meaning of the text, not what the original draftsmen intended" (Scalia 1997, 38). For Fish, in contrast, the act of interpretation is by definition the designation of an author's intention. Focusing on anything else (such as a text's contemporary significance) might be a valuable enterprise but it is not doing interpretation, which can only be the discerning of the original author's meaning. Without positing an intention for a text, an interpreter cannot determine that text's meaning, a fixed point that it is the interpreter's job to determine. According to Fish, "Justice Scalia is right to champion originalism, but he backs the wrong version of it. Textual originalism doesn't do the job because severed from intention, the words of the text can mean too many things. In order to get at the meaning, you have to bring in—no, you have to start with—intention" (Fish 2015, 183).

But more to my rhetorical point, Fish argues further that whatever the hermeneutics, such general theories dictate no specific interpretive consequences, as Scalia and most other legal theorists believe. "Justice Scalia's originalism—his insistence that the Constitution has a fixed meaning—dictates no interpretive results, conservative or otherwise. In fact, no theory of constitutional interpretation dictates an interpretive result, for theoretical accounts do no interpretive work" (Fish 2015, 181). When Fish claims that "theoretical accounts do no interpretive work," he seems to mean either that interpreters do the work, not theories (a mere truism); or that theories can't rule over interpretive practice and have no necessary practical consequences in specific interpretations (a valid antifoundationalist claim); or that theories have no influence on interpretive practice at all. I think this last exaggeration is what Fish often means.[7] I call it an exaggeration—and a misleading one—because even if theories do not have necessary, logical consequences, some theories do have contingent, rhetorical, and ultimately political consequences.[8]

For example, a rhetorical hermeneutic theory might be able heuristically to suggest places in a judge's network of interconnected interpretations where rhetorical pressure could be applied to change another part of the network and thus have political effects. Perhaps arguing with Justice Scalia over the meaning of a verse from Paul might someday have changed his view of the meaning of the Eighth Amendment. However, this would be rhetorical hermeneutic work outside the genre of court opinions as currently understood. More practically relevant is the fact that when some member of a lawyer's audience is known to hold a specific theory of constitutional interpretation, the lawyer will likely appeal to that theory. For instance, if a member of the Supreme Court holds an originalist theory, the counsel will likely cite evidence about the relevant statute's original meaning. As Justice Scalia noted, when he first joined the Supreme Court, "briefs and oral arguments . . . generally discussed only the most recent Supreme Court cases and policy considerations; not a word about what the text was thought to mean when the people adopted it." In contrast, "[r]arely, nowadays, does counsel fritter away two out of nine votes by failing to address what Justice Thomas and I consider dispositive. Originalism is in the game, even if it does not always prevail" (Scalia 2007, 44).[9] In this way, theory can have practical consequences, contingent rhetorical consequences.

Let me now turn to some of the ways the substance and form of Scalia's rhetoric interact in the practice and theory of what might be called his own rhetorical hermeneutics, his specific combination of interpretation and rhetoric, his making sense of the law through the way he uses language.

Scalia's Rhetorical Hermeneutics

What is the relation between Justice Scalia's hermeneutic theory and his rhetorical practice? What, for instance, is the relation between the interpretive substance of his legal opinions and its rhetorical expression? This way of putting the question relies on a common distinction: content versus form, what is said versus how it is said. What is the relationship between the two? The answer to this question depends on the specific text and historical context being discussed. In some cases, it is easy to separate the content and form of a discourse, but at other times it seems that these binaries tend to collapse into each other either through identification of the opposed terms or by one aspect motivating the other.

Justice Scalia's opinions often illustrate this collapse, as when interpretive substance motivates rhetorical form or when one aspect becomes the other (figuration becomes argument). That is, the rhetoric of Scalia's opinions, especially his "colorful dissents," exhibits a continuity between content and form, between what is said and how it is said, insofar as certain stylistic choices reinforce or even embody the interpretive arguments. Furthermore, this claim about the rhetoric of Scalia's interpretations (his applied practice) can also be made about his theoretical defenses of his originalist hermeneutics (his abstract theory).

So far, I seem to be making a distinction between an interpretive argument and its rhetorical embellishment, a distinction that I'm suggesting can in some instances be minimized or collapsed. Before turning to a couple of concrete examples, I want to dwell for a moment on the definition of rhetoric I'm using. Most generally, one might simply equate rhetoric with language use. A general definition of rhetoric is *the use of language in a context to have effects.* The two main effects are effects on audiences and effects on language itself. The first kind we often call persuasion, and the second, figuration. I sometimes employ this broad definition with my students to encompass as many general definitions of rhetoric as possible (Mailloux 2017). But a narrower, more contentious definition of rhetoric is that rhetoric is *the ethical and political effectivity of trope, argument, and narrative in culture* (Mailloux 1998). I think this narrower definition works especially well for understanding the relation between hermeneutic substance and rhetorical form, persuasion and figuration, in Scalia's opinions and their reception within the legal field and in the larger public sphere.

Again, form and substance, rhetoric and interpretation, cannot be easily separated. Often Scalia's substantive interpretive arguments motivate or extend his formal rhetorical tropes and vice versa. Moreover, his assumed narratives of past and present jurisprudential conflict often contextualize and prompt his polemical opinions. That is, Scalia's rhetoric of sarcasm and exaggeration is not superfluous ornamentation but substantive enhancement of his arguments.

This observation applies to his textual originalism both in practice and in theory. In the interpretive practice of his court opinions, especially his dissents, Justice Scalia doesn't just disagree with his colleagues on the bench; his rhetoric registers shock or disgust, tropologically marking the depth of his rejection of their opinions. A string of rhetorical examples from Scalia's scathing dissent in *Atkins v. Virginia* (2002) illustrates the point. He begins, "Seldom has an opinion of this Court rested so obviously upon nothing but the personal views of its members." He then goes on to ridicule "the embarrassingly feeble evidence" the majority opinion presents, concluding with his declaration that "the Prize for the Court's Most Feeble Effort to fabricate 'national consensus' must go to its appeal . . . to the views of . . . members of the so-called 'world community,' and respondents to opinion polls."

Scalia righteously rebukes his colleagues, asserting that "the Court can be so cavalier about the evidence for consensus" because it apparently presumes that, as "really good lawyers," the justices "have moral sentiments superior to those of the common herd" of the American people. "The arrogance of this assumption of power takes one's breath away."[10] Other Scalia dissents repeat the rhetorical moves. The Court majority reaches "implausible" results "on the flimsiest of grounds" as it turns to scientific studies "to look over the heads of the crowd and pick out its friends." The Court rejects the Constitution's "fixed meaning," making it "a mirror of the passing and changing sentiment of American society," thus setting a destabilizing example for lower courts that will result in "crown[ing] arbitrariness with chaos."[11]

As this last quotation suggests, the close relation between Scalia's polemical rhetoric and interpretive arguments in his juridical practice can also be seen in his philosophy of law. In theoretical moments of hermeneutic reflection, Scalia's opinions disparage those who support a "living Constitution" that changes with the times as opposed to the stable Constitution of original meaning.[12] Using the metaphor of a "living Constitution" allows Scalia ironically to support the notion of a "dead Constitution," a Constitution that is paradoxically alive precisely because its meaning is dead and buried once and for all in the past and only needs to be carefully excavated and preserved again and again in the present and future.[13]

Conclusion

A review of *The Originalist*, a 2015 drama based on the life of Justice Scalia, declared that its main character is "arguably among the most polarizing jurists of his stature in American history, and inarguably the most combative justice currently on the court" (Isherwood 2015). In demonstrating how this is so, the play has the character Scalia reference the two intertwined issues I have examined in this essay. "I'm not an ideologue. I'm an originalist," he says at one point; and later he notes concerning one of his opinions, "I used rhetorical exaggeration to make a legal point." We might say that both the popular and the professional legacies of Justice Scalia thus include a particular version of rhetorical hermeneutics: a distinctive combination of originalist interpretive argument, its rhetorical incarnation, and their theoretical articulation. Viewed as a form of interpretive politics, the Scalia brand of jurisprudence often makes it as difficult to distinguish his ideological commitments from his hermeneutic performance as it does to separate his interpretive arguments from their rhetorical embodiments.

References

Burke, Kenneth. 1970. *The Rhetoric of Religion: Studies in Logology.* Berkeley: University of California Press.

Dorf, Michael C. 2012. "The Undead Constitution." *Harvard Law Review* 125, no. 8, 2011–55.

Fish, Stanley. 1989. *Doing What Comes Naturally: Change, Rhetoric, and the Practice of Theory in Literary and Legal Studies.* Durham, NC: Duke University Press.

———. 1999. *The Trouble with Principle.* Cambridge, MA: Harvard University Press.

———. 2015. *Think Again: Contrarian Reflections on Life, Culture, Politics, Religion, Law, and Education.* Princeton NJ: Princeton University Press.

Gorsuch, Neil M. 2016. "Of Lions and Bears, Judges and Legislators, and the Legacy of Justice Scalia." *Case Western Reserve Law Review* 66, no. 4, 905–20.

Isherwood, Charles. 2015. "Review: 'The Originalist,' About Scalia, Opens in Washington." Online at https://www.nytimes.com/2015/03/28/theater/review-the-originalist-about-scalia-opens-in-washington.html.

Mailloux, Steven. 1989. *Rhetorical Power.* Ithaca, NY: Cornell University Press.

———. 1998. *Reception Histories: Rhetoric, Pragmatism, and American Cultural Politics.* Ithaca, NY: Cornell University Press.

———. 2006. *Disciplinary Identities: Rhetorical Paths of English, Speech, and Composition.* New York: Modern Language Association of America.

———. 2017. *Rhetoric's Pragmatism: Essays in Rhetorical Hermeneutics.* University Park: Pennsylvania State University Press.

Mootz, Francis J., III. 2010. *Law, Hermeneutics and Rhetoric.* Burlington, VT: Ashgate.

Murphy, Bruce Allen. 2014. "The Dead Constitution Tour." In *Scalia: A Court of One*, chap. 19. New York: Simon and Schuster.

Posner, Richard A. 2003. *Law, Pragmatism, and Democracy.* Cambridge, MA: Harvard University Press.

———. 2008. *How Judges Think.* Cambridge, MA: Harvard University Press.

Scalia, Antonin. 1989. "The Rule of Law as a Law of Rules." *University of Chicago Law Review* 56, no. 4, 1175–88.

———. 1997. *A Matter of Interpretation: Federal Courts and the Law.* Princeton, NJ: Princeton University Press.

———. 2002. "God's Justice and Ours." *First Things* (May). Online at https://www.firstthings.com/article/2002/05/gods-justice-and-ours.

———. 2007. "Foreword." In *Originalism: A Quarter-Century of Debate*, edited by Steven G. Calabresi. Washington, DC: Regnery.

9

Rhetoric, Jurisprudence, and the Case of Justice Scalia; Or, Why Did Justice Scalia, of All Judges, Write Like *That*?

DARIEN SHANSKE

Introduction

Justice Scalia was the rare judge who also developed a sophisticated jurisprudence. Scalia advocated for a textual approach to the interpretation of statutes and the Constitution. His preferred approach is grounded on an argument about the proper—and modest—role for judges in a constitutional democracy. Given his principled advocacy of textualism, one might have thought that Justice Scalia's judicial rhetoric would be characterized as somberly legalistic, thus demonstrating that *this* is how a judge is to operate as a judge— namely, as a textual engineer, carefully applying the various canons. Needless to say, this would not be the way anyone would describe Justice Scalia's characteristic rhetorical style. To be fair, Scalia's jurisprudence certainly did not logically entail a certain style. Furthermore, it is not the case that all of Justice Scalia's opinions are characterized by the rhetorical pyrotechnics for which he is known. Nevertheless, I will demonstrate how exploring this tension between jurisprudence and style can be fruitful.

I argue that the case of Justice Scalia's rhetoric is suggestive—and only can be suggestive—of three broad jurisprudential conclusions, none of which would presumably have been particularly congenial to Justice Scalia. First, Scalia's rhetorical style often underscores the need for courts to exercise judgment as to contested—and novel—matters of political philosophy. Thus in a broad way Scalia demonstrates the merit of Ronald Dworkin's original critique of H. L. A. Hart's picture of law in *The Concept of Law* (Dworkin 1977). Second, Scalia's rhetoric demonstrates the depth of disagreement that can be accommodated within the law. This demonstration also illustrates the contentious point made somewhat later by Ronald Dworkin that law is a social practice that somehow can accommodate extraordinary diversity as to its fundamental premises (Dworkin 1986).

Finally, Scalia's rhetoric illustrates a possible resolution of the tension between the rule of law and democracy. The tension is that the rule of law does not permit a democratic majority always to get its way. Scalia the jurisprudential thinker argued—or rather assumed—that the rule of law in a constitutional democracy requires a textual—and formal—approach to law. Again, such an approach should rather plausibly have led Scalia the judge to a very staid rhetorical style. That Scalia the judge eschewed this style in favor of one far more outward-facing is an indication that adherence to original public meaning is not in fact what the rule of law in a democracy must always—or ever—consist in. Perhaps self-government under law requires publicly contesting that which is contested. This has the whiff of paradox, but it should not. How is it consistent with the rule of law for judges to impose controversial interpretations of basic constitutional principles on the basis of an also controversial methodology? The rule of law also requires that the people living under the law recognize it as their own. Perhaps Justice Scalia's rhetoric reached out to the public on controversial matters for just this reason.

Put another way, Scalia's outward-facing rhetoric and arguments are perhaps essential features of his jurisprudence. Scalia himself famously observed that if a parent were to treat two siblings unfairly in regard to watching television, then one "will feel the fury of the fundamental sense of justice unleashed" (Scalia 1989, 1178). He therefore urges a method of judging that he believes is most consonant with that fundamental sense of justice. I think it reasonable to suppose that Scalia also perceived, if more inchoately, that the fundamental sense of justice, at least of a self-governing people, also requires that the law not be an alien imposition. Thus, even as he argued that the rule of law demanded that we be ruled by the original public meaning of others, discovered by an obscure and controversial methodology, Scalia was also very concerned to persuade us that this law was, in fact, our own, and we would choose it for ourselves—if we could.

Scalia's Jurisprudence in a Nutshell

So far as I know, Justice Scalia never articulated a position on the most abstract questions of jurisprudence, and thus I do not know, for instance, whether he considered himself a positivist, much less an exclusive positivist. Justice Scalia did, however, go to some lengths to develop a position on the role of the judge in a constitutional democracy—in particular, a democracy that had passed a great many statutes.

As for the federal Constitution, Scalia argued that the judge should be constrained by the original public meaning of a constitutional provision (Scalia 1998, 38). This approach to the Constitution has at least two important advantages. First, the original public meaning has democratic legitimacy because a democratic majority actually ratified that sense of the constitution's key terms. Second, the original public meaning limits permissible interpretations of the Constitution, thereby preventing unelected judges from imposing their will.

As for statutes, judges should interpret them fairly on the basis of their plain meaning (Scalia and Garner 2012, 3). Specifically, Scalia's preferred "fair-reading" approach "determine[s] the application of a governing text to given facts on the basis of how a reasonable reader, fully competent in the language, would have understood the text at the time it was issued" (33). More dynamic approaches to statutory interpretation give too much power to judges. For instance, if courts are allowed to root through legislative history, then they will be able to find more material to interpret statutes in a manner consistent with their own preferences.

Scalia does not question that there will still be hard cases. His distinctive approach to jurisprudence indicates two further judicial techniques. First, he thinks judges should rely on canons of interpretation. As with plain meaning and original public meaning, reliance on a stable set of canons hems in judges and constrains their use of discretion. Second, he thinks judges — and particularly justices of the Supreme Court — should frame their decisions in the form of rules as much as practicable (Scalia 1989). *One* significant advantage of a rule is that it binds lower-court judges as well as justices who consider themselves bound by stare decisis.

Scalia's Puzzling Rhetoric

Given Scalia the judge's background commitments, one might have assumed that his opinions would be characterized by sober workmanship. After all, as just explained, an important underlying justification for Scalia's preferred judicial approaches is that in a democracy the people and not judges should make decisions on matters of policy. Thus, even on contentious issues, a judge starts from the plain meaning/original public meaning, applies a canon or two, articulates a clear rule for the future, and then moves on.

Courts in other jurisdictions, including powerful constitutional courts, do write opinions in more or less this manner.[1] To be sure, adopting a particular style does not follow from Scalia's commitments, but there is certainly a sense not only that such a style would have been consistent with his commitments, but would also have amounted to a demonstration—a performance, to use jargon—of his point. *This* is how a judge in a democracy decides matters, because here is a judge attending to the boring task of parsing the meaning of words rather than wading into the contentious issues of the day.

To say that Scalia's rhetorical style does not perform his jurisprudence in this way would be an understatement. It is not merely that Scalia's opinions, particularly his dissents, reflect a more common-law tradition of what a judicial opinion looks like; rather, his opinions are celebrated—or excoriated (or both)—for their distinctive rhetorical features and most particularly for biting and broad assaults on the ethos of his colleagues.

In order to be precise, my focus is not on the use of the art of rhetoric to craft a more persuasive argument. Hence aspects of Scalia's decisions such as clear and vivid language, foregrounding of stronger arguments, appealing— at least sotto voce—to pathos as well as logos, while they are of great interest, are not my focus.[2] After all, all communications have an intended audience that one is trying to persuade. The German Constitutional Court's decisions surely can be analyzed for their rhetoric, even if there is a studied attempt to appear to use no rhetoric.

Rather, what I am focusing on are those passages in Justice Scalia's opinions that are extraneous to his "fair-reading" methodology but also consistent with making an argument, on grounds beyond the text, for his preferred approach or outcome. Those rhetorical flourishes that target the reasoning of his colleagues in a way that is very unlikely to persuade those colleagues, or even lawyers generally, are especially strong examples of Scalia the judge eschewing the modest role that Scalia the jurisprudential thinker would have judges take in a democracy. But they are not the only relevant passages.

Let me offer one example of the many that would be possible. As is well known, a few terms ago (2015) a statutory interpretation question came to the Court concerning the Affordable Care Act—Obamacare.[3] The question was, basically, how to interpret four words—"established by the State." This was a case tailor-made for the use of canons. On the one hand, there was the antisurplusage canon, which indicated that these words must be given significance.[4] On the other hand, there are the whole-text canon and the anti-absurdity canon,[5] which indicate that a statute should be read as a coherent whole—if the four words were given specific significance, then the impact would be essentially to undermine the whole statutory scheme. I think this should have been an easy case for Justice Scalia, as he makes clear that the antisurplusage canon is not absolute, and he generally argues—sensibly—that courts must primarily look to interpret statutes *fairly*.[6]

A majority of the Court agreed with me that the antisurplusage canon needed to yield; Justice Scalia did not. *That* he did not is one additional data point indicating that Scalia the jurisprudential thinker was wrong to believe that a set of canons could meaningfully restrain judges from reaching their preferred policy conclusions.[7] But this is not my point here. Scalia could have reached the conclusion he did through patient demonstration of why these four words should be allowed to unravel a major piece of legislation, and he does do that to some extent,[8] but his opinion is also filled with passages such as the following:

> Under all the usual rules of interpretation, in short, the Government should lose this case. But normal rules of interpretation seem always to yield to the overriding principle of the present Court: The Affordable Care Act must be saved.[9]

> The Court's next bit of interpretive jiggery-pokery involves other parts of the Act that purportedly presuppose the availability of tax credits on both federal and state Exchanges.[10]

> Having gone wrong in consulting statutory purpose at all, the Court goes wrong again in analyzing it. The purposes of a law must be "collected chiefly from its words," not "from extrinsic circumstances."[11]

> The Court's decision reflects the philosophy that judges should endure whatever interpretive distortions it takes in order to correct a supposed flaw in the statutory machinery. That philosophy ignores the American people's decision to give Congress "[a]ll legislative Powers" enumerated in the Constitution. Art. I, § 1. They made Congress, not this Court, responsible for both making laws and mending them. This Court holds only the judicial power—the power to pronounce the law as Congress has enacted it. We lack the prerogative to repair laws that do not work out in practice, just as the people lack the ability to throw us out of office if they dislike the solutions we concoct.[12]

These examples—far from atypical—run the gamut of the aspects of the decisions I want to focus on. First, and starting at the end, note that Scalia the justice is expressly appealing to the theories of Scalia the jurisprudential thinker. That is, he emphasizes interpretation that relies on the original meaning of terms as a method appropriate for a judge in a democracy. Yet, Scalia the justice performs this philosophy in a manner that is at times dismissive of his colleague's arguments and ethos, often in a highly quotable package. The "package" part here is important. As Aristotle teaches, the heart of rhetoric is the enthymeme.[13] Whatever precisely Aristotle means by enthymeme, his broad point is clear. In a public persuasive context, arguments must be truncated and contain hidden, but reasonable (seeming) premises. The claim here is not that there is something amiss in having hidden — or political — premises per se; rather, what we are noting is that Scalia the justice engages in explicitly rhetorical practice so freely.

Easy Answers

One could just dismiss this rhetoric as idiosyncrasy, of course, and, to be sure, Scalia's rhetoric is no necessity. We will see if Justice Gorsuch, who seems to embrace a similar jurisprudential perspective, is also drawn to such rhetoric.[14] We might also point to various aspects of American legal practice likely to be explanatory, and which long predate Scalia, such as signed opinions and dissents, the construction of constitutional law case books,[15] and much more.

That much of Scalia's most pyrotechnic rhetoric appears in dissents is worthy of further discussion. After all, one might reasonably argue that the stakes in dissents are lower. There is no need for a judge writing a dissent to make sure there is no unfortunate ambiguity hidden in dicta. Moreover, a dissent, by definition, is not law and is a persuasive exercise. Why should we be surprised if Justice Scalia engages in fiery rhetoric in a persuasive context? There are a few answers to this, although first it must be conceded that this does mitigate our puzzle.

There are several reasons why we should not let matters rest with the observation that the passages in which Scalia the judge most departs from the preferred methodology of Scalia the jurisprudential theorist appear in dissents. First, Scalia's characteristic rhetoric is not wholly limited to dissents. Remember, what we are concerned with is not just passages that are acerbic, but passages that bring in matters extraneous to settling a case based on a "fair reading." Scalia for the majority will engage in weighing policy arguments,[16] constructing novel structural constitutional arguments,[17] and adopting new constitutional rules for reasons that at least partially resonate with his preferred mode of jurisprudence.[18]

Second, even if the rhetoric we are interested in were so cabined, the question would remain why Scalia, of all justices, chose to adopt such a style in his dissents. After all, if, as he so often asserts, his colleagues have gone wrong in understanding the nature of their job, why not demonstrate the way? Again, the particular point of view Scalia seems most eager to advance is that judges should pursue their limited role modestly. They are not to engage in political philosophy.

Finally, as we have seen, Scalia himself saw a connection between his opinions, including his dissents, and his jurisprudence. He would certainly not have wanted us to discard his dissents as "mere" rhetoric, and so we will consider their rhetoric and structure, along with similar, if fainter aspects of his majority opinions.

Three (Possible) Jurisprudential Implications

THE ROLE OF CREATIVE POLITICAL JUDGMENT

In many ways, I teach a traditional class in jurisprudence. At the heart of the class is the Hart-Dworkin debate. I assign Scalia's article "The Rule of Law as a Law of Rules" (Scalia 1989) after the Hart-Dworkin debate. Every time I teach the class, my students and I have the experience that the Justice Scalia of that article is engaging in as much a herculean enterprise as Brandeis in *The Right to Privacy* or Cardozo in *MacPherson v. Buick Motor Co.* Consider one of Scalia's key points: that the interpretation of a law that protects unpopular groups, such as criminal defendants, should be written in rules that are as clear as possible so that judges cannot fudge matters at a moment of crisis (Scalia 1989, 1180). Let's leave aside various limits to this argument;[19] I think it is an excellent argument. Yet from whence does this argument emerge? It is partly an argument from political philosophy about the importance of protecting unpopular minorities, partly an argument about political economy, and partly an argument about judicial behavior.

Thus, already buried in Scalia's jurisprudence is an indication that judges are going to have a hard time avoiding straying into political philosophy (and more)—even when he is making the argument about why and how judges should avoid straying into political philosophy. This, of course, is not just an isolated instance. We have already seen Justice Scalia's appeal to these external considerations in *King v. Burwell.* Other examples abound. For instance, there is Scalia's celebrated dissent from the decision upholding the independent prosecutor statute. There, Scalia argues, among other things, that creating an independent prosecutor is not only a violation of separation of powers because the prosecutor is not accountable to the president, but is also fundamentally unfair and unwise because the prosecutor is being set up to have no perspective on the alleged wrongs of the person she is called upon to prosecute.[20]

In wrapping up this subsection, it is worth noting the extent to which I believe Justice Scalia provides succor for a broadly Dworkinian approach to law. It is often maintained that inclusive legal positivism neuters the early Dworkinian critique of positivism because it is not inconsistent with (inclusive) positivism that a legal system—such as, arguably, ours—to have the social practice of appealing to principles outside the law for determination of cases, especially hard constitutional cases.[21] And yet the counter to this counter is that it is decidedly ad hoc just to say that such practices can be included. To be sure, in Dworkin's original critique of Hart, he does primarily offer principles that could easily have been found in a treatise on equity, and so it makes a lot of sense to say that we have a practice of creatively including certain broad principles in our law (Dworkin 1977, 23–24). Yet the examples from Scalia illustrate the great diversity and novelty of principles that our legal system seems to take on board—or that Scalia argues *should* be taken on board. Scalia's accurate warning about the independent prosecutor represents a novel insight, grounded in individual psychology, institutional dynamics, and so forth. There is no general principle, long known in the law (that I know of), that prosecutors should be given broad discretion and many responsibilities in order to protect citizens from being prosecuted for minor offenses.

Examples can be proliferated. Take the dormant Commerce Clause. As an originalist, Scalia was no fan of the clause but he took the position that he would enforce it as a matter of stare decisis.[22] This was a reasonable decision, but certainly one that required balancing the import of originalism with the rule-of-law values embodied by stare decisis, as well as perhaps some consideration of the value of the dormant Commerce Clause as facilitating commerce in the United States.[23] The limits of stare decisis are by no means self-executing, of course, and so consider a major dormant Commerce Clause case decided late in Scalia's career—*Wynne v. Comptroller*.[24] The majority in this case insisted that its decision followed directly from precedent. Even better, the majority found that precedent also provided a bright-line rule. As an added bonus, the rule was hardly arbitrary, but recommended by economists.

Yet Justice Scalia dissented from the majority opinion, which was written by Justice Alito and joined by justices Roberts, Kennedy, Breyer, and Sotomayor. This was a 5–4 decision in a nonideological case, or at least a nontraditional one. Scalia's dissent was one of three; there was one by Justice Thomas and one by Justice Ginsburg. Justices Scalia and Kagan joined Justice Ginsburg's dissent, while only Justices Scalia and Thomas joined one another's dissents. Scalia denied that this case was covered by precedent, but he offered other principled reasons for not joining the majority. The lack of a textual anchor for the dormant Commerce Clause is one major reason Scalia refused to embrace the clear rule offered by the majority.[25] Also in the background is a federalism concern, as the dormant Commerce Clause is a cudgel by which federal law, as ultimately interpreted by the federal judges of the Supreme Court, impacts fundamental state policies as to revenue collection.[26] Thus it seems to me that Scalia reads the dormant Commerce Clause precedents more narrowly than the majority at least in part because of these background concerns. In any event, it is only because of his background concern about the clause that Scalia is fundamentally opposed to applying it beyond what precedent requires.

The key here is not whether or not Scalia is correct, but to note another necessarily creative balancing of (sometimes novel) principles on his part. The rule of law might be a law of rules, but in this case Scalia thought that textualism and federalism ought to win out over the articulation of a clear rule.

LAW AS INTERPRETIVE CONCEPT

The Dworkin of *Law's Empire* moves on to a different, related critique of the positivism of *The Concept of Law*. Dworkin's key argument is that law cannot be an agreed-upon social practice when there are such deep theoretical disagreements about the law (Dworkin 1986, 45–46). Scalia's repeated engagement in debates about the law in which he challenges the fundamental understanding of his colleagues would seem to be a primary example of what Dworkin has in mind.

Let's return to *King v. Burwell*. Scalia could have framed the debate in the mundane terms of statutory interpretation, but ultimately he does not. He claims—accurately I believe—that there are in fact foundational differences in vision as to the role of courts in a democracy that are motivating how he and the majority use the ordinary tools of statutory interpretation. Remember that Scalia claims that the majority is seeking to "save" the Affordable Care Act, which is to say that Scalia understands that ruling against the government is tantamount to undermining a gigantic piece of legislation that affects tens of millions of people. As I already noted, I think that the ordinary tools of statutory interpretation presented by Scalia indicate clearly that the majority in *King v. Burwell* was correct. Yet, to be sure, one could use different tools and arrive at another conclusion, and one reason not to reach this weaker conclusion is precisely the reason Scalia offers: namely, why go to so much trouble to undermine the result reached by means of the democratic process? Presumably Scalia is guided by other metaprinciples, perhaps something along these lines:[27] The product of democratic legislatures must be interpreted strictly, indeed right up to the point of absurdity, in order to (1) encourage legislatures to do their jobs better and (2) prevent judges from being given the power to interpret poorly written statutes. If these are Scalia's metaprinciples, I confess to finding them somewhat appealing, though not terribly compelling in the context of a statute like the ACA. In any event, the jurisprudential point is that these are deep differences, and they would seem to reflect differences in political philosophy.

There is a deep tension, at least as an initial matter, between the rule of law and the norm of majority control that is central to a democracy. In the context of American legal thought, this problem is known as the counter-majoritarian difficulty.[28] There are many answers to this tension, such as Ely's famous argument in *Democracy and Distrust* that what unelected judges can legitimately do is to ensure that the political process is fair so that the will of the majority is legitimate (Ely 1980, 102–03).

Another kind of answer argues that the seeming contradiction can be dissolved in some way; for instance, one might argue that the rule of law and democracy are codetermined. Habermas offers an argument of this sort, arguing, roughly, that one only arrives at a legitimate democracy through rule of law and that the rule of law requires democracy.[29] Applied to the role of judicial review, Habermas explains that

> in my view, a constitution that is democratic—not just in its content but also according to its source of legitimation—is a tradition-building project with a clearly marked beginning in time. All the later generations have the task of actualizing the still-untapped normative substance of the system of rights laid down in the original document of the constitution. According to this dynamic understanding of the constitution, ongoing legislation carries on the system of rights by interpreting and adapting rights for current circumstances (and, to this extent, levels off the threshold between constitutional norms and ordinary law). (Habermas 2001, 774)

It goes without saying that Scalia would not agree with Habermas about how constitutions work in a democracy. And yet Scalia's public-engaging rhetoric,[30] making broad philosophical claims, itself seems clearly aimed at "actualizing the still-untapped normative substance of the system of rights laid down in the original document of the constitution."

One can illustrate this point in a different way. In arguing for a modest judicial role, Scalia echoes progressive legal scholars from the early twentieth century, such as Roscoe Pound. Both Scalia and Pound agree that it is not appropriate for judges in a democracy to use free-wheeling common-law methods to limit statutes passed by legislatures (Pound 1908). In the same vein, Pound also argued that the Old Court's commitment to laissez-faire constitutionalism was undermining the rule of law (Pound 1907, 911–15). Part of Pound's insight here was surely grounded on the contention that laissez-faire constitutionalism is not a good interpretation of our Constitution. Scalia could presumably agree with Pound about this too.

Yet it is also part of Pound's argument that there is a limit to the tolerance of a democratic people for the imposition of an alien law, whatever its exegetical merit. On this point, Scalia the jurisprudential thinker cannot agree with Pound, and we have seen that Scalia makes a strong argument that we sometimes want courts to uphold "alien" laws against the will of the democratic majority. But I presume that Pound would argue that the details and degree matter. Holding the line on protections for an unpopular group at a moment of crisis is one thing; striking down swaths of popular social legislation is quite another, though the line is blurry. I think the practice of Scalia's rhetoric indicates that Scalia the judge intuits this point. That is, as for matters that are truly contentious, Scalia's rhetoric indicates that he knows about the public controversy and understands that he will need to win the day through outward-facing appeals. The rule of law also requires consent of the ruled: democracy, and rule of law seems to be codetermined, as Habermas suggests.

Conclusion

Let me conclude by taking an even broader step back. The first democracy, Athens, has been critiqued since antiquity as lacking the rule of law. The critique was easy to level. Athens had relatively little written law, much less a written constitution, and much of the evidence we have of Athenian legal practice—the speeches of the orators—are full of ad hominem attacks and other tendentious information that seem to underscore that the law of Athens was what the majority of Athenians said it was. And, of course, the most famous trial in Athenian history resulted in the death of Socrates. Even a leading modern commentator concludes that the Athenians essentially chose to have the rule of the majority over the rule of law (Lanni 2009, 721–22).

There are at least two problems with this gloss on Athens: the Athenians themselves apparently valued the rule of law (Carugati, Hadfield, and Weingast 2015), and the Athenian polity—and economy—functioned well for almost two centuries (Ober 2008), which suggests that the rule of law rhetoric was not "mere" rhetoric. What then was going on? At least one powerful approach argues that there was rule of law, but it was enforced informally.[31] That is, citizens did have notice of what was expected of them in the absence of extensive formal law precisely because of all of the extraneous norms that were hashed out in public courtroom speeches. This was how the rule of law could be maintained while also being democratic.

I have little doubt that Justice Scalia would not have appreciated the idea that his acerbic rhetoric illustrates that there is a way other than his preferred method to solve the problem of the rule of law in a democracy, but there you have it. The rule of law need not be a law of rules, but it does need to be the law that the people author for themselves. This process requires outward-facing rhetoric that engages in contested issues of political philosophy. On this model, the public rhetoric of Justice Scalia is a *feature* of judging in a democracy, not just an idiosyncratic bug.

References

Asenas, Jennifer J., and Kevin A. Johnson. 2017. "Justice Scalia's Communication Legacy: Going Public and the Republican Rhetorical Style." *Communication Law Review* 16:22–40.

Bickel, Alexander M. 1962. *The Least Dangerous Branch*. New Haven, CT: Yale University Press.

Burnyeat, M. F. 1996. "Enthymeme: Aristotle on the Rationality of Rhetoric." In *Essays on Aristotle's Rhetoric*, edited by Amelie Oksenberg Rorty. Berkeley: University of California Press.

Carugati, Federica, Gillian K. Hadfield, and Barry R. Weingast. 2015. "Building Legal Order in Ancient Athens." *Journal of Legal Analysis* 7:291–324.

Dworkin, Ronald. 1977. "The Model of Rules." In *Taking Rights Seriously*. Cambridge, MA: Harvard University Press.

———. 1986. *Law's Empire*. Cambridge, MA: Harvard University Press.

Ely, John Hart. 1980. *Democracy and Distrust*. Cambridge, MA: Harvard University Press.

Eskridge, William N., Jr. 2013. "The New Textualism and Normative Canons." *Columbia Law Review* 113:531–92.

Gamage, David, and Darien Shanske. 2014. "Why the Text of the Affordable Care Act Authorizes Tax Credits on the Federal Exchanges: A Response to Adler and Cannon." *State Tax Notes* 71:229–234.

Greenhouse, Linda. 2017. "Trump's Life-Tenured Judicial Avatar." *New York Times*, July 6. Online at https://www.nytimes.com/2017/07/06/opinion/gorsuch-trump-supreme-court.html ?_r=0.

Habermas, Jürgen. 2001. "Constitutional Democracy: A Paradoxical Union of Contradictory Principles?" Translated by William Rehg. *Political Theory* 29:766–81.

Kommers, Donald P., and Russell A. Miller. 2012. *The Constitutional Jurisprudence of the Federal Republic of Germany*. Durham, NC: Duke University Press.

Lanni, Adriaan. 2009. "Social Norms in the Courts of Ancient Athens." *Journal of Legal Analysis* 9:691–736.

Ober, Josiah. 2008. *Democracy and Knowledge*. Princeton, NJ: Princeton University Press.

Pound, Roscoe. 1907. "The Need for a Sociological Jurisprudence." *Annual Report American Bar Association* 31:911–26.

———. 1908. "Common Law and Legislation," *Harvard Law Review* 21:383–407.

Scalia, Antonin. 1989. "The Rule of Law as a Law of Rules." *University of Chicago Law Review* 56:1175–88.

———. 1998. *A Matter of Interpretation.* Princeton, NJ: Princeton University Press.

———, and Bryan Garner. 2012. *Reading Law: The Interpretation of Legal Texts.* St. Paul, MN: Thomson/West.

Shapiro, Scott. 2007. "The 'Hart–Dworkin' Debate: A Short Guide for the Perplexed." In *Ronald Dworkin,* edited by A. Ripstein. Cambridge: Cambridge University Press.

No Reasonable Person

GEORGE H. TAYLOR, MATTHEW L. JOCKERS,
AND FERNANDO NASCIMENTO

Introduction

It is a commonplace that the late Justice Antonin Scalia advocated in general that legal interpretation must be based on an originalist textualism. Interpreters, including courts, must restrict themselves to interpretation of a statutory or constitutional text—instead of extraneous legislative history and purpose—and must interpret textual meaning as understood at the time of enactment. Justice Scalia claimed that originalist textualism restricted judicial discretion and so, as a matter of separation of powers, heeded the legal values established by the legislative branch in a statutory or constitutional provision. On the basis of an examination of Justice Scalia's rhetoric, we challenge his thesis. To test the merits of his interpretive approach on its own terms, we accept for the sake of argument the framework of Justice Scalia's originalist textualism. We also accept that Justice Scalia can write opinions that have considerable legal erudition, sophistication, and insight. Yet an analysis of his opinions indicates that he frequently uses rhetorical moves to assert that only one judicial interpretation is available, while in fact greater interpretive play is at work that he denies. Examination of his rhetoric evidences that he often is engaged not in the reduction but rather the enhancement of judicial discretion—his own.

We begin with a brief summary of Justice Scalia's originalist textualism, including his advocacy of a "fair reading" of the legal text. We then turn, also briefly, to representative evidence of the various kinds of rhetorical strategies he uses in his Supreme Court opinions to criticize opposing views and enhance the legitimacy of his own. We then choose as representative of this rhetoric his frequent criticism of other views as "absurd" and spend most of our analysis evaluating this usage. We offer what we perceive to be three distinct contributions here. First, we set the stage by examining the implications of the rhetorical enhancement of judicial discretion in a famous case. We argue that key rhetorical passages in the concurrence in the Supreme Court case of *Bush v. Gore*[1] exemplify the fallacious rhetorical accusation of opposing views as absurd, and we maintain that linguistic evidence and patterns of word use typical of Justice Scalia suggest that these passages reflect his rhetorical style rather than the concurrence's formal author, Chief Justice William Rehnquist. We contend, then, that there is evidence to suggest that Justice Scalia may have contributed to key phrases and passages in the concurrence. Second, we address more analytically the nature of Justice Scalia's criticism of other views as "absurd." What does he mean when he attributes absurdity to these other interpretive stances? To our knowledge, we are the first to undertake this inquiry in any detail. Third, as we elaborate, his critique is quite different from more customary attention to the "absurdity" doctrine. In that doctrine, advocates either argue that a literal interpretation is not legitimate and needs to be amended because the results would be absurd, or (as Justice Scalia often does), that a "plain" reading is not absurd. By contrast, Justice Scalia more frequently criticizes *other interpreters'* views as absurd and in so doing seeks to underscore his own interpretation as the sole legitimate interpretation of a contested statutory or constitutional passage. We exemplify his approach and its implications with a number of examples drawn from his opinions.

We argue, then, that Justice Scalia's rhetoric highlights the interpretive consequences of a mode of analysis that claims to limit judicial discretion but instead employs a rhetoric that enhances its own interpretive choice. Whether we prove to be correct about Justice Scalia's role in the rhetoric of the *Bush v. Gore* concurrence, our analysis of the plethora of his other opinions where he invokes the absurdity of other views provides independent confirmation of the interpretive discretion afforded by his rhetorical style. We conclude with some general observations that Justice Scalia's rhetoric owes more to his interpretive preference for a jurisprudence of rules, which results from his perspective as an interpreter rather than as a requirement of a legal text, and that contested legal texts more often require interpretive judgment, which permits—and requires—judicial discretion.

Justice Scalia's Originalist Textualism and His Rhetoric

Justice Scalia claims that interpretive adherence to the original meaning of a statutory or constitutional text is required as a matter of separation of powers: an originalist approach allows the values of the enacting legislature to pre-

vail and restrains a court's imposition of its own values on the case. He insists that his employment of originalist textualism leads to a "fair reading" of
the contested text. He criticizes and rejects a narrow form of textualism that
engages in "strict constructionism" and "hyperliteralism." (Scalia and Garner 2012, 39–41). Within our assumed boundaries of originalist textualism,
there is much to commend in a "fair-reading" interpretive stance. Our concern lies in those moments, particularly evidenced in his rhetoric, where Justice Scalia seems to betray a fair reading—which may allow for diverse interpretive assessments—and instead insists upon his own. He often does seem
hyperliteralist.

In his opinions Justice Scalia often utilizes rhetorical phrases that rebuke
opposing interpretive approaches not simply as differing interpretive judgments but as falling at a far, irresponsible end of the interpretive spectrum.
He often criticizes opposing views as being: "absurd,"[2] "implausible,"[3] "nonsense,"[4] "irrational,"[5] "inconceivable,"[6] and "unquestionably wrong."[7] In contrast, he uses the following kind of rhetorical vocabulary to endorse the inexo-
rability of his own interpretive approach: it is the "best" and "only plausible"
interpretation,[8] an interpretation of which there is "no doubt;"[9] it follows "ineluctably"[10] to the proper interpretive conclusion. As mentioned, we concentrate our attention particularly on Justice Scalia's characterization of an opposing interpretive view as *absurd*, and we argue that his usage of this term
exemplifies his rhetorical style and an interpretive excess that expands rather
than constrains his judicial discretion.

The *Bush v. Gore* Concurrence

In considering Justice Scalia's characterization of an opposing view as absurd,
we begin with what we consider to be a most illuminating judicial example:
the concurrence in *Bush v. Gore*. Although the concurrence was formally authored by Chief Justice Rehnquist, we contend that the rhetorical language in
a decisive passage shows many of the hallmark features of Justice Scalia's rhetorical style. The significance of the case highlights the potential consequences
of the rhetorical method. In that case, as many will recall, the Supreme Court
had to decide whether a Florida presidential recount should continue. The
case's conclusion was decisive for the resolution of the 2000 presidential race,
because halting the recount, as the Court did, would give the Florida popular vote, the Florida electoral college vote, and the presidency to candidate
Bush. Most of the commentary on the Court decision has focused on the five-
member majority's decision to stop the recount on Equal Protection grounds,
but we concentrate here on the three-member concurrence's attention to the

language of Florida state law. This concurrence is a significant marker for our larger thesis, because it claims to be interpreting in a straightforward fashion Florida state law—and so not engaging in judicial discretion of its own—while castigating and rejecting what it views to be an abuse of judicial discretion by the Florida Supreme Court, whose decision it is reviewing.

The concurrence argues that Article II of the federal Constitution requires each state to appoint electors for the electoral college as the state legislature provides. The concurrence contends that while federal courts ordinarily defer to state court interpretations of state law, the constitutional requirement here imposes special significance on the Court's adherence to the text of the state election law. We do not enter the debate about whether the concurrence's interpretation of the Article II requirements is justifiable, except to note that the other two members of the Court majority—Justice Kennedy and Justice O'Connor—do not join the concurrence, and the *Bush v. Gore* dissent strenuously disagrees with the concurrence's analysis.

Given our own emphasis on judicial rhetoric, we elide much of the concurrence's argument about relevant details of Florida state election law and focus on a central passage in the opinion whose rhetorical tones seem very much in accord with Justice Scalia's patterns and habits of word usage. In this section, the concurrence is reviewing and rejecting the Florida Supreme Court's distinction in the relevant Florida statute between a "vote tabulation" and a "vote tabulation system." The Florida court argued that the difference in terms allowed a recount to proceed in order to correct the "vote tabulation" due to human errors in marking punch card ballots, even if the "vote tabulation system"—the electronic voting system—functioned properly. The concurrence vigorously differs. In three telling rhetorical phrases, the concurrence contends that "[n]o reasonable person" would conclude there was an error in vote tabulation if the vote tabulation system worked and that the argument raised by the Florida court was "of course absurd" and "inconceivable."[11] In the view of the concurrence, the Florida decision is not just mistaken but beyond the bounds of reason; it is absurd and inconceivable.

Note the implications. The concurrence was unwilling to defer to the Florida court's interpretation of its state law and instead pronounced its own judgment on the meaning of state law. The rhetoric suggests a widening of an interpretive space—interpretive discretion—for the concurrence and a limiting of a space for the Florida court's reasoning. And the argument supported the denial of the continuation of the recount, to candidate Bush's advantage.

What evidence, though, do we have that Justice Scalia may have played a hand in the rhetoric of this passage? Initially, we were so struck by the anecdotal similarity of the passage quoted to rhetorical moves used by Justice

Scalia in other opinions that we wondered whether Chief Justice Rehnquist might have delegated portions of the concurrence to Justice Scalia. To explore this possibility empirically, we compiled a corpus of Supreme Court opinions from each of the three justices and then built a machine classifier that analyzed and compared how each author used the most frequently occurring words in the collection of documents. In blind, tenfold cross-validation, the model achieved 93% accuracy in identifying the three authors, and then predicted with an 80% probability that the most likely author of the concurrence was Chief Justice Rehnquist.[12] If everything about the usage of language in the concurrence were perfectly consistent with the language usage typical to Chief Justice Rehnquist, then we could perhaps expect a 100% probability for the Chief Justice. That we did not observe such a result suggested the possibility that another hand was at work in the document. In this case, the second most likely of the three justices was Justice Scalia, with a 19% probability.

This evidence was certainly not enough in itself to claim that Justice Scalia contributed to the concurrence, but it did open the door for deeper exploration. Instead of looking only at the usage of high-frequency words, we expanded our analysis to identify words that are frequent in one author's documents but comparatively absent from the others. Of special interest here was the machine's identification of a number of relevant rhetorical terms that Justice Scalia used at a rate quite above the mean use of his colleagues in the concurrence. His usage of the word *absurd* (or variants, such as *absurdity*) was, for example, 3.78 times greater than the mean usage of that term in opinions by Justices Rehnquist and Thomas. Further, his use of *inconceivable* was 3.07 times greater than that of his two colleagues. None of the three justices employed the phrase "no reasonable person" very often, but the phrase may still register some possible associations with Justice Scalia. As we shall see later in his extrajudicial writing, he defines absurdity in relation to an interpretation that "no reasonable person" could endorse.

For further context, consider that Justice Scalia uses the term *absurd* in some 121 opinions (13%)[13] — across almost every year that he was on the Supreme Court bench — including in 7 opinions in 2000, the year of the *Bush v. Gore* concurrence. Chief Justice Rehnquist employs the term *absurd* in only 21 (2%) cases, and Justice Thomas, in only 28 (4%). Justice Scalia uses the term *inconceivable* in 30 (3%) of his opinions, Chief Justice Rehnquist in 19 (1%), and Justice Thomas in 4 (0.5%). In 10 of Justice Scalia's opinions, he uses both *inconceivable* and *absurd*, while Chief Justice Rehnquist does so in only 1, and Justice Thomas never does. On the basis of this quantitative analysis, we contend, then, that there is significant evidence to suggest that the rhetoric in the central passage in the *Bush v. Gore* concurrence came at the instigation of Justice Scalia. In a case of national importance, this rhetoric did not limit but allowed the expansion of judicial discretion.

We cannot know with certainty whether we are correct in our evaluation of Justice Scalia's role in the concurrence's rhetoric, but the evidence is compelling and forms the predicate for the remainder of our analysis. We go on to argue that these habits of word usage are quite reflective of Justice Scalia's interpretive approach across his opinions. This larger examination also responds to a potential critique that whoever inserted the rhetorical language into the *Bush v. Gore* concurrence may have been doing so as a singular event occasioned by the import of the ultimate decision. Instead, we find considerable consistency across a significant swath of Justice Scalia's opinions, and we find that these rhetorical habits tend to diminish opposing views and exalt his own as definitive.

The Absurdity Doctrine in Contrast to the
Critique of Interpretive Views as Absurd

Justice Scalia's characterization of an opposing interpretive view as "absurd" is not simply a colloquialism. He appears intentionally to be drawing upon the absurdity doctrine and its long lineage. In a footnote to his opinion in *K Mart Corp. v. Cartier, Inc.*,[14] for instance, he notes the doctrine as a "venerable principle," quoting an 1869 Supreme Court decision that in turn cited examples from the seventeenth-century German jurist Samuel Pufendorf and the sixteenth-century English jurist Edmund Plowden of absurd implications of laws that would not be enforced precisely because they were absurd. In *King v. Burwell*,[15] Justice Scalia quotes the 1819 opinion of Chief Justice Marshall in *Sturges v. Crowninshield*,[16] that a court should reject as absurd and so not impose the seeming meaning of a provision whose consequence is "'so monstrous, that all mankind, would, without hesitation, unite in rejecting the application.'" In his book with Bryan Garner, *Reading Law*, Justice Scalia cites Blackstone to similar effect. (Scalia and Garner 2012, 234, and n. 1.) Aside from his citation of *Sturges v. Crowninshield*, however, it is unusual for Justice Scalia's opinions to define what it actually means for an interpretive approach to be "absurd." The definition of *absurdity* is central to our argument regarding his rhetorical excess in using the term. As we have anticipated, we want to distinguish between the definition of *absurdity* in the absurdity doctrine and what we argue is in fact quite a divergent usage when Justice Scalia criticizes an alternate interpretation to his own as absurd.

For the purposes of this chapter, we do not engage in a debate about the merits of the absurdity doctrine, and we accept—and indeed emphasize—Justice Scalia's definition of the doctrine in his academic writing. In the several-page discussion of the doctrine in *Reading Law*, he and coauthor Garner define the doctrine as follows: "A provision may be either disregarded or judicially corrected as an error (when the correction is textually simple) if failing to do so would result in a disposition that *no reasonable person* could approve" (Scalia and Garner 2012, 234; emphasis added). We stress three elements or implications of this definition. First, as we have highlighted, for a disposition to be absurd, it must be one that "no reasonable person" could accept. A reviewing court should normally not second-guess the rationale of an enacting body, even if the disposition is odd or anomalous. The court must accept a wide range of reasonableness from a provision's enactors and should restrain against imposing its own values, its own judicial discretion. Only when the disposition is one to which no reasonable person would agree should the court rewrite or refrain from enforcing the provision. This stance is consistent with the language of Chief Justice Marshall, cited earlier, that the consequence must be so extreme that all of humanity would "without hesitation, unite in rejecting the application." In a few judicial contexts where Justice Scalia has defined absurdity, he has commented that a result is, for example, "beyond imagination" and "impossible to believe"[17] or an "unthinkable disposition."[18] The equation between the absurd and the endorsement of "no reasonable person" is one to which we will continue to return, and its significance has led to our chapter's title. In his criticism of other interpretive views as absurd, he seems to allow his rhetoric to get away from him, implying that "no reasonable person" could endorse a view contrary to his own. The interrelation of the terms also may provide additional reinforcement for the suggestion that the presence of "absurd" and "no reasonable person" in the *Bush v. Gore* concurrence may have something to do with their conjunction for Justice Scalia.

A second element of the absurdity doctrine is that the focus of evaluation is primarily on the enacted provision and only secondarily and consequentially on the result. As Justice Scalia maintains in his definition, it is the provision that may be disregarded or judicially corrected if it leads to an absurd consequence. His judicial references to the absurdity doctrine sound similar: "[A] provision decrees an absurd result."[19] The results are absurd as arrived at by "a straightforward reading of the statute"[20] or by giving enacted terms their "normal meaning."[21] The difficulty needing redress is the meaning of the provision, and the absurd results simply exemplify this problem. A standard example for Justice Scalia where application of the absurdity doctrine would be appropriate is a scrivener's error—a flaw in the text such as a misprint or elimination of a needed "not."[22] The text is problematic, as witnessed by its absurd implications. We shall shortly return to the consequences of this point when assessing by contrast Justice Scalia's critique of other interpretive views as absurd.

The third implication of the absurdity doctrine is that it is appropriately invoked only rarely, when the meaning of a provision is one that no reasonable person could endorse. We know of only one case where Justice Scalia accepted that the "normal meaning" of a statutory provision was indeed absurd and so required rewriting.[23] More typically, Justice Scalia instead insists that no need exists to invoke the absurdity doctrine, because the contested statutory meaning is not absurd. He has reached this conclusion in twenty-seven of his opinions. In these cases, a "straightforward" reading leads to results that show some sign of reasonableness, even if anomalous or odd. These conclusions protect Justice Scalia's textualism; they claim to defer to a legislative judgment, regardless of whether the judiciary accepts the reasoning as its own. As commentators agree, the absurdity doctrine is "reserved only for exceptional cases" (Manning 2003, 2407). Only if, again quoting Chief Justice Marshall, all of humanity would "unite in rejecting the application" is the doctrine appropriately referenced.

The absurdity doctrine raises some interesting methodological questions in itself. As commentators have recognized, the doctrine may implicate the rationale of textualism, because it arguably requires a differentiation between the meaning of an enacted provision—which in the relevant circumstance is absurd—and a separable legislative intention, which the court's renovation of textual meaning seeks to protect (Dougherty 1994, 132; Manning 2003, 2392). Textualism does not want to grant legal legitimacy to legislative intention unless present in an enacted text. In response, textualist commentators such as Dean John Manning (himself a former Scalia clerk) have sought to reorient the authority of the absurdity doctrine by moving away from legislative intention to the norms of a "relevant linguistic community" (Manning 2003, 2457–58, 2486).

Our concern, however, lies not with the integrity of the absurdity doctrine, a subject we do not take the time to debate, but with the contrast between the elements of the absurdity doctrine and Justice Scalia's criticism of other interpretive approaches as absurd. Here we see the significant role of his rhetoric and its excess. Justice Scalia's criticism of other views as absurd flips the analysis undertaken in the absurdity doctrine. We raise three objections. First, recall his definition of the doctrine: "A provision may be either disregarded or judicially corrected as an error (when the correction is textually simple) if failing to do so would result in a disposition that *no reasonable person* could approve." In critiquing the absurdity of others' views, on the contrary, Justice Scalia's emphasis is no longer on the questionableness of legislative meaning in the text which is made manifest in its absurd implications but on the absurdity of the implications of others' interpretations, which supports his own defense of the text's textualist meaning. The focus is not on whether the meaning of the text itself is absurd, requiring reworking, but on whether an interpretation of the text is absurd. The results of the other interpretation are "so intolerable as to be absurd."[24] An interpretation is to be rejected if it produces "such absurd results."[25] If the interpretation of the text is absurd, then Justice Scalia's interpretation of the text—the "straightforward" reading—survives. Unlike under the absurdity doctrine, the text is not critiqued to raise questions about the legitimate interpretation; the interpretation is critiqued to save the meaning—his meaning—of the text.

Our second objection to Justice Scalia's critique of other views as absurd is that, again contrary to the absurdity doctrine, his recourse to this critique is not rare or exceptional but frequent. Justice Scalia engages in such critique in eighty-five of his opinions, and, as we mentioned at the outset, this frequency simply typifies similar rhetorical vocabulary that he uses on multiple other occasions. Our objection here correlates with our third criticism, that in these many opinions rejecting opposing views as absurd, he appears to be claiming that these views are ones that "no reasonable person" could draw, that they offer interpretive resolutions that humanity would unite in rejecting. The space he demarcates for what "no reasonable person" could conclude is not narrow but significantly broadened, and the space is enhanced in these multiple judicial opinions. We do not dispute that Justice Scalia's judicial analyses can be insightful and well-delineated. But it is something else again for him to assert the absurdity not only of the views of parties to a dispute but of those of his colleagues on the Supreme Court bench. He may have legitimate disagreements with his colleagues, but it is difficult to accept that theirs are absurd and therefore so extreme that they are ones to which "no reasonable person" could consent. It should be noted too that these accusations of absurdity often appear in a Scalia opinion when he is not writing for the majority but supplementing the majority decision with an independent take as a concurrence or criticizing the majority in a dissent. In many of his judicial assertions of absurdity, then, he is not even in the majority among the members of the Court.

It might be claimed that there is no necessary correlation between whether in a particular case Justice Scalia writes in the minority and whether his argument is indeed the legally correct one. In the next section, we respond to this criticism by offering more detailed, substantive elaboration of these criticisms of Justice Scalia's approach through examination of several of his opinions where he claims opposing views are absurd. For now, our claim is that the expansiveness of his critique of other interpretations as absurd, as without reason, documents his own rhetorical excess. His rhetoric widens the space for his own judgments; he enhances rather than delimits his own judicial discretion. To our knowledge, our evaluation of Justice Scalia's critique of other interpretations as absurd is distinct. His critique's divergence from the absurdity doctrine and its own character, rhetoric, and implications for judicial discretion are not elsewhere analyzed, whether by Justice Scalia himself in his opinions, or in his extrajudicial writings, or by secondary commentary.

Analysis of Justice Scalia's Critique
of Views as Absurd in His Opinions

In this section we draw upon an illustrative sampling of Justice Scalia's opinions to test whether the logic of these opinions permits his evaluation that opposing views construe a statute or constitutional provision in ways that produce absurd results, ones that "no reasonable person" could endorse. In most instances, we believe that a brief presentation of the differing views in a case suffices to show, contrary to Justice Scalia's absurdity claim, that some reasonable grounds exist for the disputed interpretations. We examine at greater length, for its salience, the debate in one recent case, *King v. Burwell.* We proceed in chronological order, from a case in 1989 early in Justice Scalia's tenure on the Court to the *Burwell* decision in 2015, and we include a range of issues, both in statutory and constitutional dimensions and in differing levels of visibility.

In *Texas Monthly, Inc. v. Bullock,*[26] the Court held unconstitutional, as a violation of the Establishment Clause, a Texas statute that exempted religious periodicals from the state sales tax. In his three-member dissent, Justice Scalia argued that there was no violation of either the Establishment Clause or the First Amendment's Press Clause, which forbids Congress from making a law abridging the freedom of the press. To accommodate religion under the Freedom of Religion Clause, he maintained that it was "absurd," "beyond imagination," and "impossible to believe" that the state could not tax a secular magazine more than a religious periodical.

In *Roper v. Simmons,*[27] the Court held that it was a violation of the Eighth Amendment prohibition against cruel and unusual punishments for an adolescent criminal defendant to be sentenced to death. The Court reached this conclusion in significant part on the basis of scientific and sociological evidence of the immaturity and recklessness of the adolescent brain. Writing for a three-member dissent, Justice Scalia argued that it was "absurd" to compare laws restricting driving, drinking, voting, marrying, or serving on a jury on the basis of age to knowledge that murder is deeply wrong.

In *Romer v. Evans*,[28] the Court struck down as a violation of equal protection a 1992 Colorado amendment to its state constitution that forbade municipalities from providing protections against discrimination on the basis of sexual orientation. The Court majority held that the law bore no rational relation to a legitimate government end and indeed conversely seemed motivated by "animus toward the class it affects." Writing for a three-member dissent, Justice Scalia contended that the majority's denial as unconstitutional of a democratic procedure was a "facially absurd proposition."

In *District of Columbia v. Heller*,[29] the Court debated whether the Second Amendment's right to bear arms protected that right for individuals or restricted the right in connection with service in a militia. As is well known, the Second Amendment provides that "[a] well regulated Militia, being necessary to the security of a free state, the right of the people to keep and bear Arms, shall not be infringed." Writing for the Court majority, Justice Scalia held that the Amendment granted the right to bear arms to individuals. In countering the dissent's interpretation, Justice Scalia asserted that the dissent's conjunction of "bear arms" with military service led to a definition that was an "absurdity." As Justice Scalia acknowledged, his views were disputed not only by the four justices in dissent but by an amicus brief authored by professors of Linguistics and English.

Finally, in *King v. Burwell*,[30] the Court addressed elements of the Patient Protection and Affordable Care Act ("Obamacare"). The Affordable Care Act appeared to be predicated upon three interlocking requirements: insurance coverage of preexisting conditions (including premiums assessed on the basis of community ratings, not individual conditions); mandates of individual insurance participation; and tax credits for participation for individuals of lower income. The tax credits depended in part on whether a taxpayer had enrolled in an insurance plan through "an Exchange established by the State," and the question before the Court was whether tax credits were available in states that had federal Exchanges rather than state Exchanges. Writing for the six-member majority, Chief Justice Roberts argued that the phrase "established by the State" was ambiguous, given the larger statutory context. And, he continued, the broader design of the statute led the Court to a holding that tax credits were available in states with federal Exchanges. Quoting prior precedent in the *United Savings Association* case, the Court reaffirmed: "'A provision that may seem ambiguous in isolation is often clarified by the remainder of the statutory scheme . . . because only one of the permissible meanings produces a substantive effect that is compatible with the rest of the law.'"[31] In the Court's view, a contrary ruling could have fatally undermined the congressional scheme. It was unlikely that Congress would have meant for a "sub-sub-sub section of the Tax Code" to affect the viability of the Affordable Care Act. Again quoting precedent in support, here from the *Whitman* case, Chief Justice Roberts maintained that Congress "'does not alter the fundamental details of a regulatory scheme in vague terms or ancillary provisions.'"[32] For our purposes, it is of interest—and, to our knowledge, little commented upon—that the *United Savings* and *Whitman* decisions quoted by the chief justice were authored by Justice Scalia.

In his three-member dissent, Justice Scalia strongly objected to the Court's interpretation. In response to the Court's claim that an Exchange "established by the State" includes a federal Exchange, his opening paragraph was quite direct: "That is of course quite absurd." While agreeing with the Court that statutory context matters in interpretation of a contested passage, Justice Scalia criticized the Court for using context not to understand the law but as an excuse for rewriting it. In his view, the statutory design is relevant only to clarify ambiguity, and the contested passage was not ambiguous. Recognizing the majority's challenge that the Act sought to require tax credits to ensure the Act's viability, Justice Scalia responded that evidence of congressional meaning comes only "from the terms of the law, and those terms show beyond all question that tax credits are available only on state Exchanges." Justice Scalia also seemed aware that his own interpretation might itself be regarded as absurd given its conclusions, but he disallowed that the contested passage was open to the absurdity doctrine's limitation to a scrivener's error or misprint decreeing "an absurd result," one so monstrous that all humanity would reject its application.

As throughout this chapter, it is not our purpose to decide in *King v. Burwell* or in the other cases discussed whether one side is legally correct and the other legally wrong. It suffices if we raise as a substantial question whether Justice Scalia is accurate in maintaining that opposing views were absurd and therefore ones that no reasonable person could hold. In *King v. Burwell* it seems particularly instructive that Chief Justice Roberts quotes in support of his holding arguments about the integration of statutory context that come from prior majority decisions by Justice Scalia. We raise more generally the question of whether in his practice Justice Scalia's rhetoric enhances rather than reduces his judicial discretion. We question whether he adheres to his claim of a "fair reading" of a legal text or instead does engage in "hyperliteralism" and "strict constructionism."

Conclusion

We contend, then, that the evidence we have gathered shows that Justice Scalia frequently invokes rhetorical terms criticizing other views as "absurd" or to similar ends when plausible arguments are raised on the other side. If absurdity requires that "no reasonable person" could agree with an outcome, then the opposing views are not absurd. Our conclusion has significant methodological consequences, as they implicate Justice Scalia's claims that his originalist textualism imposes substantial constraint on judicial discretion. We find instead that Justice Scalia's rhetoric permits him an expansion of his own discretion by way of narrowing the seeming reasonability of opposing stances. This expansion of discretion is relevant to critique both in more ordinary cases of interpretation and in more visible and consequential cases, such as the *Bush v. Gore* decision, where the concurrence, we argue, asserted judicial discretion in significant part due to rhetorical language in a decisive passage that has all the linguistic hallmarks of Justice Scalia's unique style and rhetorical excess. We hope that our quantitative "distant reading" (Moretti 2013) of Justice Scalia's corpus of opinions, conjoined with a more traditional "close reading" of individual opinions, has offered a unique and fruitful perspective on Justice Scalia's patterns of rhetorical word use. It may be that the quantitative tools of text mining will find increasing merit in legal analysis, as they have already done in other disciplines.

At the horizon of our analysis lies a concern that Justice Scalia's effort to reduce opposition to absurdity may rest less in the claimed univocality of the legal text than in his goal, as interpreter, to establish a law of rules (Scalia 1989). In contrast, we find more often occasions where interpretive judgment of a disputed statutory or constitutional provision is required. Reorientation of legal interpretation from an initial framework of interpretive rule to interpretive judgment would require greater attention to the nature—and limitations—of judgment, a subject we continue to pursue in work on legal hermeneutics and understandings of Aristotelian practical judgment (Taylor 2017; Nascimento 2014; Ricoeur 2000).

References

Dougherty, Veronica M. 1994. "Absurdity and the Limits of Literalism: Defining the Absurd Result Principle in Statutory Interpretation." *American University Law Review* 44:127–66.

Manning, John F. "The Absurdity Doctrine." 2003. *Harvard Law Review* 116:2387–486.

Moretti, Franco. 2013. *Distant Reading*. London: Verso.

Nascimento, Fernando. 2014. "Narrative, Mimesis, and Phronetical Deliberation." *Storyworlds: A Journal of Narrative Studies* 6, no. 2, 29–48. Online at https://doi.org/10.1353/stw.2014.0010.

Ricoeur, Paul. 2000. "Interpretation and/or Argumentation." In *The Just*, translated by David Pellauer, 109–26. Chicago: University of Chicago Press.

Scalia, Antonin. 1989. "The Rule of Law as a Law of Rules." *University of Chicago Law Review* 56:1175–88.

———, and Bryan A. Garner. 2012. *Reading Law: The Interpretation of Legal Texts*. St. Paul, MN: Thomson/West.

Taylor, George H. 2017. "Practical Hermeneutics: The Legal Text and Beyond." *Journal of the British Society for Phenomenology* 48, no. 3, 257–74. Online at https://doi.org/10.1080/000 71773.2017.1303121.

Justice Scalia and Family Law

BRIAN H. BIX

Introduction

Justice Antonin Scalia had a long and influential judicial career,[1] having a lasting impact both on the current understanding of the United States Constitution and various federal statutes, and, more generally, on originalism and statutory interpretation (Scalia 1989; 1997). This chapter explores the language Justice Scalia uses to describe and analyze family law, sexuality, and family life. The language is drawn from six cases: *Michael H. v. Gerald D.*[2] (rights of nonmarital biological fathers); *Planned Parenthood of Southeastern Pennsylvania v. Casey*[3] (abortion); *Romer v. Evans*[4] (state law prohibiting local anti-gay discriminatory laws); *Lawrence v. Texas*[5] (criminalization of homosexual sodomy); *Adoptive Couple v. Baby Girl*[6] (Indian Child Welfare Act); and *United States v. Windsor*[7] (Defense of Marriage Act). Through the language Justice Scalia chose, one can see how his distinctive view of law and society shaped his conclusions regarding the scope and limits of the United States Constitution's application to families and family law. Justice Scalia's support for culturally conservative views on the family, and his sharp dismissal of any claim to find other sorts of family structures protected by the U.S. Constitution, are well known. What this article is investigating is something more subtle: the view of human nature, morality, and family life implicit in Justice Scalia's language.

Justice Scalia's Language

MICHAEL H. V. GERALD D.

Michael H. v. Gerald D. involved a child born to a married woman and a man who was not her husband. For a while, those two raised the child together, but eventually the mother went back to her spouse. The biological father's legal effort to obtain continued contact with the child was opposed by the married couple. The state court had sided with the married couple, grounding its decision on a state law marital presumption (presuming a child born to an intact marriage is a child of that marriage). On appeal, the Supreme Court affirmed. In his Opinion for the Court, Justice Scalia repeatedly refers to the plaintiff, Michael H. as an "adulterous father."[8] In contemporary legal and academic writing, a person in that position would more likely be called "the biological father" or "the natural father," both of which clearly avoid the obvious negative connotation of "adulterous" (even "extramarital" would have carried far less of a negative charge).

Judges with whom I have spoken have consistently emphasized that a central task of judges in writing their opinions is to convince readers (whether the general public, the lawyers for the case, or a reviewing court) that the outcome was the right one. If one were to write an opinion in favor of the plaintiff in *Michael H.*, one would likely have emphasized a caring (biological) father kept from his child. It is perhaps not surprising that Justice Scalia, writing an opinion *rejecting* the plaintiff's claim, emphasized "adultery" (sinner, home-wrecker) rather than "father." Seeing the world through the "adultery" lens inclines us toward appropriate (Biblical) punishment for the wrongdoer, in contrast to the view through the "father" lens, where the sympathies would have been with keeping genetically related people together. (There is one place in the opinion where Justice Scalia uses the label "adulterous natural father";[9] the tension between the clearly negative valence of "adulterous" and the generally positive sound of "natural" (and "father") makes the phrase almost poetic.)

PLANNED PARENTHOOD OF SOUTHEASTERN PENNSYLVANIA V. CASEY

Casey involved a challenge to state-law restrictions on abortion. It received a lot of attention at the time because of the belief that the Court might use the case as an occasion to overrule *Roe v. Wade*.[10] Instead, the Court reaffirmed a constitutional right to abortion, with an influential plurality opinion emphasizing the importance of stare decisis. In Justice Scalia's dissent, he objected to the majority's treatment of the state's interest in abortion decisions as relating to "potential life" rather than to "[fully] human life."[11] *Alive* and *potentially alive*, in relation to the abortion debate, are ways of seeing the world that signal and justify outcomes (as does the terminology choice between *fetus* and *unborn child*), with neither term being a helpful description of the underlying reality. A fertilized embryo is alive, as are sperm and egg cells in the human body, as are human cells grown in test tubes. However, the living (not "dead") nature of all of these entities tells us nothing about the constitutionality of laws restricting what pregnant women can do. The choice of terminology signals one's position on the morality of (all, or at least some kinds of) abortions, and, like the use of "adulterous father" versus "biological/natural father" in *Michael H.*, inclines the reader to a normative conclusion — without offering reasoned arguments for it.

Later in his *Casey* dissent, Justice Scalia observes that the way that the plurality opinion foregrounds the political pressure on the Court on this issue will simply encourage more of it. "As long as this Court thought (and the people thought) that we Justices were doing essentially lawyer's work up here, . . . the public pretty much left us alone. . . . [However, if] the 'liberties' protected by the Constitution are, as the Court says, undefined and unbounded, then the people *should* demonstrate, to protest that we do not implement *their* values instead of *ours*."[12] The contrast between "lawyer's work" and "unbounded" political decision-making calls upon a distinction that Justice Scalia both assumes and in part rejects. The assumed position is that what judges do is simply "find the law," using doctrinal analysis and other forms of legal reasoning. At least, that is what Justice Scalia would say that judges *should do*, and the best ones actually do. Throughout his time on the bench (and in a number of the cases covered in this chapter), Justice Scalia, in dissent, would accuse the judges in the majority of doing un-judgelike things, imposing their own policy preferences on the country, in the guise of legal and constitutional analysis.[13] Of course, the question of whether judges can ever avoid (consciously or unconsciously) legislating is a debate that flows through much of legal scholarship, from the American legal realists and the European free law movement, through the legal process movement, critical legal studies, and the works of Ronald Dworkin, just to offer a small sample. There is obviously no time to rehearse the arguments here, beyond noting the way that one side of the debate appears in the language chosen by Justice Scalia.

ROMER V. EVANS

In *Romer v. Evans*, the Court invalidated a state referendum that had enacted an amendment to the state constitution: that amendment prohibited municipalities from passing antidiscrimination ordinances protecting homosexuals. The Court's decision was grounded in part on the conclusion that the referendum had been motivated (the majority claimed) by animus against homosexuals. Justice Scalia's dissent began, "The Court has mistaken a Kulturkampf for a fit of spite."[14] His basic point was that the purpose of the amendment was not a "'bare . . . desire to harm' homosexuals," but "a modest attempt by seemingly tolerant Coloradans to preserve traditional sexual mores against the efforts of a politically powerful minority to revise those mores through use of the laws."[15]

While Justice Scalia might have had a point, one must keep in mind the general picture on which it is based: that it is or should be acceptable to support (a particular view of) appropriate sexual behavior by condoning employment or housing discrimination against those who do not follow the prescribed standards (or, more precisely, by preventing any government body from trying to stop such discrimination).[16] Perhaps this *is* a more civilized response than making unconventional sexual practices subject to serious criminal punishment (like the death penalty that has been provided for in some countries, even, on rare occasions, to this day),[17] but relative leniency hardly rises to moral, or constitutional, persuasiveness.

One should focus also on Justice Scalia's reference to "traditional sexual mores." For Justice Scalia, over the course of his opinions, family and sexual norms seem to have two different aspects, which are in tension. On one hand, such norms are natural and independent of us; on the other hand, they are subject to social change and political choice. Implied in the idea of states protecting "traditional [sexual] morality" is the view of that morality as monolithic and unchanging, although history and sociology teach us that what counts as ("traditional" or "conventional") sexual morality changes greatly over time, and remains variable across people at any given time. On the other hand, at least in his later opinions, Justice Scalia seems quite conscious that (conventional) sexual morality has changed and is continuing to change. In his dissent in *Lawrence v. Texas*, he stated as much: "Social perceptions of sexual and other morality change over time, and every group has the right to persuade its fellow citizens that its view of such matters is best."[18]

Also, in his *Romer* dissent, Justice Scalia follows a standard trope of conservative commentators in characterizing antidiscrimination ordinances as "preferential laws" offering "*special* treatment of homosexuals."[19] The point he was trying to make (echoing an argument made by those defending the law) was that homosexuals remained protected by "general laws and policies that prohibit arbitrary discrimination in government and private settings."[20] Of course, in the legal context in question, it would have been clear that being treated worse *because of one's sexual orientation* would not be considered "arbitrary discrimination." Gays were thus no more seeking "special treatment" in an antidiscrimination law than were racial or religious minorities in their antidiscrimination laws. To speak of "special treatment" is to make it sound as if homosexuals were seeking to be treated *better* than others, when they would have said that they only wanted (with the help of antidiscrimination laws) to be treated the same.[21]

LAWRENCE V. TEXAS

In *Lawrence v. Texas*, the Supreme Court held that states could not criminalize homosexual sexual acts between consenting adults. In his dissent, Justice Scalia famously complained that the Court, "which is the product of a law-profession culture, . . . has largely signed on to the so-called homosexual agenda."[22] As with the reference in *Romer* to "preferential laws" offering "*special* treatment of homosexuals,"[23] one might wonder if the same sort of wording — reference to a "homosexual agenda" — would have been used in relation to other groups that have been historically oppressed in this country, like African Americans, Mormons, or Jews.

Justice Scalia accused the majority of having "taken sides in the culture war, departing from its role of assuring, as neutral observer, that the democratic rules of engagement are observed."[24] Again, the comparison with race issues may be instructive. The chief justice for the early part of Justice Scalia's time on the Supreme Court was William Rehnquist. When Rehnquist was a mere law clerk at the Supreme Court, back in 1955, he famously advised Justice Jackson that the Court should not (in *Brown v. Board of Education*[25]) overturn *Plessy v. Ferguson*,[26] because to do so would just be to repeat the mistake of *Lochner v. New York*, of judges' reading their preferences into the Constitution.[27] The attitude and phrasing of William Rehnquist, as Supreme Court clerk talking about racial desegregation in 1955, is not that different from Antonin Scalia, as Supreme Court justice talking about same-sex marriage, in 2013.

ADOPTIVE COUPLE V. BABY GIRL

In *Adoptive Couple v. Baby Girl*, a mother sought to give up a child for adoption after the father seemed to have abandoned his claim to the child. The father later changed his mind, and brought a suit for custody under the Indian Child Welfare Act (ICWA) against the couple who had sought to adopt the child.[28] The Court rejected the father's claim, reading the ICWA narrowly, and emphasizing that adoption would be in the best interests of the child in question. In his dissent, Justice Scalia wrote,

> The Court's opinion . . . needlessly demeans the rights of parenthood. It has been the constant practice of the common law to respect the entitlement of

those who bring a child into the world to raise that child. We do not inquire whether leaving a child with his parents is "in the best interest of the child." It sometimes is not; he would be better off raised by someone else. But parents have their rights, no less than children do. This father wants to raise his daughter and the statute amply protects his right to do so. There is no reason in law or policy to dilute that protection."[29]

This language is worth noting, primarily for the contrast with the language in *Michael H.*, discussed above. Obviously, the facts and legal context are different. However, as noted, in *Michael H.*, Justice Scalia downplayed the narrative of a biological parent wanting continued contact with his child as a prelude to rejecting the parent's claim, while in this case he made that same narrative salient, as part of an argument for upholding the claim. In *Adoptive Couple*, one could have spoken of the "abandoning father" as easily as one could speak of the "adulterous father" in *Michael H.*

UNITED STATES V. WINDSOR

In *United States v. Windsor*, the Court invalidated a law that refused to recognize same-sex marriages for the purpose of rights and benefits under federal law. In his dissenting opinion in *United States v. Windsor*, Justice Scalia begins with an attention-grabbing sentence: "This case is about power. . . ."[30] What he meant was that the Court's power to pronounce the law in constitutional review cases inevitably comes at the expense of "the power of the people to govern themselves."[31] In part, his complaint was related to a concern about whether the Court should have heard the case at all, where the president refused to defend the federal law.[32] The reference to "power" is a little jolting used in this way in a judicial opinion. As in Justice Scalia's dissent in *Casey*, it invokes a contrast with the Court's properly confining itself to "lawyer's work."

Elsewhere in the *Windsor* dissent, Justice Scalia objects to the majority's analysis that the federal law must be rejected because based on "animus." Justice Scalia insisted that "to defend traditional marriage is not to condemn, demean, or humiliate those who would prefer other arrangements."[33] The majority, according to Justice Scalia, has effectively imposed societal change and has done this "by adjudging those who oppose it [as] enemies of the human race."[34] Against the majority's view that the legislation was motivated by a "bare . . . desire to harm,"[35] Justice Scalia argued that "the Constitution does not forbid the government to enforce traditional moral and sexual norms," whether this be in the area of same-sex marriage, no-fault divorce, polygamy, or the consumption of alcohol.[36] Beyond the picture of "traditional sexual morality," already discussed in connection with Justice Scalia's *Romer* dissent, here we also see (again, as in *Romer*) the notion that one can view an activity or lifestyle as unworthy of recognition or support, or perhaps even properly subject to exclusion and punishment, without this being equivalent to a disparagement of those who practice that activity or lifestyle. In other words, one can "hate the sin, but love the sinner." It is a view commonly asserted, but also commonly contested, and Justice Scalia is clearly on one side of the debate (and the majorities in *Romer* and *Windsor* on the other).

Conclusion

In exploring the language and vision of Justice Scalia in family law cases, the argument of this chapter is *not* that Justice Scalia saw law, society, and humanity "through a glass darkly," while we enlightened folks see clearer and know better. "Ideology" is not something that others have, while we have none. We all see the world through a set of concepts and assumptions.[37] The purpose of the chapter is to use the words of Justice Scalia's family law opinions to show the outlines of his worldview, while acknowledging that all of us have different, equally distinctive and equally contestable, worldviews.

References

Bearok, Max, and Daria Cameron. 2016. "Here Are the 10 Countries Where Homosexuality May Be Punished by Death." *Washington Post*, June 16, 2016. Online at www.washingtonpost .com/news/worldviews/wp/2016/06/13/here-are-the-10-countries-where-homosexuality -may-be-punished-by-death-2/?utm_term=.54f62032aeac.

Foucault, Michel, 1984. "Truth and Power." In *The Foucault Reader*, edited by Paul Rabinow. New York: Pantheon.

Scalia, Antonin. 1989. "Originalism: The Lesser Evil." *University of Cincinnati Law Review* 57: 849.

———. 1997. *A Matter of Interpretation*, edited by Amy Gutmann. Princeton, NJ: Princeton University Press.

Schleiermacher, Friedrich (1813) 2012. "On the Different Methods of Translating." In *The Translation Studies Reader*, 3rd ed., translated by Susan Bernofsky, edited by Lawrence Venuti. London: Routledge.

Snyder, Brad, and John Q. Barrett. 2012. "Rehnquist's Missing Letter: A Former Law Clerk's 1955 Thoughts on Justice Jackson and *Brown*." *Boston College Law Review* 53:631.

Thayer, James B. 1893. "The Origin and Scope of the American Doctrine of Constitutional Law." *Harvard Law Review* 7:129.

PART 4

Rhetorical Criticism of *Heller*

Guns and Preludes

EUGENE GARVER

Antonin Scalia's greatest rhetorical triumph was declaring that he followed an originalist method of interpretation and getting people to believe him. Convincing people both that there is such a method and that he did, and most others did not, practice it are both remarkable achievements, regardless of whether either of these theses is true. All three of those terms, *originalist*, *method*, and *interpretation* deserve attention. First, a quick look at *Heller*—and I will give it more than a quick look—is enough to show that Justice Scalia is no more and no less an originalist than those he opposes.[1] Therefore I turn instead to method and interpretation.

With respect to method, in *Heller* at least, the originalist method leads in this instance to conflicting conclusions. Whether this is a strength or weakness turns on the relation between method and result: is originalism the right method because it leads to the right results? If so, then leading to conflicting conclusions is a deep flaw. To take an easy example, if a deductive system led to conflicting conclusions, either the method or its initial principles would be inadequate and contradictory. If, on the other hand, results are right because they are products of the right method, we have to be open to the possibility that those results might not be what we desire on nonlegal grounds. The scientist is committed to following out the consequences of a method, regardless of whether they agree with common sense or tradition. A judge would be mad to follow the scientist in this respect.[2]

Between these two options, Scalia's rhetoric employs a bait-and-switch strategy: to his wider political audience, as when he rails against the culture wars, he recommends originalism because it leads to all the conclusions any right-thinking conservative would like. To the legal audience, he argues that constitutional interpretation—the nature of judging or the nature of the Constitution—demands originalism, and that whether it leads to politically consistent conclusions is beside the point, as he voted against prohibiting flag burning and frequently sided with criminal defendants. The difference between the appeals to distinct audiences is covered by the following rhetorical argument: since terrible things follow from failure to observe the method, it follows that observing the method will produce good things. It is for this reason that the method of originalism cannot be consistently and determinately used in constructing arguments; its real power is in refutation.

To the extent that the practice of originalism is a method, it is, for Scalia, a method of constraint, or deference, rather than of interpretation. More exactly, *because* it is a method of constraint, it is not a method of interpretation. Avoiding error and producing truth are distinct enterprises. Methods of constraint resemble what philosophers of science sometimes call the method of proof, which constrains the conclusions one can draw from given premises, while methods of interpretation resemble methods of discovery, where the practitioner must find the hypothesis to be tested by the method of proof. Philosophers of science have long debated whether a method of discovery is possible. If it is, "method" will not have the codification that makes the logic of proof so powerful.

In the legal case, if there is a method of interpretation, it will not, as a method of constraint does, exclude *ethos*, judgment, practical reason, or a flexible response to circumstances, which lie at the heart of a method of constraint. Whether excluding practical reason is a feature or a flaw remains to be seen. Mostly, declaring that one has a method is, again in Scalia's hands, a stick with which to beat one's opponents for being irrational. The restraint of method makes unnecessary any ethical restraint by a judge. Thinking oneself rational entitles one to be unreasonable. The vitriol of Scalia's dissents and his inability to understand anyone who disagrees with him come from the lack of ethical restraint.[3]

While I think *originalism* is of little interest, and have to set *method* aside for this brief paper, I think we can learn something about the nature of *interpretation* by focusing on *Heller*. Judicial opinions are a perfect place to examine the nature of interpretation, because hermeneutics is the opposite face of rhetoric; interpretation concerns the reception of texts, and rhetoric, their production. The judge is both hermeneut and rhetor, interpreting the Constitution and persuading an audience of the rightness of that interpretation. A typical text, like a law, is simultaneously an interpretation of a prior text and an object for further interpretation. Preambles, including the preamble to the

Second Amendment, are very unusual objects of interpretation, and a fuller following out of my argument would also show that constitutions are unusual objects as well.

In *Heller* Scalia claims that the preamble to the Second Amendment is surplusage, while the dissenters see it as essential to determining the meaning of the right to keep and bear arms. The justices argue over whether one should consider the preamble before or after determining the meaning of the "operative clause." It should seem strange to anyone not thoroughly socialized into the legal profession that whether or not one has a right to own a gun depends on the precise relation between preamble and operative clause, almost as odd as whether the state of Colorado could prevent municipalities from passing ordinances prohibiting discrimination based on sexual orientation should turn on whether a proper interpretation of a passage from Plato's *Laws* should be done in accordance with one or another edition of the Greek lexicon.[4]

The Constitution itself starts with a preamble, and so one might think that that preamble would be a guide to figuring out what to do with the preamble to the Second Amendment.[5] No justice tries to do that, and with good reason. The preamble to the Constitution names itself a preamble, while the preamble to the Second Amendment does not, and so identifying it as one is a decision, not a datum. It is Scalia, not Madison, who divides the Second Amendment into a "prefatory clause" and an "operative clause."[6] Rather than use scare quotes throughout, I will for the sake of argument accept Scalia's terminology and ask the reader to remember that the Second Amendment says no such thing. While preambles to constitutions are, if not obligatory, at least expected, the preamble to the Second Amendment is an anomaly—unique in the Bill of Rights—and explaining its anomalous presence must be part of understanding its purpose, meaning, and force—something none of the justices in *Heller* tries to do.[7] We need to know not only how the preamble to the Second Amendment is "operative" or not, but also why only the Second Amendment has a preamble. If original understanding includes the structure of the Constitution and not just individual words, all interpretations in *Heller* fail.

Sticking to the U.S. Constitution alone to understand preambles offers too small a sample size. Starting with a focus on preambles lets me build a theory of interpretation from the objects being interpreted, instead of starting with an overall theory. Preambles are an odd set of objects, and seeing how to interpret them will show something about interpretation in general. While a General Theory of Preambles sounds like a chapter in *Tristram Shandy*, I think a wider view can help.

Preludes in the Great American Songbook

American popular songs, especially those that originate in Broadway or movie musicals, often have preambles that are discarded in subsequent performances. They are no longer part of the song. Musical practice seems to be on Scalia's side, downgrading the importance of preludes. Seeing what happens when preludes are deleted shows something about how they work.

Here are two examples, chosen because I think what we normally think of as "the song" would not be anticipated by someone who listens to the preamble, and these are songs with very different emotional tone: "Pick Yourself Up" and "Hello Young Lovers" (www.youtube.com/watch?v=AGUsRGuZb6k and www.youtube.com/watch?v=IsVTj6LNGFU).[8] These preludes are not like overtures to operas or musicals that give quick selections of the music to follow. Their main function is to contextualize the song, to integrate it into the larger whole of a musical or film. The song's meaning is then what the character singing it means. Removing the preamble makes the song autonomous, to be interpreted in a variety of ways for different purposes by different musicians, the difference between what is meant by a text and by a speaker. Preambles are intrusions of history into the declaration of an absolute truth, in Scalia's Second Amendment, a natural right.

The first moral to draw from these examples is that the identity of an object, in this case a song, is not a neutral datum, in contrast to its multiple interpretations. What constitutes a song's identity is the product of an interpretative decision. Instead of assuming that there can be a neutral statement of the law that allows different interpretations, the identity of the law depends on its interpretation. That there is no neutral object called a song or a law prior to interpretation is old news to philosophers of science, who have been arguing for decades against the idea of neutral data. It is also old news to interpreters of the Bible, since how to mark off the boundaries of the text(s) called the Decalogue or Ten Commandments, and indeed what to call them, are contested and not given.[9]

Second, the deletion of a prelude not only makes the song more universal in meaning; it also becomes more universal in who can sing it. There is both gain and loss in this universalizing. "Hello Young Lovers" can now be sung by anyone, man or woman, but the emotional poignancy of Deborah Kerr's presentation is lost when I sing it. Because there is both gain and loss, there can be no general principle that preambles either are or ought to be part of the laws. And with the generalizing of the speaker comes a generalizing of audience; a prelude may be direct address, like a soliloquy, breaking the fourth wall of the theater, but the musical performance severed from dramatic context can have multiple or indeterminate audiences, as can legal texts.

The universalizing that comes from deleting the preamble is at work in Scalia's opinion in *Heller*, which states that "the 'militia' in colonial America consisted of a subset of 'the people'—those who were male, able bodied, and within a certain age range. Reading the Second Amendment as protecting only the right to 'keep and bear Arms' in an organized militia therefore fits poorly with the operative clause's description of the holder of the right as 'the people.' We start therefore with a strong presumption that the Second Amendment right is exercised individually and belongs to all Americans" (580–81).[10] Even more indicative of the universalizing power of deleting prologues is Scalia's account of his difference from Justice Breyer:

> It is therefore entirely sensible that the Second Amendment's prefatory clause announces the purpose for which the right was codified to prevent elimination of the militia. The prefatory clause does not suggest that preserving the militia was the only reason Americans valued the ancient right; most undoubtedly thought it even more important for self-defense and hunting. But the threat that the new Federal Government would destroy the citizens' militia by taking away their arms was the reason that right—unlike some other English right—was codified in a written Constitution. Justice Breyer's assertion that individual self-defense is merely a 'subsidiary interest' of the right to keep and bear arms . . . is profoundly mistaken. He bases his assertion solely upon the prologue—but that can only show that self-defense had little to do with the right's *codification*; it was the *central component* of the right itself. (661–62)[11]

If Breyer, according to Scalia, bases his assertion on the prologue alone, Scalia bases his not on the text at all but on what most Americans at the time "undoubtedly thought." An odd assertion for a textualist, but this is not an area where consistency is an ultimate value. Even if he's right about the facts—that this was the main reason Americans valued "the ancient right"—it does not follow that that reason is central to the right protected by the Second Amendment. The Second Amendment doesn't protect the ancient right. It protects those aspects of the right that its authors or ratifiers thought were or could be threatened by the federal government. Thus Breyer's dissent: "There is no indication that the Framers of the Amendment intended to enshrine the common-law right of self-defense in the Constitution" (637).[12]

Scalia argues that the universal, or natural, right precedes the protection of the right whose purpose is announced in the preamble. There is a harmony between universalizing a text and believing oneself to have an objective, impersonal method of interpretation, as both focus on the meaning of an utterance rather than of a speaker, and a proposition rather than a speech act. Admitting the possibility that texts have meaning, not reducible to what they mean *to* someone, rescues us from the false dilemma Scalia imposes: that the Second Amendment must either mean what it meant to people in 1791 or to people in 2008.

And yet Scalia assumes that meaning is not the meaning intended by a speaker, or meaning embodied in a text, but meaning *to* someone, the some-one who he insists is the reader of 1791.[13] In this case, Scalia claims that we first have the right, and then one aspect of it needs protecting, but what really counts is the protection of the whole right. The operative clause precedes the preamble in our order of understanding, even though the two are reversed in order of exposition. And so when Breyer accuses Scalia of putting the opera-tive clause before the preamble, he wasn't just talking, as Scalia took it, in terms of order of exposition, but of reasoning. Scalia argues that one first in-spects the operative clause, and only if it is ambiguous does one then turn to the preamble for help in interpretation.[14]

But whether an utterance is ambiguous depends on what uses are made of it: ambiguity is often a property of *parole*, as well as of *langue*. A brief ex-ample from a completely different sort of textual interpretation clarifies the difference. In Plato's *Charmides*, Critias says that the definition of temperance is knowledge of knowledge, that *sôphrosynê* is *epistêmê hêautou*. A quick look at the Greek dictionary is enough to show that Critias didn't know Greek, since *epistêmê hêautou* doesn't come close to any of the definitions offered in Liddell-Scott-Jones (*A Greek-English Lexicon*). But Plato is a competent writer of Attic Greek, and the character Critias in the *Charmides* is depicted as a competent speaker. And the dictionary isn't incompetent or wrong either. Critias speaks correctly, if not truly, and the dictionary reports accurately. And yet they don't match up. The fault is not in Plato, and not in Liddell and his successors, but in a reader who thinks that the dictionary offers a sort of help it isn't designed for. The obvious reply to my tendentious example is that a Platonic dialogue is different from the Constitution. But that makes my point. Genre is relevant to interpretation.[15] Words are not automatically, as Scalia assumes, the unit of interpretation.

The difference between the ambiguity of *langue* and of *parole* makes the search for meaning rhetorical rather than lexicographic. As Madison put it in *Federalist 37*, "All new laws, though penned with the greatest technical skill, and passed on the fullest and most mature deliberation, are considered as more or less obscure and equivocal, until their meaning be liquidated and ascertained by the series of particular discussions and adjudications." Inter-pretation as liquidation is a rhetorical idea in which meaning emerges only in controversy or, more broadly, when a text is *used* to address some problem, to make a problematic situation determinate.[16] The need for interpretation does not come from a defect in the text, such as vagueness or ambiguity. And so Scalia's assertion that constitutions are designed to prevent change is pure assertion.[17]

The example of preambles destroys that naive epistemology even further. A prelude can be omitted or sung; therefore the identity of a song is a decision, a choice between contextualizing and universalizing. But in addition, in the case of preambles, each enactment is a distinct speech act, not a token of a type, in a way not true for statutes or constitutional operative clauses, just because it is direct address. If some other nation were to adopt the preamble to the U.S. Constitution (almost) verbatim, it wouldn't have the same meaning and so wouldn't be a single text that made two distinct appearances, but two distinct texts. Some nation can adopt bicameralism or a strong or weak executive from our Constitution, but the preambles to different constitutions are *sui generis*. Preambles, then, are the most illiberal aspects of constitutions. The sentiments they express might be universal—who could object to justice and domestic tranquility?—but they are acts of expression by a particular people at a particular time, unlike the body of the Constitution, which comprises commands and prohibitions that are not voiced by anyone in particular, and so can be adopted or rejected on their merits by any nation.

A preamble has a speaker's meaning, a meaning intended by a speaker to be understood by an audience, not an utterance meaning, and so can't be appropriated. The power of laws comes from the ability of readers to abstract from their conditions of utterance. Preambles are recalcitrant to such abstraction.[18] Since Scalia believes that he is recovering an "original public understanding" as opposed to the intentions of authors, or the meaning of the text itself, the preamble cannot have meaning for him.[19]

Whether or not interpretation has a *method*, it does have a *principle*: the principle of charity or equity. Originalism, literalism, textualism, levels of generality—these are not productive ways to talk about constitutional interpretation. They only have polemical value. A more substantive way to understand constitutional interpretation and interpretation more generally is through the principle of charity. That principle has two principal forms: I can interpret a text under the assumption that it is a meaningful utterance, or under the much stronger assumption that it is a truthful utterance. When I try to understand Critias's definitions of temperance in the *Charmides*, I don't assume that whatever he says must be true, but I do presuppose that he's a competent speaker of Greek and, sincere or not, intends to be understood by Socrates as saying something meaningful enough to be cross-examined. When I ask for street directions in a strange city, I don't just assume that the person I ask is not speaking gibberish, but that she is telling the truth. Augustine teaches how to interpret the Bible in *de Doctrina Christiana*: since the Bible is the Word of God, it is true. The task of interpretation is to figure out how what it says is true.

But when we interpret law, the situation is slightly different. We're interpreting commands rather than statements. Instead of occupying a continuum between trying to determine meaning and truth, the range goes from seeing a law—and especially the Constitution—as an act of will to seeing a law as an act of reason.[20] As an act of will, it is tied to its situation of utterance; an act of reason floats free of its origins.

I draw three morals from this extended analogy between legal preambles and musical prologues. First, as I've already noted, that prologues can be omitted in performance shows that songs are not given, stable objects; their identity as objects depends on interpretation and is not prior to it. Second, the outstanding function of a prologue is to tie a song to its context, and removing the prologue is a way of universalizing the song, including universalizing who can sing to whom. Third, prologues are unusual hermeneutic objects, because their interpretations do not become texts open to further interpretation in their own right. They are neither paradigms for imitation nor instances of a general type. They are pure *paroles*, and never become *langue*. Understanding what makes preambles atypical hermeneutic objects can help us to see what unusual objects constitutions are, and what an unusual activity constitutional interpretation is. Justice Marshall famously said, "In considering this question, then, we must never forget, that it is a *constitution* we are expounding." In considering the first phrase of the Second Amendment, we must never forget, that it is a *preamble* we are expounding.[21]

However, I don't have space here to do that. Instead I want to conclude by going back from interpretation to method. I've argued that Scalia's method of interpretation—indeed, calling what he does a method—has rhetorical, polemical value but no substantive meaning. His method rather contains a substantive ambiguity, an ambiguity that allows for cheating. Practical reason should be a place for productive ambiguity in the relation between method and result. No practical person can say, "Follow a method and let the chips fall where they may." *Fiat justitia, ruat coelum*. No practical person can simply reinforce her preferences with rationalization. It is in the interplay between method and result, moving in both directions of inference, where practical wisdom and good judgment are found.

Of Guns and Grammar:
Justice Scalia's Rhetoric

PETER BROOKS

There are many full-throated moments of operatic rhetoric in Justice Scalia's opinions. One of the most notable comes at the end of his dissent in *Planned Parenthood v. Casey*, the 1992 case that largely reaffirmed the holdings of *Roe v. Wade*. Scalia evokes the portrait of Chief Justice Taney that hangs in the Harvard Law School. For Scalia, it suggests Taney's recent decision in *Dred Scott v. Sandford* (1857):

> [The portrait was] painted in 1859, the 82d year of his life, the 24th of his Chief Justiceship, the second after his opinion in *Dred Scott*. He is all in black, sitting in a shadowed red armchair, left hand resting upon a pad of paper in his lap, right hand hanging limply, almost lifelessly, beside the inner arm of the chair. He sits facing the viewer and staring straight out. There seems to be on his face, and in his deep-set eyes, an expression of profound sadness and disillusionment. Perhaps he always looked that way, even when dwelling upon the happiest of thoughts. But those of us who know how the lustre of his great Chief Justiceship came to be eclipsed by *Dred Scott* cannot help believing that he had that case — its already apparent consequences for the Court and its soon-to-be-played-out consequences for the Nation — burning on his mind. I expect that two years earlier he, too, had thought himself "call[ing] the contending sides of national controversy to end their national division by accepting a common mandate rooted in the Constitution."[1]

I think the proper name for Scalia's trope here might be *ekphrasis*, the verbal recreation of a painted image (though it also has elements of *prosopopeia*, attributing speech to the eminent dead). It might remind us of famous ekphrastic moments in classic novels, such as Lucy Snowe's encounter with the fleshy portrait of Cleopatra in Charlotte Brontë's *Villette* or Milly Theale's discovery of her mortality before a Bronzino portrait in Henry James's *The Wings of the*

Dove. Such moments inevitably set up mirrorings: the living beholder receives back some self-knowledge from the stasis of the art work beheld. It harbors a truth about the human condition suddenly revealed. For Scalia in *Planned Parenthood v. Casey*, that truth is a negative one: attempts by the Court to resolve great national controversies in a "common mandate rooted in the Constitution" are bound to fail. Just as *Dred Scott* led to Civil War, *Casey*, following *Roe*, will lead to an increasingly dire culture war. "We should get out of this area, where we have no right to be, and where we do neither ourselves nor the country any good by remaining," he writes in the final sentence of his opinion.

It's not clear to me that the ekphrasis of the Taney portrait works quite as Scalia intends. His position in dissent seems actually to resemble closely Taney's in the majority, and indeed Taney sounds very much like a Scalian originalist in his reasoning: "No one, we presume, supposes that any change in public opinion, or feeling, in relation to this unfortunate race, in the civilized nations of Europe or in this   country, should induce the court to give to the words of the Constitution a more liberal construction in their favor than they were intended to bear when the instrument was framed and adopted. Such an argument would be altogether inadmissible in any tribunal called on to interpret it."[2] Ekphrastic portraits, like constitutions, require interpretation. They don't automatically provide the symbolic representations that you are seeking. Perhaps Taney is mirroring Scalia himself more than the authors of the controlling Joint Opinion in *Casey* (Justices Kennedy, O'Connor, and Souter). One can somewhat more easily conceive of the brooding Scalia, rather than the relatively cheerful authors of the Joint Opinion, face to face with the brooding Taney. Scalia's finale in *Casey* is impressive but, to me at least, inconclusive in the vector of its application.

I am, of course, using Scalia's ekphrastic moment to suggest what I have often found amiss in Scalia's rhetoric and in the praise so often heaped on it. It can be sonorous and momentarily impressive, but its aim often seems uncertain, and its effect tends to dissipate when you look at it carefully. Scalia presents himself as the Supreme Court justice who knows rhetoric and has studied interpretation—on which he published two well-known books. Yet his rhetorical fireworks often seem to go off in the wrong directions. This problem seems to me related to his claim to interpret with a greater fidelity to the "original understanding" of the Constitution than anyone else: the interpretive moves and the rhetorical flourishes seem to reinforce one another to produce a result that is more imposed than textually justified. I find the whole "originalist" claim to be largely incoherent and incompatible with Scalia's professed adherence to "textualism" in any event: the rules of interpretation, and the limits he wishes to impose on interpretation, seem largely arbitrary. I want to pursue this argument through attention to one of his most consequential majority opinions, that in *District of Columbia v. Heller* (2008).

I choose *Heller*, which overturned the District's gun-control laws, in part because it deals with a crucial interpretative issue in the Bill of Rights, and also because it seems a good test of Scalia's claims as a theoretician of inter-pretation. In his major statement on the subject, in the book *A Matter of In-terpretation* (1997)—more vigorously polemical than the later *Reading Law* (2012)—he laments that courts have "no intelligible, generally accepted, and consistently applied theory of statutory interpretation."[3] He wants to promote strict canons of interpretation, to rule out any consideration of legislative his-tory, the crutch usually relied on by courts when the "plain meaning" of a statute isn't so plain, in favor of a close attention to the text itself. Interpreters should restrict their attention to "the intent that a reasonable person would gather from the text of the law" (at 17). When he comes to constitutional inter-pretation, he argues that one should not search for the intent of the framers—which would be a pretextualist approach—but seek out the "original under-standing" of the text, how it was first interpreted, consulting *The Federalist*, for instance, and views of delegates to the Constitutional Convention. This is the notion that now goes under the label "original meaning"—though that phrase seems to me to beg the very question that needs answering, whereas the more modest "original understanding" at least points toward where one is to look for an answer. Original meaning is glossed in his later book, *Reading Law*, as follows: "In their full context, words mean what they conveyed to reasonable people at the time they were written—with the understanding that general terms may embrace later technological innovations."[4]

The "reasonable person" reading statutory texts is eclipsed, when we come to the Constitution, by a reasonable 1787er: only meanings conveyed to readers of the founding generation are acceptable. Scalia explicitly rejects the notion that the "*current* meaning" of the text has any relevance at all, since he believes that constitutions are designed precisely to *prevent* change (*A Matter*, 38). Scalia would like to get rid of layers of constitutional interpretation that have accreted over the ages and get back to what the text first meant, though he accepts, as "an exception to textualism, . . . born not of logic but of neces-sity," the requirements of stare decisis (*Reading Law*, 424). In constitutional interpretation, his textualism is bounded by originalism: he cannot let us read beyond the lexicon and semantics of what words "conveyed . . . at the time they were written": all past tense.

Scalia concludes that in constitutional interpretation, the "originalist at least knows what he is looking for: the original meaning of the text" (*A Mat-ter*, 45). I think the "what" of "what he is looking for" is far more problematic than Scalia allows. As moderns, we cannot wholly renounce what we have learned since the eighteenth century. Scalia's textual originalism might benefit from some consideration of what we literary scholars call "reception aesthetics," which tracks the evolving horizon of the reading of texts, showing that they inevitably change over time. *Madame Bovary* in 2017 is not and cannot be exactly what it was in 1857: we as readers, and the contexts of our reading, have inevitably evolved. I doubt that we can wholly reinvent the reading, or the psychology, of a 1787er, even if we think it's a useful exercise. Scalia's "original understanding" of the Constitution has to depend on an act of historical reconstruction that is itself the interpretive act of an interpreter.

In *Heller*, everything turns on the "original understanding" of the Second Amendment.[5] Even Justice Stevens in dissent seems to play on that same terrain. The object of interpretive scrutiny here is, of course, the famously vexing language of the Second Amendment: "A well regulated Militia, being necessary to the security of a free State, the right of the people to keep and bear Arms, shall not be infringed." The long-standing debate here concerns the linkage of the different propositions in this sentence. After a brief recitation of the facts of the case, Scalia begins his opinion: "We turn first to the meaning of the Second Amendment."[6] Note that he does not speak of the "interpretation" of the Amendment, or of its "possible meanings," or of the reconstruction of the context of its reading and understanding, or of anything of the sort that would acknowledge that he is embarked on an interpretive enterprise. He offers us rather "the meaning" of the Amendment, which turns out to be an individual right to keep and bear arms for self-defense—a right that seems to fit better into twenty-first-century than eighteenth-century controversies.[7] Over pages 4 to 19 of his opinion, he isolates details of the single sentence that forms the Amendment, parsing "the right of the people" and "keep and bear arms" in a myriad of other contexts that don't seem directly pertinent to the case at hand. But these somehow give him the authority to claim by page 19, "Putting all of these textual elements together, we find that they guarantee the individual right to possess and carry weapons in case of confrontation." I'll return to that redefined right. Note for now that its derivation requires some assembly—having first splintered the sentence into discrete parts—but with no apparent tools needed.

The most enigmatic of "textual elements" in the Amendment has always been the relation of the first phrase, on the "well regulated militia, being necessary to the security of a free State," to the right to bear arms—an enigma enhanced by the strange, eighteenth-century punctuation of the sentence. Scalia briskly solves the problem by calling the first phrase a "prefatory clause" (it is not in fact grammatically a clause but an adverbial phrase), whereas the rest of the sentence becomes "the operative clause"—which essentially allows him to discount any limiting effect of part one of the sentence on part two. Later, he will recharacterize part one as a "prologue," trivializing it still further (at 2790, n. 4). Note that "prefatory" and "prologue" are his words, not those of the Amendment. [8]

Now, Scalia is clearly aware of an amicus brief in this case—he cites it, but then ignores its argument, though one senses a covert polemic with it throughout his opinion—that was filed on behalf of a group of "Professors of Linguistics and English," in "an effort to assist the Court in understanding eighteenth century grammar and the historical meaning of the language used in the Second Amendment."[9] That sounds exactly like something an "original understanding" jurist should welcome. The brief is in fact of the greatest interest to anyone concerned with reconstructing past contexts for interpretation. The professors argue that "under long-standing linguistic principles that were well understood and recognized at the time the Second Amendment was adopted," the "well regulated militia" phrase provides the reason for the "keep and bear arms" clause. Part one of the Amendment, "A well regulated militia, being necessary to the security of a free state," is a Latinate construction, an English version of what in Latin is called an "ablative absolute." If you studied Latin, you will recall that this construction in the ablative case does not agree grammatically with any noun in the main part of the sentence but rather modifies it all, representing a condition of cause, or manner, or temporal context. We don't generally use absolute constructions today, except in stock phrases such as "that being the case," and "weather permitting," and "all things being equal" (occasionally in the Latin original *ceteris paribus*)—they smack too much of the dangling modifier. We would today find such a construction grammatically faulty, but it was utterly commonplace in eighteenth-century English, where most literate people were trained in Latin translation and composition, and indeed derived their stylistic models from Latin. Reading and writing for those who were in a position to postulate the "original understanding" of the Constitution was essentially a matter of mastering Latin grammar and rhetoric. The professors cite a number of ablative absolutes from James Madison's pen, for instance, including his first draft of the Second Amendment, which inserts the absolute phrase on the militia in the middle of the sentence.

A standard textbook, *Essentials of Latin*, tells us, "In translating an ablative absolute, one must use judgment in selecting a translation that is consistent with the meaning of the main verb."[10] The Amendment should thus be construed to mean: "*Because* a well regulated Militia is necessary to the security of a free state, . . ." If that is the case, the right to bear arms is clearly tied to service in a militia: it is its logical entailment—as Justice Stevens will argue in his dissent (though he doesn't take what is in my view the logical next step, which is to decide that with the demise of state and local militias, the Second Amendment simply has no application today). Scalia doesn't dispute the "Because" translation—but he then does not truly seek consistency between the "prefatory clause" and the rest of the sentence (if he recognized it as a phrase rather than a clause, he might be obligated to see a tighter fit between them). Instead, he drives a deeper wedge between the two principal parts of the sentence, then patches them together with connectives of his own making. He derives from the Amendment a "right of the people" to self-defense that denies any force to the "militia" phrase. While dismissing Justice Stevens's interpretations as "grotesque" and "worthy of the mad hatter," he arrives, after a number of twists and spins, at this rhetorical dodge: "The prefatory clause does not suggest that preserving the militia was the only reason Americans valued the ancient right; most undoubtedly thought it even more important for self-defense and hunting" (at 2801). Maybe not the only reason, but surely the only reason stated in the Second Amendment. Watch out for "undoubtedly's"—along with the reiteration of "unambiguously refer" and the like—which return insistently in the opinion. Scalia's claim to originalism here parts company with the text itself.

Scalia sweeps the argument of the amicus brief aside with the claim, "Normal meaning may of course include an idiomatic meaning, but it excludes secret or technical meanings that would not have been known to ordinary citizens in the founding generation" (at 2788). It is hard to credit his good faith here. His declaration sounds democratic, even populist, but he must know that "ordinary citizens" in the founding generation who could read and write would not have found Latinate constructions "secret or technical," but, on the contrary, the stuff of everyday public oratory and writing. Who does he think participated in public affairs—including the ratification debates—in 1787? Scalia's opinion in fact unfolds, as I suggested, in a series of interpretations that are more philological coups d'état than attempts at textual explanation, description, or explicitation. He pulls out of other constitutional clauses the inference that the right involved in the Second Amendment is "unambiguously" individual, not collective. A few pages later, I noted, it becomes "the individual right to possess and carry weapons in case of confrontation" (at 2797). Wherever did the notion of "confrontation" come from? I fail to find any textual basis for it. Then a few pages after that, "individual self-defense" has become, in italics, "the *central component* of the right itself" (at 2801). This is really a personal obsession posing as a textual reading; I see no justification for it in the text or context of the Amendment. At the last, for Scalia, the right guaranteed by the Second Amendment comes to be about "the inherent right to self-defense" (at 2817): this is beginning to sound more like some Hobbesian version of natural law than textual interpretation. Finally, in Scalia's interpretation, the Second Amendment is to be read as a constitutional bar to the prohibition of "handguns held and used for self-defense in the home" (at 2822). It appears that the interpretation of constitutional language has been effaced, usurped by some appeal to natural law or perhaps sociobiology.

I don't claim to be the first to criticize Scalia's interpretive reasoning in *Heller*. In particular, former allies in the conservative camp were harsh. J. Harvie Wilkinson asserts that the Constitution says no more about rules for handgun ownership than it does about trimesters of pregnancy—conflating *Heller* with *Roe*, in the ultimate conservative gesture of rejection. Richard Posner refers to Scalia's opinion as "faux originalism."[11] A year following *Heller*, Judge Frank Easterbrook, in turning back the NRA's challenge to Chicago gun-control laws, asserted that: "The way to evaluate the relation between guns and crime is in scholarly journals and the political process, rather than invocation of ambiguous texts that long precede the contemporary debate."[12] That is, I think, a good sentence to set against Scalia's "We turn first to the meaning of the Second Amendment." And it suggests that textual originalism has inherent limits.

The point I wish to stress is this: if you are going to base a major decision (overturning acts of legislatures, invalidating a municipality's attempt to regulate violent crime) on acts of linguistic interpretation, you need to know what you are doing. You live and die by your interpretive mastery. You need more than declarations of what "original meaning" consists in; you also need principles and methods of interpretation, and when you are dealing with texts from more than two centuries ago, you need to have philological understanding as well. The professors of linguistics at least have principles for their interpretation, and at least they understand that they are engaged in an *act* of interpretation, of construal: that the meaning of the sentence needs to be constructed, not simply read off. Scalia's act of reading finally appears to be not so much authoritative as authoritarian—like Humpty Dumpty's claim to Alice, in *Through the Looking Glass*, that words mean what he chooses them to mean:

"There's glory for you!"
"I don't know what you mean by 'glory,'" Alice said.

Humpty Dumpty smiled contemptuously. "Of course you don't—till I tell you. I meant 'there's a nice knock-down argument for you!'"

"But 'glory' doesn't mean a 'nice knock-down argument,'" Alice objected.

"When *I* use a word," Humpty Dumpty said, in rather a scornful tone, it means just what I choose it to mean—neither more nor less."

"The question is," said Alice, "whether you *can* make words mean so many different things."

"The question is," said Humpty Dumpty, "which is to be master—that's all."[13]

When legal interpretation depends on the mere assertion of mastery, perhaps it is time to bring in the professors of literature.

Those professors appear to understand that the act of interpretation is an act of translation, of mediation. The interpreter, etymologically, is one who "speaks between," who translates a message: an ambassador of meanings. The act of historical interpretation always has an archaeological dimension: the reconstruction of context from remains that may be fragmentary. And reconstruction always involves the hypothetical construction of the missing portion. We turn to history in an attempt to understand the acts and thoughts of the past. But of course history itself never simply gives us the answer: it must itself be used in what is an interpretive act—as *Heller* surely demonstrates.

I am not arguing that legal and literary interpretation are the same. Clearly they are bounded by different horizons. Legal interpretation, as Robert Post has argued, takes place within a pragmatic horizon: "Knowledge," he writes, "is always produced by the organization of a discipline that is itself arranged so as to accomplish given ends."[14] Legal interpretation intends to produce a workable understanding of language within legal practice, whereas literary interpretation would simply produce an understanding that seeks to have the text itself "make sense" as a whole, as a satisfactorily complete and persuasive statement. And yet the two types of interpretation share this situation: that there is a need to interpret, that the message and its applications are not wholly transparent. Legislators and constitution makers may think they are writing language of complete limpidity (though clearly the makers of the U.S. Constitution did *not* believe this), but the fact that they are using language at all dictates that this will never be the case. There is much to be said for "plain meaning" in the interpretation of statutes and other texts, but rarely is language wholly plain. The problem that so often arises in law, I think, is the refusal of legal actors to acknowledge that they are dealing with a medium where exactitude is never wholly determinable. Meaning always depends on what I. A. Richards called "the interanimation of words." The advantage that the literary reader holds over the legal reader is that the former knows that this interanimation will take unexpected and uncontrollable forms.

Scalia, as someone well-versed in language and rhetoric, should know as much. I see his hectoring of his opponents—Justice Stevens as "mad hatter," for instance, or Justice Breyer as speaking "gobbledy-gook"—as the sort of bluster that may most of all speak to his repression of inconvenient truths about language and meaning.[15] His dismissive and, I would argue, bad-faith treatment of the amicus brief in *Heller* seems to speak of a need to scorch the earth of anyone who does not accept his imposition of a single meaning on a famously vexed, eighteenth-century text. If Shakespeare scholars behaved in the manner of Scalia, there would be no further room for maneuver for directors and actors, not to mention scholarly interpreters: there could be only one *Hamlet*. One can once again acknowledge that the purposes of legal interpretation are different, that there needs to be a pragmatic outcome. But that does not justify imposing a single, arbitrary, calamitous meaning on the Second Amendment. Nobody, with the possible exception of the National Rifle Association, needed that.

Rereading today such Scalia opinions as *Michael H. v. Gerald D.*—where Scalia for the majority bans the biological father of a child from any visiting rights—or *Lawrence v. Texas*, where his dissent quite viciously stigmatizes homosexuality while defending the decision in *Bowers v. Hardwick*, I am struck as always by Scalia's pugnaciousness and, beyond that, by what one might see as his need to deny any interpretive standing to his opponents' arguments. An interesting and disturbing instance comes in the 2007 case, *Scott v. Harris*, where Scalia is firmly in control—an eight-to-one decision, with only Justice Stevens dissenting—but nonetheless on the warpath.[16] Victor Harris, guilty of exceeding the speed limit, responded to police pursuit by speeding up and leading a high-speed chase over rural Georgia roads late at night. Eventually, Officer Timothy Scott radioed for permission to "take out" Harris, intending originally to use a "Precision Intervention Technique"—to put Harris's car into a spin—but then deciding instead to bump his car from behind. The pursuit ended when officer Scott "applied his push bumper to the rear of respondent's vehicle. As a result, respondent lost control of his vehicle, which left the roadway, ran down an embankment, overturned, and crashed. Respondent was badly injured and was rendered quadriplegic."[17]

I quote here from Scalia's Opinion of the Court. In prior proceedings, Harris had sued Scott for violating his Fourth Amendment rights by use of excessive force, resulting in an unreasonable seizure; Scott had claimed qualified immunity and moved for summary judgment; the district court had denied the motion, finding that there were issues of fact that required submission to a jury; and the Eleventh Circuit Court of Appeals, on interlocutory appeal, had affirmed, allowing Harris's Fourth Amendment claim to go to trial. The Supreme Court now reverses, denying Harris's claim. Normally the facts of the case would be judged on the appellate level in the light most favorable to the party asserting the injury, as indeed the Eleventh Circuit did. But, says Scalia, there is in this case "an added wrinkle: . . . existence in the record of a videotape capturing the events in question," and "[t]he videotape quite clearly contradicts the version of the story told by respondent and adopted by the Court of Appeals" (at 5). In a footnote, disputing Stevens's dissent, Scalia says, "We are happy to allow the videotape to speak for itself" (at 5, fn. 5). And, in refutation of the opinion from the Eleventh Circuit, he says, "The videotape tells quite a different story" (at 6). The Court can set aside the normal rule of viewing the facts in the light most favorable to Harris because his version of events "is blatantly contradicted by the record, so that no reasonable jury could believe it . . ."; and, he repeats, "Respondent's version of events is so utterly discredited by the record that no reasonable jury could have believed him. The Court of Appeals should not have relied on such visible fiction: it should have viewed the facts in the light depicted by the videotape" (at 7–8).

The Court in this case takes the unusual step of posting the pursuit video — recorded by dashboard cams on the two police cruisers — on its website, in apparent justification of its refusal to credit Harris's case. To Scalia, the video depicts "a Hollywood-style car chase of the most frightening sort, placing police officers and innocent bystanders alike at great risk of serious injury" (at 7). The respondent poses an "extreme danger to human life" (at 10); "it is clear from the videotape that respondent posed an actual and imminent threat to the lives of any pedestrians who might have been present"; "how does a court go about weighing the perhaps lesser probability of injuring and killing numerous bystanders against the perhaps larger probability of injuring or killing a single person?" (at 11). It was, after all, Harris who produced "the choice between two evils that Scott confronted." Scalia is caught up in the chase, which has become a version of the streetcar moral dilemma. It's exciting stuff.

It is only in Stevens's lone dissent that things calm down a bit. He notes that when the chase begins, Harris is driving on a four-lane stretch of Highway 34. His speed is clocked at 73 miles per hour in a 55 mph zone when the first officer initiates the chase, which then generates speeds up to 85 mph. Officer Scott picks up the chase on his radio — he does not know why Harris is being pursued — and joins in, then makes himself the lead car, and eventually decides to put an end to it, and to Harris's mobility forever. Stevens argues that a careful viewing of the video in fact "confirms, rather than contradicts, the lower courts' appraisal of the factual questions at issue." And it "surely does not provide a principled basis for depriving the respondent of his right to have a jury evaluate the question whether the police officers' decision to use deadly force to being the chase to an end was reasonable" (at 2).

Now we have Stevens's analytic reading of the video. It's one that I largely agree with, and I predict that most viewers will too.[18] He makes the point that Harris is at all times in control of his car, that he pulls out to pass other cars only when it is safe to do so, and uses his turn signals, and that the cars he passes seem to have already pulled onto the shoulder, no doubt from the blazing lights and shrieking sirens of the chase, and the two intersections with traffic lights he crosses show only stationary vehicles. Stevens offers a kind of analytic driving lesson to his colleagues. In an interesting footnote, he debunks the majority's "Hollywood chase" designation: "I can only conclude that my colleagues were unduly frightened by two or three images on the tape that looked like bursts of lightning or explosions, but were in fact merely the headlights of vehicles zooming by in the opposite lane. Had they learned to drive when most high-speed driving took place on two-lane roads rather than superhighways—when split-second judgments about the risk of passing a slowpoke in the face of oncoming traffic were routine—they might well have reacted to the videotape more dispassionately" (at 2, fn. 1). Learn to drive, guys, and stop being so impressed by the Hollywood-style visible fiction.

Stevens also points out that when the cars momentarily move into a mall parking lot, the mall is closed (it's 11:00 pm), and that all those "innocent by-standers" and "pedestrians that might have been present" who worry Scalia don't exist on these rural Georgia roads deep into the night. In sum, Harris's offense is serious, but it is not "a capital offense, or even an offense that justi-fied the use of deadly force" (at 5). But Stevens makes no headway against the preemptive strike of Scalia's interpretation of the video. Here, an act of inter-pretation of visual material—material that, carefully viewed, does not seem to ratify Scalia's "Hollywood-type car chase"—utterly erases the normal bases of adjudication and denies Harris access to legal redress.

Like Humpty Dumpty, Scalia responds to interpretive alternatives as life threats, and lashes out with invective. I know there are those who find this kind of rhetorical overkill bracing and entertaining. To me it speaks of a kind of bullying that may result from a deep interpretive insecurity. What if the world of legal language were not so utterly stable as Scalia needs to maintain? What if the arts of rhetorical interpretation really are relevant in the law? Paul de Man once argued that literary studies should be taught first as "poetics and rhetoric," prior to being taught as "history and hermeneutics."[19] By that, I think he meant that we ought to pay attention to the formal structures of meaning—how meaning is made—before interpreting specific meanings and how they are linked in history. One might argue that a similar attention to the processes of how meaning is made in legal texts—the performative rhetoric in which they seek to order and control reality—could be a useful first step before indulging in imperial acts of interpretation. What about a course in rhetoric for first-year law students?

Scalia's "originalism" seems to have conquered legal thinking like the plague. As I noted, even Stevens seems to get caught in its toils in his *Heller* dissent. It's true that "new originalism," or "new textualism," might offer a more richly nuanced and less constricted reading of constitutional language, one more compatible with progressive political theory. Yet I'm not sure that these revisions of conservative originalism—revisions associated, for instance, with the work of Jack Balkin and Akhil Amar—really solve the problem of trying to wring meaning from what Judge Easterbrook called "ambiguous texts that long precede contemporary debate." James Ryan, in a useful and approving article on "new textualism," criticizes David Strauss and Cass Sunstein for rejecting originalist argument, claiming that they are "inevitably buttressing the conservative claim that the text of the Constitution, if embraced faithfully, is more in line with conservative rather than progressive values."[20] I find that "embraced faithfully" raises more problems than it solves, especially in the context of Ryan's repeated references to "what the Constitution actually means" (e.g., at 27).[21] What Ryan elsewhere appears to be saying is that progressives as well as conservatives need to argue *from* constitutional text— which is a far lesser and more acceptable claim. The parsing of constitutional text may be necessary but cannot be sufficient to an understanding of what constitutional principles "mean." They are the starting point of any interpretive gesture, but not where such a gesture ends up.

What I miss even in newer and more progressive versions of originalism is an acknowledgment that texts do not and indeed cannot mean the same thing over time. To return to the example of Flaubert's *Madame Bovary*: we can hypothetically reconstruct the "meaning" of the novel to readers when it was published, first in serial form in 1856—with some passages censored by the editors of the *Revue de Paris* in a first gesture of reader response—then as a book in 1857. We have contemporaneous book reviews, comments in letters and journals, and even, in this case, a public trial for the novel's alleged "outrage to morality" that give us a fair sense of the range of reactions it elicited. But to reconstruct those 1857 readings is not to say what it means to readers today. For one thing, we have had a century and a half of the legal and social emancipation of women since then—and yet perhaps also reinforcement of many of the stereotypes that hem in Emma Bovary. I can attest from often teaching the novel that it remains astonishingly fresh, even radical to readers today, precisely because they read it through the lens of everything that has happened—and failed to happen—since 1857. We can lead those students to consider more closely what the novel may have meant in 1857, and if we want them to be scholars of French literature, we should. But that by no means tells us what the novel means now—it can't, it shouldn't, and in any event it is a retrospective historical reconstruction that is subject to various uncertainties of its own. To paraphrase T. S. Eliot, we know more than the great poets of the past—because we know them. To discard our acquired contemporary knowledge in favor of some putative return to past understandings has all the authenticity of a Club Med reconstruction of prelapsarian paradise.

But that, largely thanks to Scalia, in fact seems to be where we are today: prisoners of a constructed "original understanding" Constitution that has been, and surely will be more and more in the future, cited to undo progressive legislation and exercise a kind of dull weight of past prejudice on the evolution of American democracy. The current right-wing obsession with deconstructing the "administrative state" stands, as I write, as the latest and most potent attempt to undo the rights and benefits guaranteed to citizens by every mature democratic regime. It is a pity that Scalia's view of constitutions as preventing change should have become so ingrained in the legal community, and that his interpretive moves should be so often accepted as good coin rather than rhetorical postures.

References

Balkin, Jack. 2011. *Living Originalism*. Cambridge, MA: Harvard University Press.

Brooks, Peter. 2016. "*Scott v. Harris*: The Supreme Court's Reality Effect." *Law & Literature*, December, 1–7.

Carroll, Lewis. (1871) 1960. *Through the Looking Glass*. New York: NAL/Signet.

de Man, Paul. 1982. "The Return to Philology." *Times Literary Supplement*, December 10.

Kahan, Dan M., David A. Hoffman, and Donald Braman. 2009. "Whose Eyes Are You Going to Believe? *Scott v. Harris* and the Perils of Cognitive Illiberalism." *Harvard Law Review* 122: 837.

Pearson, Henry Carr. 1912. *Essentials of Latin*. New York: American Book Company.

Posner, Richard A. 2008. "In Defense of Looseness: The Supreme Court and Gun Control." *New Republic*, August 27.

Post, Robert. 2004. "Law and Literature." Unpublished manuscript, on file with author.

Ryan, James. 2011. "Laying Claim to the Constitution: The Promise of New Textualism." *Virginia Law Review* 97:1523.

Scalia, Antonin. 1997 *A Matter of Interpretation*, edited by Amy Guttmann. Princeton, NJ: Princeton University Press.

———, and Bryan Garner. 2012. *Reading Law*. Saint Paul, MN: Thompson/West.

Siegel, Reva. 2008. "Dead or Alive: Originalism as Popular Constitutionalism in *Heller*." *Harvard Law Review* 122:191.

Wilkinson, J. Harvie. 2009. "Of Guns, Abortions, and the Unraveling Rule of Law." *Virginia Law Review* 95:253.

PART 5

The Rhetoric of the Past

A Separate, Abridged Edition
of the First Amendment

COLIN STARGER

In 2014, the late Justice Scalia concurred in judgment in a case called *Mc-Cullen v. Coakley*.[1] Judgment was in fact unanimous—invalidating under the First Amendment a Massachusetts law that criminalized standing on a public road or sidewalk within thirty-five feet of a reproductive health care facility. Though satisfied with the Court's decision to strike down the law, Justice Scalia bucked at the means taken to the end. His concurrence opens with these words: "Today's opinion carries forward this Court's practice of giving abortion-rights advocates a pass when it comes to suppressing the free-speech rights of their opponents. There is an entirely separate, abridged edition of the First Amendment applicable to speech against abortion."[2] Scalia then cited two prior cases that enacted the "abortion-speech edition of the First Amendment"—*Madsen v. Women's Health Center* (1994) and *Hill v. Colorado* (2000).[3] Not coincidentally, Scalia wrote forceful, separate dissenting opinions in each of those prior cases.

This chapter analyzes the rhetorical strategy pursued by Scalia across his separate opinions in the "abridged" First Amendment controversies. Initial analysis leads to a counterintuitive conclusion: that Scalia's opinions in these so-called "abortion-speech" cases are not actually about free speech at all. While they formally focus on First Amendment doctrine, the opinions' true subject is the broader and highly fraught legal discourse around abortion and choice itself. Pages of technical free-speech exposition merely frame Scalia's deeper and more essential rhetoric aimed at promoting values and arguments undermining the Court's abortion decisions from *Roe v. Wade* onward.

To break down Scalia's strategy in the abortion-speech cases, this chapter considers his opinions as exemplifying what rhetoricians call *epideictic* speech. From the time of Aristotle, epideictic speech has been understood as ceremonial in nature and lacking a sharply defined argumentative purpose. Yet modern commentators have come to understand that epideictic speech aims to move discourse over the long run by shaping the core values of participants in the discourse. As this chapter shows, Scalia's abortion-speech dissents are understood best as aiming to move constitutional discourse over the long run. While writing in dissent inherently meant that he lost the immediate First Amendment debate, Scalia used his abortion-speech dissents to promote a pro-life perspective that transcends the First Amendment context. By employing an epideictic strategy, Scalia attempts to delegitimize the Court's abortion doctrine writ large.

Agree or disagree with him on the merits of his doctrinal claims (and there is ample room for disagreement), Scalia's recourse to epideictic argument warrants our close attention. When Scalia argues that the Court's abortion doctrine is an "ad hoc nullification machine" that wreaks havoc on the rule of law,[4] he seeks to associate abortion with the erosion of core legal values. Appealing to the deepest values of a discourse is the heart of epideictic strategy. Analysis of this ancient rhetorical category can illuminate the dynamics of persuasion in legal discourse and remind us that the true axis of dispute in the Court's most controversial cases often concerns competing values (Starger 2016).

Abortion Protest, the Supreme Court, and the First Amendment

After the Supreme Court decided *Roe v. Wade* in 1973, national debate over abortion did not end. To the contrary, battles over life, choice, and women's rights only intensified after the Court "resolved" the constitutional question.[5] This intensification is at least partially explained by *Roe*'s disruption of state legislative efforts and its short-circuiting of the political process. As Justice Ginsburg (1992) has acknowledged, *Roe* "left virtually no state laws fully conforming to the Court's delineation of abortion regulation still permissible. Around that extraordinary decision, a well-organized and vocal right-to-life movement rallied" (1205).

The strategies of this right-to-life movement evolved over time and varied wildly. In legal terms, tactics have run the gamut from the clearly legal (such as letter-writing and prayer vigils) to the clearly illegal (such as firebombing clinics and even murdering doctors) (National Abortion Federation 2017).[6] For obvious reasons, the violent actions of criminal "activists" occupy a prominent place in public debates over the right-to-life movement. In Supreme Court debates, however, the fanatical fringe lurks in the background of the discourse. This is because pro-life protesters whose cases have reached the Court generally have pushed the legal boundaries of free speech rather than engaged in outright violence. The most relevant context for the Court's "abortion-speech" cases is thus militant, pro-life civil disobedience.

This civil disobedience tradition began on a small scale in the 1970s, often led by leftist Catholics who had cut their teeth in earlier civil rights and anti-war movements (Keleher 2002, 839–40). By the late 1980s, militant civil disobedience had become widespread. Radical pro-lifers employed direct-action tactics, such as sit-ins and entrance blockades, in their efforts to shut down abortion clinics. Groups such as Operation Rescue directly courted arrest, and this outcome was common. In 1988, for example, there were 188 clinic blockades, resulting in more than eleven thousand arrests ("Safety Valve Closed: The Removal of Nonviolent Outlets for Dissent and the Onset of Anti-Abortion Violence" 2000, 1218).

As charged scenes of confrontation and chaos played out in front of clinics around the country, the women's rights movement mobilized. In addition to organizing grassroots clinic defense, pro-choice activists turned to the law to combat disruptive direct action. In courts and legislatures, abortion-rights advocates sought injunctions against specific pro-life groups as well as the passage of laws to protect clinic access.[7] Legal wrangling over the space outside of clinics led to cat-and-mouse games where lines would be drawn to prevent pro-life protesters from interfering with clinic functions, then protesters would find ways to skirt or avoid the lines, and then new lines would be drawn. Eventually, some of this wrangling ended up in the Supreme Court.

The Supreme Court cases that directly adjudicated pro-life protesters' First Amendment rights are properly understood as the "abortion-speech" cases. During Justice Scalia's thirty-year tenure on the Court from 1986 to 2016, the Court decided five abortion-speech cases: *Frisby* (1988),[8] *Madsen* (1994),[9] *Schenck* (1997),[10] *Hill* (2000),[11] and *McCullen* (2014).[12] To be clear, the Court decided numerous other cases that dealt with abortion and even abortion protest during this thirty-year period.[13] But only *Frisby, Madsen, Schenck, Hill,* and *McCullen* directly ruled on pro-life protesters' First Amendment rights. Since they provide the source material for this chapter's rhetorical analysis, a snapshot view of these disputes and the doctrinal questions implicated is in order.

Frisby concerned a facial challenge to local law in Brookfield, Wisconsin, that prohibited all picketing in front of residential homes. The law was passed after protesters had repeatedly gathered at the home of a local doctor who performed abortions and disturbed neighborhood quiet. After protesters challenged the law on First Amendment grounds, a 6–3 majority of the Supreme Court upheld it. Even though abortion protest provided the impetus, the law itself prohibited *all* residential picketing in front of a single house and thus was "content-neutral." Though he did not write an opinion, Justice Scalia notably voted with the majority. Dissent only came from the Court's liberal wing, which objected to the broad sweep of the antipicketing law.

Six years after *Frisby*, the Court decided *Madsen*. After the Aware Woman Center for Choice in Melbourne, Florida, obtained an injunction prohibiting activists from directly interfering with access, protests nonetheless continued. These actions featured loud noise, disturbing images, and harsh exchanges aimed at clinic employees and patients. Further litigation ensued, and the district court eventually broadened the existing injunction by imposing various buffer zones around the entire clinic and ordering limits on noise and observable images. A 6–3 majority of the Supreme Court upheld parts of the injunction and struck down others.[14]

Writing for the majority, Chief Justice Rehnquist found the new injunction to be a "content-neutral" restriction directed only at protesters who had violated the initial injunction. Rehnquist approved those buffer zones and noise limitations that were necessary for the clinic to function. However, he found the injunction violated the First Amendment when it prohibited the display of graphic images and created buffer zones in places irrelevant to preserving access to the clinic. Justice Scalia dissented. He began, "The judgment in today's case has an appearance of moderation and Solomonic wisdom, upholding as it does some portions of the injunction while disallowing others. That appearance is deceptive."[15] Per Scalia, the entire new injunction violated the First Amendment because it was a content-based restriction directed at those who expressed antiabortion sentiments.

Decided three years after *Madsen*, *Schenck* involved similar facts and provoked a similar debate. The case once again involved an injunction against pro-life activists who had blockaded clinic entrances and engaged in aggressive "sidewalk counseling." The district court issued an injunction that prohibited demonstrations within fifteen feet of clinic entrances and parking lots ("fixed buffer zones") and prohibited demonstrators from coming within fifteen feet of patients coming to the clinic ("floating buffer zones"). By a vote of 6–3, the Supreme Court upheld the fixed buffer zones but struck down the floating buffer zones as violating the First Amendment. Once again, Chief Justice Rehnquist penned the majority opinion and once again Justice Scalia dissented from that part of the decision that upheld portions of the injunction.[16]

Next in the series, *Hill* is possibly the most controversial abortion-speech case. Decided in 2000, *Hill* involved a statute rather than an injunction. The Colorado law prohibited those standing within one hundred feet of a health care facility's entrance from approaching people going to the facility and passing them leaflets without their consent. The law also limited within one hundred feet displaying signs and engaging in protest, education, or counseling. In another 6–3 decision with the exact same lineup as in *Madsen* and *Schenck*, the Court upheld the statute against a First Amendment challenge.

Justice Stevens wrote for the majority and classified the law as a content-neutral time, place, and manner restriction. Per Stevens, the law did not discriminate based on viewpoint and served legitimate government interests in ensuring ingress and egress to medical clinics. Scalia dissented, hotly disputing the majority's content-neutrality analysis: "I have no doubt that this regulation would be deemed content-based *in an instant* if the case before us involved antiwar protesters, or union members seeking to 'educate' the public about the reasons for their strike. . . . But the jurisprudence of this Court has a way of changing when abortion is involved."[17] This quotation reflects both Scalia's concern with content-neutrality doctrine and his rhetorical strategy of accusing the Court of double standards when it comes to abortion.

Before examining that strategy in earnest, the final case in the abortion-speech line requires brief exposition—*McCullen*. This 2014 case involved a Massachusetts law that criminalized knowingly standing within thirty-five feet of an abortion facility (other than a hospital). The law was an undeniably aggressive response to antiabortion protest. The Court unanimously struck down the law on First Amendment grounds. Chief Justice Roberts authored the majority opinion. Roberts reasoned that although the Massachusetts law was content-neutral, it was also overbroad because it prohibited too much protected speech.

Scalia concurred in judgment only and wrote separately. In his concurrence, Scalia argued that the Massachusetts law was not at all content-neutral and castigated the Court for what he saw as its continued distortion of free-speech doctrine. It was in this final opinion in the line that Scalia accused the Court of applying "an entirely separate, abridged edition of the First Amendment applicable to speech against abortion."

Scalia's Rhetoric Attacking Legitimacy

Justice Scalia's separate opinions in the abortion-speech cases span dozens of pages of the U.S. Reports. The great bulk of the ink spilled is devoted to what might be fairly characterized as technical analysis—close readings of the factual record before the Court and of relevant First Amendment precedent. This is as it should be. The majority opinions in these cases were likewise centered on conventional argument over the record and precedent. The main First Amendment flashpoint concerned content-neutrality doctrine.

For the purpose of this rhetorical analysis, it does not matter who is "right," or who is "wrong" about the finer points of content-neutrality doctrine. Different plausible interpretations of the First Amendment based on different plausible readings of case law are possible; even if one side is "truer to the doctrine," reasonable jurists could (and certainly did) disagree on the merits. What matters for our analysis is the nature of Scalia's nontechnical argument—his more essential rhetoric. This deeper rhetoric maintained that the only *real* explanation for the majority's doctrinal positions was its ideological commitment to abortion and its bias against pro-life protest. Despite occupying less opinion space than technical doctrinal analysis, Scalia's attacks on the majority's basic legitimacy form the crux of his argument.

From the outset, Scalia faced a significant rhetorical obstacle in painting his opponents as driven by an ideological commitment to abortion and a bias again pro-life protest. This is because the interpretative divide in the abortion-speech cases never fell along classic liberal/conservative lines. Indeed, the first case in this line—*Frisby*—saw a conservative majority that included Scalia himself (!) uphold regulations drawn up to stop antiabortion home picketing. Then came the clinic-access cases *Madsen*, *Schenck*, *Hill*, and *McCullen*. While Scalia was invariably joined by Justices Kennedy and Thomas in his separate opinions in those cases, the competing majority coalitions always attracted conservative justices—at first Rehnquist and O'Connor and later Roberts. None of these conservative justices could be fairly accused of a pro-abortion ideological bias.

Scalia's response to this awkward reality was to bob and weave.

In *Madsen*, Scalia bobbed by throwing his opponents' words back in their faces. Specifically, Scalia opened his own dissent by block-quoting another dissent from "long ago" in "another abortion-related case": "This Court's abortion decisions have already worked a major distortion in the Court's constitutional jurisprudence. Today's decision goes further, and makes it painfully clear that no legal rule or doctrine is safe from ad hoc nullification by this Court when an occasion for its application arises in a case involving state regulation of abortion."[18] The block quotation came from O'Connor in her dissent—joined by Justice Rehnquist—in a mainline abortion case (*Thornburgh*), where the majority invalidated state informed-consent and reporting regulations. Now that Rehnquist and O'Connor were in the *Madsen* majority, Scalia declared, "Today the ad hoc nullification machine claims its latest, greatest, and most surprising victim: the First Amendment."[19]

Here Scalia implicitly branded Rehnquist and O'Connor as hypocrites. Never mind that the hypocrisy charge makes little sense. (Given that Rehnquist and O'Connor favored abortion regulation in *Thornburgh*, it seems unlikely that anti-pro-life sentiment guided their First Amendment analysis in *Madsen*). The larger point Scalia strives to make is that abortion confuses Court doctrine. To make this point, Scalia creates heat through explosive accusation of hypocrisy. Labeling the majority opinion as the latest result of an "ad hoc nullification machine" creates rhetorical confusion by attacking basic legitimacy. In this confusion, the majority's argument seems shakier than it might in a more reasoned debate.

In *Hill*, Scalia weaved around the legitimacy issue by deploying a time-tested trope: repetition. In page after page, Scalia charged the majority with bias. "Having deprived abortion opponents of their political right to persuade the electorate that abortion should be restricted by law," he begins, "the Court today . . . expands its assault upon their individual right to persuade women contemplating abortion that what they are doing is wrong."[20] Later he muses, "There is apparently no end to the distortion of our First Amendment law that the Court is willing to endure in order to sustain this restriction upon the free speech of abortion opponents."[21] And then finally: "Does the deck seem stacked? You bet."[22] Through repetition, the charge of illegitimacy gains momentum.

Scalia amplifies his charge through familiar accusations of hypocrisy. Since Justice Stevens wrote the *Hill* majority opinion, Scalia sets his sights on Stevens's prior dissents (including *Frisby*), wherein Stevens had argued against antipicketing restrictions because they hindered vital persuasive communications. "Today, of course," barbed Scalia, "Justice Stevens gives us an opinion restricting not only handbilling but also one-on-one conversation of a particular content."[23] For Scalia, this about-face proves ill will. (Never mind that Scalia voted with the majority in *Frisby* in upholding antipicketing restrictions burdening pro-life protest; Scalia ignores his own about-face).

As a liberal, Stevens made an easy target. Yet Scalia's rhetorical posture once again failed to come to grips with the fact that the *Hill* majority garnered votes from conservative pro-life justices. Specifically, Chief Justice Rehnquist joined the *Hill* majority, even though he voted with Scalia to uphold the so-called "partial birth abortion ban" in *Stenberg v. Carhart*, a massively controversial case decided *on the very same day* as *Hill*.[24] Hypocrisy, bias, and a desire to stifle antiabortion speech simply cannot explain Rehnquist's First Amendment analysis in *Madsen* and *Schenck* or his vote in *Hill*.

Although Scalia ignored the Rehnquist problem in his *Hill* dissent, he did not ignore *Stenberg*. Far from it. In *Stenberg*, a 5–4 majority struck down the "partial birth abortion" restrictions, and so Scalia (and Rehnquist) both dissented. In his *Hill* dissent, Scalia argued extensively that the majority methods in *Hill* and *Stenberg* contradicted each other, thus revealing hypocrisy. The appeal to hypocrisy must now be put aside, for it is Scalia's references to *Stenberg* itself that hold the key to understanding the rhetorical strategy driving all his abortion-speech dissents. He writes,

> The public forum involved here—the public spaces outside of health care facilities—has become, by necessity and by virtue of this Court's decisions, a forum of last resort for those who oppose abortion. The possibility of limiting abortions by legislative means—even abortion of a live-and-kicking child that is almost entirely out of the womb—has been rendered impossible by our decisions from *Roe v. Wade* to *Stenberg v. Carhart*. For those who share an abiding moral or religious conviction . . . that abortion is the taking of a human life, there is no option but to persuade women, one by one, not to make that choice. And as a general matter, the most effective place, if not the only place, where that persuasion can occur is outside the entrances to abortion facilities.[25]

The pathos of Scalia's writing here jumps off the page. He clearly shares the view of "those who oppose abortion" that the practice is immoral. By his reference to a live-and-kicking child, it is equally clear that *Stenberg* pains him. Frustrated by defeat in that mainline abortion case, Scalia implies that his First Amendment analysis must be right because it protects the only effective way left to persuade women not to choose abortion.

This remarkable argument provides evidence for the counterintuitive conclusion foreshadowed in this chapter's introduction—that Scalia's abortion-speech opinions do not fundamentally concern free speech at all. Rather, Scalia's true subject is abortion. He aims to delegitimize the Court's mainline abortion doctrine by associating it with erosion of the rule-of-law values elsewhere in the Court's jurisprudence. Accusations of hypocrisy advance the notion that abortion causes the Court to disregard neutral decision-making and principled consistency. Neutrality and consistency are, of course, hallmarks of the rule of law.

Again, we need not evaluate the accuracy of Scalia's accusations regarding the Court's neutrality and consistency. The point is to recognize that Scalia's deeper rhetoric does not seek to "win" the technical First Amendment argument. Instead, Scalia uses his abortion-speech dissent to intervene in mainline abortion discourse. His ostensible First Amendment arguments are really pro-life value arguments. This kind of "argument really about another argument" may seem strange to the literal-minded, but rhetoricians have a concept that explains its function: epideictic. Seen through an epideictic lens, Scalia's abortion-*speech* dissents can be understood as part and parcel of long-term rhetorical strategy to influence the Court's mainline abortion doctrine.

Scalia's Rhetoric as Epideictic Speech

The concept of epideictic speech originates from the systematic study of rhetoric in ancient Greece. In his field-defining treatise, Aristotle (2007) specifically identified three species of rhetoric: deliberative, judicial, and epideictic (47–49). Each of these rhetorical species represents a genre of oratory or speech. Deliberative (also known as political) speech seeks to persuade an audience about future action. Debates before legislative bodies—Should we go to war? Should we provide health care for all?—typify the future-looking deliberative genre. By contrast, judicial (also known as forensic) speech seeks to persuade an audience to make a judgment about the past. A lawyer's argument before a court—Did the plaintiff make a valid contract? Did the defendant commit a crime?—exemplifies judicial speech. Epideictic is the third and final of these rhetorical speech categories.

According to Aristotle, epideictic speech has the present as its subject. In its classical formulation, epideictic speech praises or blames a person, place, or idea. Such present-centered reflections often occur at events like weddings or graduations, and so epideictic is sometimes dubbed ceremonial speech. Canonical examples of epideictic speech include funeral eulogies as well as oratorical panegyrics performed at ancient festivals or games.

Academic commentators recognize epideictic as the most elusive of Aristotle's speech categories and have long debated the genre's significance to rhetorical theory. Unlike deliberative or forensic speeches, the argumentative purpose of epideictic discourse is hard to pin down. Pure epideictic speech does not put a concrete proposition or course of action before an audience for its acceptance or rejection. Because of its ceremonial character, epideictic speech has been dismissed as just-for-show oratory, or "a degenerate kind of eloquence with no other aim than to please" (Perelman and Olbrechts-Tyteca 1969, 48).

Yet modern rhetorical theory understands that the epideictic genre deeply affects how persuasion operates in discourse. Contemporary theory builds on the work of Chaïm Perelman and Lucie Olbrechts-Tyteca, authors of *The New Rhetoric*. Perelman and Olbrechts-Tyteca's basic insight is that epideictic speech "strengthens the disposition towards action by increasing the adherence to the values it lauds" (1969, 50). Actors within any given discourse make many decisions over time and respond to new arguments based on their own prior values and beliefs. Epideictic speech aims to influence those prior values and beliefs.

Decisions are not made—or cases decided—in a vacuum. The specific facts and particular rules at issue in any given argument are necessarily viewed through the lens of prior prejudgments and prejudices (Gadamer 2004, 272).[26] Though it is not easily done, persuasion can move prejudgments. Epideictic speech is one way to affect prejudgment and prejudice. By promoting certain values while attacking others, what might appear to be nonpropositional ceremonial speech actually primes actors in a discourse to choose one course of action above another. Value hierarchies affect choices.

By increasing the intensity of adherence to values, epideictic speeches thus lay foundations for deliberative and judicial rhetoric. While deliberative and judicial arguments aim to persuade audiences to make specific judgments at specific points in time, epideictic "arguments" are not so tethered. As Perelman and Olbrechts-Tyteca note, "Whereas these two kinds of speeches [deliberative and judicial] make use of dispositions already present in the audience, and values are for them means that make it possible to induce action, in *epideictic* speech, on the other hand, the sharing of values is an end pursued independently of the precise circumstances in which this communion will be put to the test" (1969, 53). The precise judgment urged in a deliberative or judicial speech may be thought of as the short game in discourse. Epideictic speech always plays the long game.

Returning to Scalia and his abortion-speech opinions, we can now appreciate how he uses an epideictic approach to play the constitutional long game on abortion. Though the judicial arguments he presses in his separate opinions concern First Amendment doctrine, his deeper epideictic appeals paint abortion jurisprudence as undermining the rule of law writ large. Scalia's claim that there is "an entirely separate, abridged edition of the First Amendment applicable to speech against abortion" works with his "ad hoc nullification machine" charge to suggest that abortion is bad because it distorts the Court's jurisprudence beyond the abortion context.

Yet it is the abortion context itself—not what is beyond—that drives Scalia's rhetoric. He asserts that the majorities in abortion-speech cases fear the *content* of pro-life speech and then gives voice to that content. A striking passage from *Hill* reveals just how Scalia can pivot from discussion of First Amendment regulation to epideictic speech articulating pro-life values. In this passage, Scalia confronts the majority argument that Colorado's limits on sidewalk "counseling" do not prevent pro-life protesters from communicating their message via megaphones outside clinics. Scalia then writes,

> The availability of a powerful amplification system will be of little help to the woman who hopes to forge, in the last moments before another of her sex is to have an abortion, a bond of concern and intimacy that might enable her to

persuade the woman to change her mind and heart. The counselor may wish to walk alongside and say, sympathetically and as softly as the circumstances allow, something like: "My dear, I know what you are going through. I've been through it myself. You're not alone and you do not have to do this. There are other alternatives. Will you let me help you? May I show you a picture of what your child looks like at this stage of her human development?"[27]

Through the hypothetical protester, Scalia speaks directly to his audience. For a moment, he holds his caustic tongue and tries to persuade us "sympathetically and as softly as the circumstances allow" to change our minds and hearts about abortion.

Agree or disagree with his perspective on abortion or choice, Scalia's epideictic strategy deserves recognition. He is consciously appealing to values and associating the value of free speech and rational persuasion with the values of the pro-life movement. (Of course, Scalia does not imagine a protester throwing fake blood, screaming "murderer," or holding a poster of a doctor seen through a rifle scope.) Since he wrote in dissent, Scalia knew he had lost the battle in *Hill*. Nonetheless, he wrote separately both to rally troops for the ongoing war and to convince others to join his side. And Scalia's real war concerned abortion rather than free speech.

This epideictic lens shows how Scalia's separate opinions in the abortion-speech cases can function as "arguments really about other arguments." The pro-life and pro-choice movements have clashed in many Supreme Court cases implicating many different constitutional discourses. Yet the value hierarchies affecting how justices (and the general public) view any given conflict cut across all doctrine. Scalia is trying to persuade at this deeper level of value. For Scalia, First Amendment doctrine about free speech abstractly is less important than the concrete pro-life speech the Amendment could protect.

Conclusion

Is there an "abridged edition of the First Amendment applicable to speech against abortion"? Given the doctrine's subjective and normative nature, the merits of Scalia's claim cannot be proved or disproved. However, his argument that the Court's free-speech analysis in the abortion-speech cases has been motivated by a desire to stifle pro-life messages, to borrow a phrase Scalia loved, "blinks reality." For it is objectively true that abortion protesters have often prevailed in the Supreme Court.

Besides total victory in *McCullen* (where Scalia concurred) and partial victories in *Madsen* and *Schenck* (where portions of injunctions were struck down), pro-life protesters won the day in *Bray v. Alexandria Women's Clinic* and in the *Scheidler v. National Organization for Women* cases.[28] In those cases, the Court—joined by Scalia—struck down attempts by pro-choice organizations to make pro-life groups liable under civil conspiracy theories. Had anti-pro-life bias really infected the Court, these cases would have gone the other way.

In the final analysis, the accuracy of Scalia's claims about the Court's hypocritical First Amendment jurisprudence are beside the point. Scalia's essential rhetoric in abortion-speech cases was never aimed at vindicating timeless claims about free speech. Rather, he used the occasion of dissent to make epideictic appeals that promoted pro-life values. Scalia knew his dissents were not going to change the outcomes of the cases already decided. Where judicial argument had failed, Scalia employed epideictic argument to shape future constitutional discourse.

This rhetorical analysis of Scalia's abortion-speech dissents suggests a broader truth—all Supreme Court dissents might be regarded as having an epideictic aspect. By definition, it is always true that the author of a dissent has lost the instant judicial battle. Perhaps most dissenters also hope to win a long-term war. They dissent to speak to that longer game. Even though most Supreme Court cases do not involve as controversial an issue as abortion, and while not every dissenter can boast the flourish of Scalia, all students of constitutional law and rhetoric can learn from studying these cases.

References

Aristotle. 2007. *On Rhetoric: A Theory of Civic Discourse.* 2d ed. Translated by George A. Kennedy. New York: Oxford University Press.

Gadamer, Hans-Georg. 2004. *Truth and Method.* 2d rev. ed. Translated by Joel Weinsheimer and Donald Marshall. London: Continuum.

Ruth Bader Ginsburg. 1992. "Speaking in a Judicial Voice." *New York University Law Review* 67: 1185–1209.

Keleher, Christopher. 2002. "Double Standards: The Suppression of Abortion Protesters' Free Speech Rights." *DePaul Law Review* 51:825–910.

Perelman, Chaïm, and L. Olbrechts-Tyteca. 1969. *The New Rhetoric: A Treatise on Argumentation.* Translated by John Wilkinson and Purcell Weaver. Notre Dame, IN: University of Notre Dame Press.

Starger, Colin. 2016. "Constitutional Law and Rhetoric." *University of Pennsylvania, Journal of Constitutional Law* 18:1347–79.

National Abortion Federation. 2017. "Violence Statistics and History." Online at https://pro choice.org/education-and-advocacy/violence/violence-statistics-and-history/.

"Safety Valve Closed: The Removal of Nonviolent Outlets for Dissent and the Onset of Anti-Abortion Violence." 2000. *Harvard Law Review* 113:1210–27.

Rhetorical Constructions of Precedent:
Justice Scalia's Free-Exercise Opinion

LINDA L. BERGER

> Not only does the past inform the present case, but the decision in the present case changes the past.
>
> LINDA ROSS MEYER, *The Justice of Mercy* (2010)

This chapter examines the making and unmaking of precedent as a rhetorical process. How does a Supreme Court justice constitute the present case "as" precedent? What rhetorical methods are used to construct the past that informs the present case? And how do those rhetorical methods influence the subsequent reconstitution of the opinion as precedent over time?

The specific precedential question of the chapter is the interpretation of the Free Exercise Clause of the Constitution: "Congress shall make no law . . . prohibiting the free exercise (of religion)." Relying first on close reading, the chapter analyzes Justice Antonin Scalia's 1990 majority opinion determining that the correct interpretation of free exercise is this one: "The right of free exercise does not relieve an individual of the obligation to comply with a 'valid and neutral law of general applicability on the ground that the law proscribes (or prescribes) conduct that his religion prescribes (or proscribes)'" (*Employment Division v. Smith*, 494 U.S. 872 [1990] [quoting *United States v. Lee*, 455 U.S. 252, 263 n. 3 (1982)] [Stevens, J., concurring]). Relying on a form of computational analysis derived from distant reading, the chapter next explores the subsequent quarter-century's treatment of the precedential rules established in *Smith*.

As constructed and as reconstituted, *Smith* remains immediately relevant to the constitutional tipping point for purposes of the First Amendment's religion clauses: When does accommodating religious believers become establishing religion? It also relates to the idea that Justice Scalia enacts his vision of the rule of law through his rhetorical framing. Unlike many Scalia opinions, the *Smith* majority has been harshly criticized not for its rhetoric (by "rhetoric," these critics mean memorable images and word choices), but for its content. And not only does its content appear antithetical to Justice Scalia's ideological and interpretive preferences, but the harshest criticism of the *Smith* opinion has shifted over time from one end to the other of the political spectrum. Perhaps most important, while the *Smith* opinion has some of the hallmarks of a Scalia opinion—a clearly stated and memorable categorical rule, a disdain for balancing—others are missing. The textual argument is barely there; the opinion refers not at all to history or original meaning; and the reasoning is built entirely around a lawyer-like, but rhetorically extreme, argument based on case precedent.

Precedent Defined

In this chapter, I define *precedent* as including any written "rule" derived from an opinion that a practicing lawyer might cite as authority in a later persuasive brief. To put it another way, precedent includes all the statements that an advocate would feel comfortable repeating with the assertion that those statements represent what the opinion in *Smith* "meant," or "stood for," or "held."

The inclination to follow what worked in the past takes on authoritative tones and predictive quality in legal decision-making. In some circumstances, precedent is even said to become "binding" or "mandatory." The view that precedent actively constrains judging coincides with the formalistic view that it is a simple matter to uncover or find the law (precedent) and follow its dictates. But there is play in the joints of even the formalistic view. As Frederick Schauer noted, "The word 'precedent' is capacious [enough that it] encourages the failure to distinguish genuinely constraining precedents from those previous decisions of various courts that either did not deal with precisely the same question or did not emanate from a court whose decisions are binding on the court deciding the current case" (Schauer 2012, 122). Even if precedent provides less constraint than sometimes imagined, "it provides a foundation for an evolving body of doctrine, . . . a constitutional regime stable enough to support the rule of law, but flexible enough to adapt to changing constitutional visions" (Farber 2006, 1203).

Judges differentiate vertical precedent (following the courts above) from stare decisis (let the decision stand, or horizontal precedent). Given the basic idea that there is a "(not necessarily conclusive) obligation of a decision-maker to make the same decision that has been made on a previous occasion about the same or similar matters," vertical precedent is like obeying your parents (Schauer 2012, 123). Stare decisis, on the other hand, is the court's responsibility to follow a prior decision made by the same court. "Horizontal precedent is about treating temporal priority as sufficient grounds for authoritativeness in its own right" (Schauer 2012, 124). Justice Scalia often rejected the horizontal form of precedent as inconsistent with his obligation to properly interpret and apply the Constitution: "The whole function of [stare decisis] is to make us say that what is false under proper analysis must nevertheless be held to be true" (Scalia 1997, 139).

Even though Supreme Court justices may not themselves treat prior decisions by their colleagues as binding precedent, the rest of us have little choice: "We treat judicial rulings, particularly those of the Supreme Court, as legitimate sources of constitutional authority" (Fisher 2016, 149). But what parts of the opinion constitute "legitimate sources" of authority? What aspects might actually bind future courts?

Among lawyers and judges, the pervasive view is that "what matters is not merely what the court said [and did], but how it said it." The words and phrases used by the court to formulate the legal rule are "regarded as consequential in (if not dispositive of) a subsequent case even if the language at issue was not directly implicated in the decision of the prior case." After all, only the text of the opinion is available "as the repository of the information to which litigants and judges refer in subsequent cases in order to determine what the law is (or might be)" (Oldfather 2008, 1328). This practical constraint on methods for determining what the law is—the need to examine the text—is reason enough to engage in close reading.

Close and Distant Reading of Precedent

The processes of close and distant reading grow out of literary theory and methods. Rather than social science or political science methodologies, they are modes of interpretation. Rather than providing answers to questions or proof of hypotheses, they most often yield mapping, explanation, and description. As used in this chapter, both close and distant reading depend on looking beneath the surface to discern patterns and associations. Close reading recognizes the significance of context but focuses on the workings of the language and structures of the current text within its particular setting. Distant reading recognizes the significance of individual texts but focuses on interpreting the images that have been generated by extracting information from multiple related texts.

Bringing the two approaches together promises to help us chart the spread of ideas across and through legal networks. In this chapter, for example, one goal is to begin to map the influence of particular rhetorical approaches on one important audience for judicial opinions: the judges of later courts. What connections can be made between the rhetorical construction of a Supreme Court majority opinion and its later significance (as measured by the level of reliance on the opinion by later courts)? If, for example, Justice Scalia's majority opinions were uniquely influential, what combination of rhetorical elements made them so?

Close reading takes a deep look at the meaning of a text like a judicial opinion. Comparing the process to reading literature, James Boyd White described the rationale for applying close reading to the law:

> To a certain kind of mind, the question in reading is simply to ask what is the main idea. But in law, as in poetry and other forms of literature, the main idea is usually rather simply stated and it is not the real point. The poet is saying I am in love, or full of grief, or in despair; the first amendment says speech is a good thing, the fourth amendment says people are to be protected against searches, and so on. But you could write a book, or teach a whole course, about the significance of *the ways in which* Shakespeare says in his sonnets that he is in love or despair; likewise, you could write a book, or teach a whole course, about *the ways in which* speech is protected under the first amendment. Life and quality are in the style, not imagined simply as a form of elegance, but as all that matters most when one uses language. (White 2011, n. 11)

If close reading looks for what matters most in an individual text, distant reading looks across texts, trading depth for breadth. In distant reading, the reader compiles data covering multiple texts, often texts collected over time. Then the data is analyzed and depicted in charts, graphs, and images. Leveraging distance and multiplicity, the interpreter steps back from a particular text in order to identify trends, perceive questions, and brainstorm hypotheses. For example, relying on a form of distant reading, Professor Bernadette Meyler has suggested that the legal vitality and effectiveness of a specific precedent depends not only on its substantive role in the outcome of subsequent decisions, but also on "the rhetorical effect of the deployment and arrangement of precedents within judicial opinions" (Meyler 2016, 91).

Rather than closely studying texts, distant reading interprets images. These images map or depict large amounts of data: "time plots, histograms, trees, networks, diagrams, scatterplots. . . . Images come first . . . because—by visualizing empirical findings—they constitute *the specific object of study of computational criticism*; they are our 'text'" (Moretti 2016, 3; emphasis in original). Although distant reading is sometimes critiqued for its use in proving conclusions rather than in sparking investigation, its most prominent proponent, Franco Moretti, emphasizes its ability to encourage encounters between "the empirical and the conceptual" (Moretti 2016, 2). This chapter's computational analysis is more modest in scope, but its purpose is the same.

Justice Scalia's Rhetorical Construction of the Past

Using the materials at hand, how did Justice Scalia construct the past? That question is the subject of this section's close reading of the background context for the *Smith* majority opinion.

Rhetorical construction frequently conceals its own rhetorical nature. In judicial opinion-writing, concealment occurs when the author successfully makes it appear that the current decision flows from the past—naturally, inevitably, and virtually without the author's intervention. One means of accomplishing the appearance of such an organic progression is to construct a long line of precedent. To do so in *Smith*, Justice Scalia went back to the nineteenth century, eluding more recent and arguably more relevant precedents. In *Reynolds v. United States*, 98 U.S. 145 (1878), the Court had upheld the federal law banning polygamy by distinguishing between religious beliefs and the practices growing out of religious beliefs. According to Justice Scalia, the *Reynolds* ruling was only the beginning, the foundation for more than a century of support for his prudential argument that allowing religious exceptions to general laws would "permit every citizen to become a law unto himself."[1]

Exercising the rhetorical power of selection to maintain the appearance that only gradual precedential accretion was in play, Justice Scalia not only realigned but omitted significant subsequent history. Relying on a supportive quotation from Justice Frankfurter's majority opinion in *Minersville School District v. Gobitis*, 310 U.S. 586 (1940) rather than the holding itself, Justice Scalia sidestepped the inconvenient overruling of *Gobitis* only three years after the decision (in *West Virginia State Board of Education v. Barnette*, 319 U.S. 624 [1943]). Professor McConnell's criticism of this characterization of *Smith*'s precedential support was typical: "Relying on *Gobitis* without mentioning *Barnette* is like relying on *Plessy v. Ferguson* without mentioning *Brown v. Board of Education*" (McConnell 1990, 1124).

Lacking authoritative support for his reconstituted line of precedent, Justice Scalia selected another unlikely authority, Justice Stevens's concurring opinion in *United States v. Lee*, 455 U.S. 252 (1982). In *Lee*, an Amish farmer argued that his religious beliefs precluded him from paying or withholding social security taxes. The majority applied the prevailing general rule, emphasized the compelling government interest in maintenance of the social security system, and found no free-exercise violation. As he concurred in the

result, Justice Stevens advanced an alternative rationale not adopted by the
majority: "There is virtually no room for a 'constitutionally required exemption' on religious grounds from a valid tax law that is entirely neutral in its
general application."² Though found nowhere as governing precedent, Justice
Scalia proclaimed that this principle—that all are subject to neutral laws of
general applicability—was in accord with the "vast majority" of prior decisions.

Having constructed a preferred rhetorical façade, Justice Scalia next
sought to preempt alternative renderings. To do so, he needed to undermine
the free-exercise balancing test established in *Sherbert v. Verner*, 374 U.S. 398
(1963) and limit its relevance to a small sliver of cases. In *Sherbert*, the first
in a line of cases, a member of the Seventh-day Adventist Church was fired
for refusing to work on the Sabbath. The Supreme Court held that when, as
in *Sherbert*, the government's action substantially burdened a religious practice, the government must demonstrate a compelling government interest and
narrowly tailored means. Justice Scalia's reconstruction of *Sherbert* as a narrow exception would join his reconstitution of the general rule to inform his
majority decision in the present case.

Justice Scalia's Rhetorical Construction of the Present

[F]or Scalia, the rule's the thing; originalism and traditionalism are means, not ends.
SULLIVAN 1992, 78

Close reading of the *Smith* majority opinion validates Kathleen Sullivan's
succinct summary of Justice Scalia's approach to precedential construction:
"[F]irst, state the general rule; second, rationalize the existing messy pattern of cases by grandfathering in a few exceptions and doing the best you
can to cabin their reach; and third, anticipate future cases in which the rule
might be thought problematic and dispose of them in advance by writing
sub-paragraphs and sub-sub-paragraphs qualifying the rule with clauses beginning with 'unless' or 'except'" (Sullivan 1992, 78). In *Smith*, two employees of a private drug rehabilitation organization were fired for their illegal
drug use. They brought before the Court the question of "whether the Free
Exercise Clause of the First Amendment permits the State of Oregon to include religiously inspired peyote use within the reach of its general criminal
prohibition on use of that drug" and thus whether the state may "deny unemployment benefits to persons dismissed from their jobs because of such
religiously inspired use." The fired employees were members of the Native
American Church, and they had ingested peyote for sacramental purposes

during a church ceremony. The Oregon Supreme Court held that the Oregon controlled substances statutes made no exception for the sacramental use of the drug, and so the two employees could be denied unemployment benefits on the basis of their firing.

As he began to construct *Smith* as precedent, Justice Scalia radically re-characterized the Court's past decisions: "We have *never held* that an individual's religious beliefs excuse him from compliance with an otherwise valid law prohibiting conduct that the State is free to regulate." Instead, "the record of *more than a century* of our free exercise jurisprudence contradicts that proposition."[3] As the source for his reasoning, Justice Scalia quoted Justice Frankfurter in *Gobitis*: "Conscientious scruples have not, in the course of the long struggle for religious toleration, relieved the individual from obedience to a general law not aimed at the promotion or restriction of religious beliefs."[4]

The "more than a century" of precedent consisted only of a quotation from *Reynolds*, decided in 1878; the Justice Frankfurter quotation from the overruled *Gobitis* majority opinion; and Justice Stevens's concurrence in *Lee*, decided in 1982. Still, Justice Scalia's claim was that the *Reynolds* foundation had been buttressed by "[s]ubsequent decisions [that] have *consistently held* that the right of free exercise does not relieve an individual of the obligation to comply with a 'valid and neutral law of general applicability on the ground that the law proscribes (or prescribes) conduct that his religions prescribes (or proscribes).'"[5]

After "rationaliz[ing] the existing messy pattern of cases," Justice Scalia "grandfather[ed] in a few exceptions" and sought to "cabin their reach" (Sullivan 1992, 78). First, he discovered the hybrid exception: "The *only* decisions in which we have held that the First Amendment bars application of a neutral, generally applicable law to religiously motivated action" did not involve the Free Exercise Clause alone. Instead, those cases raised hybrid claims of violations of the Free Exercise Clause in conjunction with other constitutional provisions, including freedom of speech, freedom of the press, or the right of parents to direct the education of their children."[6] By including *Barnette* among the decisions explained by this exception, Justice Scalia avoided discussion of *Barnette*'s overruling of *Gobitis*.

Next, Justice Scalia began narrowing the application of the generally accepted line of precedent until *Smith*, the *Sherbert* balancing test. Acknowledging that the test had been used in very similar circumstances, Justice Scalia categorized those prior cases as distinguishable because they did not involve exemptions from a generally applicable criminal law. Outside the narrow area of unemployment compensation (which critics pointed out was the precise context within which *Smith* came to the Court), Justice Scalia proclaimed that even though "we have sometimes purported to apply the *Sherbert* test in contexts other than that, we have always found the test satisfied." And, in recent years, "we have abstained from applying the *Sherbert* test" (outside the unemployment compensation field) at all. As a result, the *Sherbert* decision might be said to be limited to cases "where the State [already] has in place a system of individual exemptions." And if that claim goes too far, "[w]hether or not the decisions [in *Sherbert* and related cases] are that limited, they at least have nothing to do with an across-the-board criminal prohibition on a particular form of conduct."[7]

Having "cleaned up," organized, and explained the past, Justice Scalia announced the new rule, which, viewed in the right light from the past, was really no different from the old rule. "[T]he sounder approach and the approach *in accord with the vast majority of our precedents* was to find that the *Sherbert* test did not apply to generally applicable criminal prohibitions on conduct."[8]

Justice Scalia's final argument was that a "parade of horribles" would result from allowing religious objectors to argue that every regulation of conduct was presumptively invalid. Such a rule "would open the prospect of constitutionally required religious exemptions from civic obligations . . . ranging from compulsory military service . . . to the payment of taxes . . . and laws providing for equality of opportunity."[9] Despite this prospect, Justice Scalia himself opened up the same route, one that would be heavily traveled in the future, by noting that legislators could provide religious exemptions that were not constitutionally required. Even as he recognized that leaving exemptions to the political process would disadvantage those who practice minority religions, he argued that this "unavoidable consequence of democratic government must be preferred to a system in which each conscience is a law unto itself."[10]

The Reconstitution of *Smith*

The majority decision in *Smith* was unpopular across political, social, ideological, and religious lines. Seeking explicitly to negate *Smith* and restore the *Sherbert* balancing test, Congress enacted the Religious Freedom Restoration Act (RFRA) in 1993. Four years later, the application of RFRA to state government actions was found unconstitutional in *City of Boerne v. Flores*, 521 U.S. 507 (1997). The Court held that RFRA was unconstitutional as to the states because Congress had exceeded its power in enacting it. Congress next enacted a new RFRA to apply solely to federal laws and the Religious Land Use and Institutionalized Persons Act (RLUIPA), which imposed the same standard against state laws involving land use and prisons. (In the wake of *Boerne*, more than twenty state-based RFRAs have been enacted.)

The new RFRA was interpreted broadly. In *Burwell v. Hobby Lobby Stores, Inc.*, 134 S. Ct. 2751 (2014), the Court held that because of RFRA, corporations whose religious owners object to a reproductive health care requirement could argue that they are statutorily exempted from otherwise neutral laws of general applicability, a decision that directly contradicted the *Smith* rule. In the Court's words, "The wisdom of Congress's judgment on this matter is not our concern. Our responsibility is to enforce RFRA as written, and under the standard that RFRA prescribes, the HHS contraceptive mandate is unlawful."[11]

DATA COMPILATION AND ANALYSIS

Starting with this substantive history of the *Smith* rule and applying modified distant reading techniques, what can we learn about the influence of the rule's rhetorical construction? This exploration depends on data compilation and analysis techniques developed by Professor Eric Nystrom in collaboration with Professor David Tanenhaus.[12] Professors Nystrom and Tanenhaus characterized their work as applying a "medium-data" perspective (Tanenhaus and Nystrom 2017, 358). This perspective provides a larger and more data-driven approach than traditionally practiced by historians (or close readers), but it remains an interpretive mode.

These medium-data techniques depended first on collecting data on all the subsequent cases that cited *Smith*. The data included (*a*) citations of all the citing cases, indicating jurisdictions and years of decision; (*b*) Shepard's analysis of the treatment of the precedent case by the citing case; and (*c*) LexisNexis analysis of the portions of the precedent case relied upon by the citing case as indicated by the LexisNexis headnote numbers that had been assigned to the precedent case. Analysis and interpretation of the collected data proceeded through recursive rounds of hypothesis, computation, depiction, and further hypothesis.

Shepard's citation service, available online as part of LexisNexis, classifies by treatment categories all later citations to any case. Subsequent cases are assigned to very specific treatment categories that can be grouped into more general categories. For example, "positive" citations include those that "follow" the precedent case, while "negative" citations include those that "question" the original decision or "caution" the researcher about its use. The most common category, "cited," is sometimes characterized as essentially neutral, but the mere citation of the case has also been interpreted to indicate that the author accepted its general validity.

Incorporating both treatment citations and citations to specific headnote numbers allows for finer-grained interpretation and analysis than analyses based only on citation counts. According to LexisNexis, "LexisNexis Head-notes are key legal points of a case drawn directly from the language of the court by . . . attorney-editors." Inclusion of the headnotes in the online version of a case allows researchers to easily locate key points in what amounts to a table of contents at the beginning of the opinion. Having located the relevant headnote, "you can jump directly to the text point where each LexisNexis headnote appears by selecting the numbered headnote icon next to it." For this study, I isolated headnote numbers that correlated with discrete precedential rules whose subsequent influence I wished to track.[13]

PRECEDENTIAL STAYING POWER

Figure 15.1 is a line graph of citations to *Employment Division v. Smith* grouped by treatment category over time. This graph illustrates *Smith*'s mixed fate over time. The total number of citations remains relatively high over a series of peaks and valleys.[14] Based on the assigned treatment categories, *Smith* (like many other cases) has been more often used by later courts as a supporting reference than it has been followed as binding or mandatory authority. That is, the number of citations to *Smith* without comment ("cited by") far outruns the number of positive citations. More atypically, over time, negative and positive citations have approached a rough balance,[15] though the total positive citations still exceed the total negative ones. Negative citations overtake positive ones about the time that the first lawsuits based on RFRA (1994–96) and the later RFRA challenges to the Affordable Care Act reached appellate courts (2012–16). Most of *Smith*'s citations appear in lower federal and state court opinions. *Smith* has had little influence as horizontal precedent; fewer than a handful of Supreme Court cases follow *Smith* or instruct a lower court to do so.[16]

VARIED INFLUENCE OF RULES

Figure 15.2 is a bar chart that shows the number of citations to each of the headnotes (HN) selected for study. The headnotes are described below in the order of their frequency of citation.

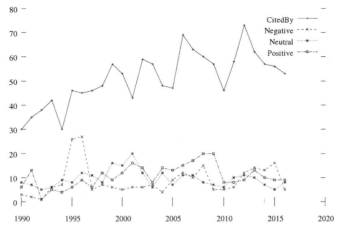

FIGURE 15.1. Citations of *Employment Division v. Smith*, 494 U.S. 872 (1990), grouped by treatment, by year (using categories following Nelson and Hinkle 2015, adjusted by the author (corrected data: March 27, 2017).

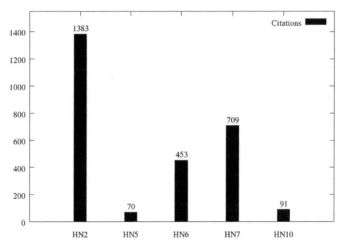

FIGURE 15.2. Bar chart of citations of *Smith*, grouped by headnote, 1990–2016 (corrected data: March 27, 2017).

Headnote 2: General Rule Framework

When they identify headnotes, the LexisNexis editors omit citations, but extract most of the actual language used in the opinion. For example, the text in the opinion that LexisNexis designated as headnote 2, establishing a general rule framework for free-exercise analysis, reads as follows:

> The Free Exercise Clause of the First Amendment, which has been made applicable to the States by incorporation into the Fourteenth Amendment, pro-

vides that "Congress shall make no law respecting an establishment of religion or prohibiting the free exercise thereof." The free exercise of religion means, first and foremost, the right to believe and profess whatever religious doctrine one desires. Thus, the First Amendment obviously excludes all "governmental regulation of religious *beliefs* as such." The government may not compel affirmation of religious belief, punish the expression of religious doctrines it believes to be false, impose special disabilities on the basis of religious views or religious status, or lend its power to one or the other side in controversies over religious authority or dogma.

As presented in the opinion (as opposed to the headnote), this rule is more obviously a "synthesized rule" because the background of precedential support that has been brought together to form the rule is clearly evidenced by the citations. As a result, the text provides a visual collection and restatement in convenient and capsule form of the rule structure that the author has derived or created, with the corresponding series of nine separate case citations adding visual and rhetorical weight. Stating a well-supported synthesized rule boosts the opinion's credibility in the present and (perhaps) far into the future. By providing a concise, complete, and memorable rule structure in an area of continuing controversy, the author has almost guaranteed that the opinion will be used to provide "authority" in future cases. The number and quality of the citations collected to support the general rule enhance these effects. In this instance, Justice Scalia framed a well-supported, noncontroversial, and helpful general rule delineating what the Free Exercise Clause means and what the government is prohibited from doing as a result. This rule is by far the most frequently cited of the headnotes selected for analysis, with 1,383 citations through 2016.

Headnote 7: Hybrid Exception

The next most-cited headnote, with 709 uses through 2016, was Justice Scalia's exception for hybrid cases: "The only decisions in which we have held that the First Amendment bars application of a neutral, generally applicable law to religiously motivated action have involved not the Free Exercise Clause alone, but the Free Exercise Clause in conjunction with other constitutional protections, such as freedom of speech and of the press . . . or the right of parents . . . to direct the education of their children." Justice Scalia supported his discovery of this exception by lining up a series of precedents, extracting helpful quotations, and—through the adept use of parentheticals—characterizing the cases as fitting exactly the quoted principles. For example, from *Murdock v. Pennsylvania*, 319 U.S. 105 (1943), which he characterized as "invalidating a flat tax on solicitation as applied to the dissemination of religious ideas," Justice Scalia pulled this quotation: "It is one thing to impose a tax on the income or property of a preacher. It is quite another thing to exact a tax from him for the privilege of delivering a sermon." As for *Wisconsin v. Yoder*, 406 U.S. 205 (1972) (invalidating compulsory school attendance laws as applied to Amish parents who refused on religious grounds to send their children to school), Justice Scalia quoted this: "When the interests of parenthood are combined with a free exercise claim of the nature revealed by this record, more than merely a 'reasonable relation to some purpose of the State' is required to sustain the validity of the State's requirement." In addition to hybrid cases involving both free exercise and another constitutional claim, Justice Scalia characterized other Supreme Court cases as having been decided "exclusively upon free-speech grounds," citing, among others, *West Virginia State Board of Education v. Barnette* (invalidating compulsory flag salute statute challenged by religious objectors).

Headnote 6: New Categorical Rule

Smith's new categorical rule was stated in the part of the opinion designated as headnote 6: "Subsequent decisions have consistently held that the right of free exercise does not relieve an individual of the obligation to comply with a 'valid and neutral law of general applicability on the ground that the law proscribes (or prescribes) conduct that his religion prescribes (or proscribes).'" Here, Justice Scalia's leading citations were *Gobitis* and the critical quotation from Justice Stevens's concurring opinion in *United States v. Lee*. Over time, this rule (considered the most significant of *Smith*'s holdings at the time of decision) has been cited less frequently than not only the general rule framework but also the narrowly framed hybrid exception, with 453 citations noted.

Headnote 10: Narrowing Strict Scrutiny

In the part of the opinion designated as headnote 10, Justice Scalia sought to confine future application of the previously well-established balancing test: "The *Sherbert* test is inapplicable to challenges to an across-the-board criminal prohibition on a particular form of conduct." This headnote has rarely been cited. Only 91 cases have been found as using this language specifically, though this small number of citing cases has remained steady across time.

Headnote 5: Rationale for New Categorical Rule

The least-cited of the opinion's headnotes over time (among those studied) is headnote 5, the part of the opinion containing the underlying rationale for the new categorical rule:

> As described succinctly by Justice Frankfurter in *Minersville v. Gobitis*, "Conscientious scruples have not, in the course of the long struggle for religious toleration, relieved the individual from obedience to a general law not aimed at the promotion or restriction of religious beliefs. The mere possession of religious convictions which contradict the relevant concerns of a political society does not relieve the citizen from the discharge of political responsibilities." We first had occasion to assert that principle in *Reynolds v. United States*, . . . where we said, "Laws . . . are made for the government of actions, and while they cannot interfere with mere religious belief and opinions, they may with practices."

When this statement of the *Smith* rationale is cited, it usually follows a citation to the new categorical rule. And, like Justice Scalia, the authors of the subsequent opinions rarely mention the overruling of *Gobitis*.

THE MOST INFLUENTIAL RULES
PREDATE AND OUTLAST *SMITH*

Like the bar chart of figure 15.2, the line graph of figure 15.3 illustrates that some rules from *Smith* have been much more cited than others. Figure 15.3 maps that finding over time by illustrating citations of *Smith* grouped together by headnote, by year. The general rule framework established in headnote 2, which was well supported by precedent, is the most cited, and it appears to play a large part in *Smith*'s overall citation trend (that is, figure 15.3 illustrates that the total number of citations and the number of citations to headnote 2 mirror one another). Headnote 6's categorical rule appears responsible for negative citations overtaking positive ones starting around 1995 (two years after RFRA was adopted) and again starting around 2010 (when RFRA challenges to the Affordable Care Act began to be heard in the courts). Indicating that subsequent courts might have found the hybrid exception helpful or more broadly applicable, the number of citations to headnote 7 regularly exceeded the number of citations to headnote 6 over time. Citations to headnote 5, stating the rationale as supported by *Gobitis* and *Reynolds*, remained low throughout.[17]

Figure 15.4 is a line graph illustrating citations following *Smith* in comparison with citations following its past precedents over time. The graph presents a preliminary look at how the decision in *Smith* may have affected the

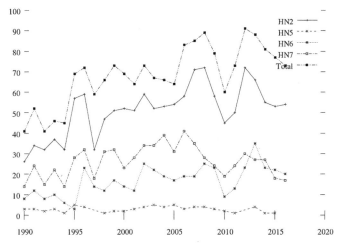

FIGURE 15.3. Line graph of citations of *Smith*, grouped by headnote, by year (using corrected data: March 27, 2017).

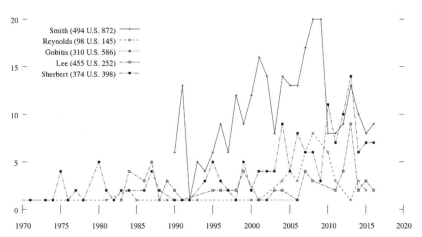

FIGURE 15.4. Citations following *Smith, Reynolds, Gobitis, Lee, Sherbert*, by year, 1970–2016 (using author-corrected Shepard's data: March 27 and May 3, 2017).

continuing influence of the precedents on which Justice Scalia relied. Despite *Smith*'s depiction of *Sherbert* as applying only within a narrow range of cases, citations to *Sherbert* began to exceed the number of citations to *Smith* in 2010 and their citation rates stayed relatively even thereafter. Once again, this result likely reflects the long-term effects of RFRA, which statutorily readopted the *Sherbert* test, and specifically the impact of RFRA on challenges to the Affordable Care Act after its adoption in 2010. *Smith*'s reliance on *Gobitis* appears to have had no positive effect on the consistently meager citation rate of the older case, while the citation trends for *Lee* and *Reynolds* are difficult to interpret in light of *Smith* because those opinions contained multiple "rules" beyond those cited in *Smith*.

Findings and Next Steps

The combination of close and distant reading used here to explore the *Smith* majority opinion provides hints about potential connections between the rhetorical methods used in opinion construction and the future development of the law. These connections have not yet received sustained attention in the proliferation of recent scholarship devoted to content and citation analyses of Supreme Court opinions. Leading researchers agree that further study is needed, but they point to the difficulty of identifying relevant rhetorical methods and tracing their influence.[18] (Cross and Pennebaker 2014; Cross 2010; Cross and Spriggs 2010, 501; Hall and Wright 2008).

This exploration of *Smith* provides additional evidence of the uncertain lasting effects of Justice Scalia's majority opinion. Despite all-but-universal early criticism and Congress's passage of legislation explicitly aimed at overturning its "new" rule, *Smith* remains mandatory precedent for all free-exercise claims brought under the U.S. Constitution. As precedent, however, the *Smith* rule covers very little. *Smith* provides far less "protection" for religious objectors than the statutory alternatives, so most free-exercise lawsuits challenging federal government action are based upon and decided under RFRA.[19] And it's likely that a majority of the free-exercise lawsuits challenging actions taken by state and local governments are based upon and decided under the Religious Land Use and Institutionalized Persons Act (RLUIPA) or a state version of RFRA. So even though *Smith* is still good law, and even though a plaintiff might allege a constitutional claim as well as a statutory claim, *Smith* is rarely the main precedent for a decision on a religious objector's free-exercise claim (see Griffin 2013; Hamilton 2016)

The application of modified distant reading techniques brought somewhat surprising results. Within a very complex setting,[20] the *Smith* majority opinion appears to have had limited influence on later courts. This contrasts with the conclusion of a comprehensive citation analysis that Justice Scalia's majority opinions have "especially high citation rates" compared with other Supreme Court justices. The study's author suggested that at least some of Justice Scalia's opinions "are apparently written in a fashion that projects greater precedential significance" (Cross 2010, 191, 202).

This chapter's close readings of Justice Scalia's majority opinion left a singular overwhelming impression: it was written as an argumentative brief. The opinion centered on arguments based on case precedent (rather than Justice Scalia's preferred modes of textualism and originalism). And the arguments stretched both factual comparisons and prior reasoning to the breaking point. It is not unusual for judicial opinions to be written as if they are not only consistent with precedent but compelled by it (Chemerinsky 2002, 2015–19). But the *Smith* opinion went further: "Its use of precedent is troubling, bordering on the shocking" (McConnell 1990, 1120). Similarly, to make it appear that the decision in the present case evolved naturally from, rather than revolutionized, the past, Justice Scalia used the rhetorical methods and techniques of an advocate afraid he is arguing a losing case. These included cherry-picking quotations and rationales; stating persuasively narrowed principles as if they were clarifying; discovering newly consistent lines of cases as if they were preexisting; and presenting mixed precedents as if they were fully supportive.

Through the use of distant reading techniques, we found that the part of the opinion supporting *Smith*'s cornerstone, that all must comply with a "neutral law of general applicability" (headnote 6), had become just another ground for argument rather than an authoritative rule. This was in contrast with the continuing positive influence on later courts of another section of the opinion (headnote 2), where Justice Scalia framed a well-supported, noncontroversial, and helpful general rule delineating what the Free Exercise Clause means and what the government is prohibited from doing as a result.

In *Smith*, Justice Scalia sought to mask his creation of a new rule by reconstructing the past rather than justifying the new. Once he reconstructed the past, he forced the present case to fit into a framework that he conceded might result in injustice to individual freedom and especially to members of minority religions. These opinion-construction decisions provide rhetorical ground for judging the *Smith* majority opinion to be "fatally incomplete and defective." That ground is what James Boyd White identified as "the virtually universal but little noted convention that the lawyer and judge alike must credibly claim that the outcome for which they argue, or which they reach, is not only called for by the legal texts in question, but is in an important sense itself just" (White 2007, 1419). Given his rhetorical construction, Justice Scalia could make no credible claim that the *Smith* majority decision was "called for by the legal texts in question" nor that it was itself just.

References

Black, Ryan C., and James F. Spriggs II. 2013. "The Citation and Depreciation of U.S. Supreme Court Precedent." *Journal of Empirical Legal Studies* 10:325.

Broughman, Brian J., and Deborah A. Widiss. 2017. "After the Override: An Empirical Analysis of Shadow Precedent." *Journal of Legal Studies* 46:51.

Chemerinsky, Erwin. 2002. "The Rhetoric of Constitutional Law." *Michigan Law Review* 100: 2008–35.

Cross, Frank B. 2010. "Determinants of Citations to Supreme Court Opinions (and the Remarkable Influence of Justice Scalia)." *Supreme Court Economic Review* 18:177.

———, and James W. Pennebaker. 2014. "The Language of the Roberts Court." *Michigan State Law Review* 2014:853.

———, and James F. Spriggs II. 2010. "The Most Important (and Best) Supreme Court Opinions and Justices." *Emory Law Journal* 60:408.

Farber, Daniel A. 2006. "The Rule of Law and the Law of Precedents." *Minnesota Law Review* 90:1173–1203.

Fisher, Louis. 2016. "The Staying Power of Erroneous Dicta: From *Curtiss-Wright* to *Zivotofsky*." *Constitutional Commentary* 31:149–208.

Griffin, Leslie C. 2013. "The Sins of Hosanna-Tabor." *Indiana Law Journal* 88:981–1018.

Hall, Mark A., and Ronald F. Wright. 2008. "Systematic Content Analysis of Judicial Opinions." *California Law Review* 96:63, 66.

Hamilton, Marci. 2016. "The Court after Scalia: The Complex Future of Free Exercise." SCOTUSblog. September 13. Online at www.scotusblog.com.

Hinkle, Rachael K. 2015. "Legal Constraint in the U.S. Courts of Appeals." *Journal of Politics* 77: 721–35.

McConnell, Michael. 1990. "Free Exercise Revisionism and the Smith Decision." *University of Chicago Law Review* 57:1109–53.

Meyer, Linda Ross. 2010. *The Justice of Mercy.* Ann Arbor: University of Michigan Press.

Meyler, Bernadette A. 2016. "The Rhetoric of Precedent." In *Rhetorical Processes and Legal Judgments: How Language and Arguments Shape Struggles for Rights and Power*, edited by Austin Sarat, 83–99. New York: Cambridge University Press.

Moretti, Franco. 2016. *Literature, Measured.* Pamphlet 12. Palo Alto: Stanford Literary Lab. Online at https://litlab.stanford.edu/pamphlets/.

Nelson, Michael J., and Rachael K. Hinkle. 2015. "Crafting the Law: How Opinion Content Influences Legal Development." *Social Science Research Network.* doi:10.2139/ssrn.2620977.

Oldfather, Chad. 2008. "Writing, Cognition, and the Nature of the Judicial Function." *Georgetown Law Journal* 96:1283–1345.

Scalia, Antonin. 1997. *A Matter of Interpretation: Federal Courts and the Law.* Princeton, NJ: Princeton University Press.

Schauer, Frederick. 2012. "Precedent." In *The Routledge Companion to Philosophy of Law*, edited by Andrei Marmor, 123–36. New York: Routledge.

Sullivan, Kathleen M. 1992. "Foreword: The Justices of Rules and Standards." *Harvard Law Review* 106:22–123.

Tanenhaus, David S., and Eric C. Nystrom. 2017. "Pursuing Gault." *Nevada Law Journal* 17:351–70.

White, James Boyd. 2011. "The Cultural Background of the Legal Imagination." In *Teaching Law and Literature*, edited by Austin Sarat, Cathrine O. Frank, and Matthew Anderson, 29–39. New York: Modern Language Association.

———. 2007. "Interview with James Boyd White." *Michigan Law Review* 105:1403–19.

Justice Scalia's Rhetoric of Overruling: Throwing Out the (Institutional) Baby with the Bathwater

CLARKE ROUNTREE

In a 1995 concurring opinion in *Hubbard v. United States*, 514 U.S. 695 (1995), a case that overruled a prior decision interpreting the federal false-statement statute, Justice Antonin Scalia explained the importance of following precedent and respecting the principle of stare decisis: "The doctrine of *stare decisis* protects the legitimate expectations of those who live under the law, and, as Alexander Hamilton observed, is one of the means by which exercise of "an arbitrary discretion in the courts" is restrained (*The Federalist No. 78*). Who ignores it must give reasons, and reasons that go beyond mere demonstration that the overruled opinion was wrong (otherwise the doctrine would be no doctrine at all)" (716) (citation omitted). Such respect for stare decisis is widely shared in American law, though that respect has proven no bar to overruling precedents. Indeed, the United States Supreme Court has overruled well over three hundred of its own precedents (*Supreme Court Decisions* 2014), and Justice Scalia has authored or concurred in more than a dozen of these reversals, which this chapter will examine.

Given the "legitimate expectations" of citizens to have consistency in the law and the judiciary's concern to avoid the appearance of ruling arbitrarily, overruling a precedent is a rhetorically fraught discourse. For an overruling court insists that what it is deciding *now* is not arbitrary, even while it admits that what it decided *before* was arbitrary, or at least flawed or otherwise problematic. Because of the corporate nature of the Supreme Court, its members commonly refer to what "we" decided in a case, whether that case was decided last year or two hundred years earlier. Thus, for the High Court to overrule a decision is to effectively say that "we" were wrong; and, if the Court was wrong then, why should we trust that they are right now?

The rhetorical challenge of this form of discourse makes it interesting, as it

requires opinion writers grappling with overruling to be inventive in addressing two distinct needs: defending the correctness of the current decision, but
also explaining why their predecessors on the bench got the precedent decision wrong. Ideally, in fulfilling the second need, the overruling court will
provide an excuse for the prior court that makes their "mistake" understandable and forgivable; for to suggest that they were careless, stupid, or driven
by extrajudicial motives is to implicate the "we" that is the High Court. In
other words, it is in the interest of members of this corporate body to protect
the standing of their institution. At a minimum, such an approach embodies
judicial decorum; above that minimum, it engages in face-saving and image
management.

Unfortunately, these two rhetorical purposes—supporting the present decision and defending the precedent court—are often at odds. For example, an
opinion writer typically wants to show that his or her own assessment of what
the law requires is obviously correct and not merely defensible, particularly
since it argues for overruling a precedent. But such an emphasis on clear and
indisputable law raises the question of how the prior court could have missed
something so obvious.

Of course some judicial philosophies support overrulings with notions
such as a "living constitution," by which courts inevitably must adapt to new
situations. It is easy to forgive the shortcomings of predecessors who could
not predict the future and how it would make problematic their legal rulings.
Judicial philosophies that highlight the open texture of law and its indeterminacy may justify judicial decisions that, in the absence of clear rules, seek the
social good (as legal realists and scholars of law and economics scholars rec-
ommend). And, insofar as social needs change, prior courts can be forgiven
for their holdings.

However much notions of a living constitution, of the open texture of law,
and of judge-sought social goods may shape the attitudes of judges, they have
not had a significant impact on the *style* of judicial rhetoric. That discourse
continues to feature a unique set of rhetorical commitments, which Gerald
Wetlaufer attributes to the rhetoric of law more generally: "These include
commitments to a certain kind of toughmindedness and rigor, to relevance
and orderliness in discourse, to objectivity, to clarity and logic, to binary judgment, and to the closure of controversies. They also include commitments to
hierarchy and authority, to the impersonal voice, and to the one right (or best)
answer to questions and the one true (or best) meaning of texts. Finally, the
rhetoric of our discipline reveals our commitment to a particular conception
of the rule of law" (1990, 1552). Such a style is well adapted to the maintenance
of the myth of objectivity in judicial decisions, which is particularly impor-

tant where judicial speakers address public audiences. Consider, for example, Chief Justice Roberts's insistence at his Senate confirmation hearing that "[j]udges and justices are servants of the law, not the other way around. Judges are like umpires. Umpires don't make rules; they apply them" (quoted in Scordato 2008, 366).

Roberts's ideal of judging reflects the impartiality and certainty typical of Wetlaufer's description of legal style—one that is at home in Justice Scalia's judicial rhetoric. Catherine L. Langford argues of the late justice, "Scalia crafted a persuasive narrative to reform judicial interpretation. The hero of Scalia's national narrative is the Constitution—perfect in construction and timeless in application—not the justice interpreting it. The villain is the activist justice who seeks to pervert the meaning of the document. Scalia's textual tale tells the story of legal decisions, bound by the confines of the constitutional text, reflecting the original meaning of the founders" (Langford 2018, 1–2). Generally, the rhetoric of judicial opinions stresses a kind of certainty that makes defending a precedent court harder. Justice Scalia's textualism and originalism make the defense of a precedent court harder still, to the extent that chaining oneself to a constitutional (or statutory) text and its original meaning presumably limits how far a judge can stray from a true understanding of the law. However, Justice Scalia recognized that other considerations had to be weighed in deciding whether or not to follow a precedent in a given case, taking him beyond a strict adherence to textualism and originalism.

A decision about whether to follow precedent involves *substantive reasoning,* whereby competing considerations are *weighed* against one another, as opposed to formal reasoning, where axiomatic or geometric rules yield clear outcomes (see, for example, Jonsen and Toulmin 1988). Thus, although Justice Scalia's originalism and textualism might seem to provide a clear rule, such as "Overrule all cases where the law in question was misinterpreted by the precedent court," such a rule, invariably applied, would lead to unacceptable consequences. Scalia acknowledges as much when he admits that the principle of stare decisis requires a "pragmatic exception" to his originalist theory (Scalia 1989, 140, n. 2). For example, as he noted at his Senate confirmation hearing, he might not overrule even an erroneous decision if it were "so woven in the fabric of law" as to make an overruling problematic (quoted in Barrett 2017, 1928). This caveat illustrates something that Scalia understands but has not articulated clearly—that is, the insufficiency of invariant principles in governing such decisions. The "wovenness" of a precedent into existing law does not describe either a categorical distinction or an antecedent rule that will handle such exceptions. Nor does it describe how deeply the relevant decisions might be embedded in the weave.

The substantive concerns that arise in judicial decision-making generally, and in the question of overruling particularly, can be usefully framed by three temporal orientations required for appropriate judgment. These temporal orientations highlight the relevant responsibilities to the past, the present, and the future. As I have argued previously, court decisions, ideally, should aspire to instill confidence on three different counts: "(1) that prior cases, long accepted legal principles, legislative statutes, administrative regulations, state and federal constitutions, and their authors (whose intentions are invoked) require the decision; (2) that the decision yields the greatest justice in the instant case (given characterizations of litigants as deserving of legal reward or punishment); and (3) that the decision creates the fairest and most efficacious results in the long run, providing clear direction and a just outcome for all foreseeable cases like it" (Rountree 1995, 168). Attention to the three temporal orientations reveals considerations, all of which matter, but none of which can be assumed to dominate. Rather, they are weighted *substantively* according to the demands of the situation.

Justice Scalia's comments on overruling can be usefully framed by this tripartite scheme to show how he balances the competing needs of past, present, and future in considering whether to overrule a precedent. His concern for the past—the law laid down—obviously is central to his originalist and textualist philosophy. As he insisted, "I try to be an honest originalist!" (quoted in Senior 2013). In respecting the past, Scalia believes it is important "how clear it is that the [precedent] decision was textually and historically wrong [in interpreting the law]." But he also weighs concerns over justice in the present case before the court. It matters to him "whether harm will be caused to those who justifiably relied on the [precedent] decision." He extends this "reliance" in a way to the larger society in weighing "whether the [precedent] decision has been generally accepted by society." His concerns over the future were particularly about the clarity of the law and the role the courts might have to play if clarity is lacking. Notably, he considered "whether the decision permanently places courts in the position of making policy calls appropriate for elected officials" (Scalia and Garner 2012, 412). That consideration involves clarity to the extent that a given decision requires repeated "policy calls." It also might be considered a concern for the past and for following law laid down to the extent that a precedent decision improperly ignores the proper division of responsibility between the political and judicial branches of government.

The remainder of this essay considers Justice Scalia's discursive practices in overruling cases, using the past-present-future framework to account for his rhetorical weighing of these competing considerations. I examine what

Justice Scalia said about overruling cases, as the author of the overruling, or in his concurrences and dissents. I consider how he defended overrulings he supported and attacked those he did not support. Finally, I look at his constructions of the overruled decisions to assess his efforts at maintaining the image of the Court, which varies with each temporal orientation.

Justice Scalia's Appeal to the Past in Overruling Cases

Justice Scalia's originalism and textualism often supported his position that a precedent court got the law wrong and must be overruled because of "error." Even William Blackstone, who was a firm believer in adhering to precedents, supported overruling where "the former decision is manifestly absurd and unjust" (quoted in Lewis 1968, 540). Justice Scalia often portrays interpretations of law with which he disagrees as absurd, if not unjust. For example, in a right to jury case whose majority opinion Justice Scalia authored, he explains why the overruled case must fall: "[T]he sole prop [remaining] for *Sinclair* is its reliance upon the unexamined proposition, never before endorsed by this Court, that materiality in perjury cases (which is analogous to pertinence in contempt cases) is a question of law for the judge. But just as there is nothing to support *Sinclair* except that proposition, there is, as we have seen, nothing to support that proposition except *Sinclair*. While this perfect circularity has a certain aesthetic appeal, *it has no logic*" (*U.S. v. Gaudin*, 515 U.S. 506, 521 [1995]; emphasis added). In a Confrontation Clause case overruling, he noted that "[m]embers of this Court and academics have suggested that we revise our doctrine *to reflect more accurately the original understanding of the Clause*" (*Crawford v. Washington*, 541 U.S. 36, 60 [2004]; emphasis added).

Justice Scalia also has shown his readiness to overrule based upon error when a majority refuses to overrule a precedent. A passionate target has been *Roe v. Wade*, 410 U.S. 113 (1973), which he called to overrule in *Planned Parenthood v. Casey*, 505 U.S. 833 (1992), despite his conservative colleagues' reluctance to follow him. In *Casey*, which reversed, in part, two prior abortion decisions while leaving *Roe*'s right to abortion intact, Justice Scalia emphasized the error of the original decision, complaining that

> [t]he authors of the joint opinion [part of which attracted a majority], of course, do not squarely contend that *Roe v. Wade* was a *correct* application of "reasoned judgment"; merely that it must be followed, because of *stare decisis*. *Ante*, 505 U.S. at 853, 861, 871. But in their exhaustive discussion of all the factors that go into the determination of when *stare decisis* should be observed and when disregarded, they never mention "how wrong was the decision on its face?" Surely, if "the Court's power lies . . . in its legitimacy, a product of

substance and perception," *ante*, 505 U.S. at 865, the "substance" part of the equation demands that plain error be acknowledged and eliminated. *Roe* was plainly wrong—even on the Court's methodology of "reasoned judgment," and even more so (of course) if the proper criteria of text and tradition are applied. (982–83)

Error in interpreting prior law is even easier to show when the Court faces two competing precedents and it is "necessary" (Blaustein and Field 1958, 168) to choose to follow one and to implicitly or explicitly overrule the other. Thus, in a concurring opinion in *Quill Corp. v. Tax Commissioner*, 504 U.S. 298 (1992), Justice Scalia invokes a conflict between two cases:

> *National Bellas Hess, Inc. v. Department of Revenue of Ill.*, 386 U.S. 753, 87 S. Ct. 1389, 18 L. Ed. 2d 505 (1967), held that the Due Process and Commerce Clauses of the Constitution prohibit a State from imposing the duty of use-tax collection and payment upon a seller whose only connection with the State is through common carrier or the United States mail. I agree with the Court that the Due Process Clause holding of *Bellas Hess* should be overruled. Even before *Bellas Hess*, we had held, correctly I think, that state regulatory jurisdiction could be asserted on the basis of contacts with the State through the United States mail. See *Travelers Health Assn. v. Virginia ex rel. State Corp. Comm'n*, 339 U.S. 643, 646–650, 94 L. Ed. 1154, 70 S. Ct. 927 (1950) (blue sky laws). It is difficult to discern any principled basis for distinguishing between jurisdiction to regulate and jurisdiction to tax. (319)

The conflicting cases argument also can be used to suggest that a precedent already has been effectively overruled. For example, consider Justice Scalia's partial concurrence and partial dissent in *United States v. Hatter*, 532 U.S. 537 (1982):

> As an initial matter, I think the Court is right in concluding that *Evans v. Gore*, 253 U.S. 245, 64 L. Ed. 887, 40 S. Ct. 550 (1920)—holding that new taxes of general applicability cannot be applied to sitting Article III judges—is no longer good law, and should be overruled. We went out of our way in *O'Malley v. Woodrough*, 307 U.S. 277, 280–281, 83 L. Ed. 1289, 59 S. Ct. 838 (1939), to catalog criticism of *Evans*, and subsequently recognized, in *United States v. Will*, 449 U.S. 200, 227, 66 L. Ed. 2d 392, 101 S. Ct. 471, and n. 31 (1980), that *O'Malley* had "undermined the reasoning of *Evans*." The Court's decision today simply recognizes what should be obvious: that *Evans* has not only been undermined, but has in fact collapsed. (582)

Opinions that rely on this form of argument get the best of both worlds: First, the opinion that effectively overruled a precedent can avoid the challenges of actually overruling by not explicitly owning up to it, and thereby dodging the rhetorical heft needed to justify a reversal. Second, the later case can own up to the effective overruling and also dodge the justification by insisting it is a *fait accompli.*

Justice Scalia also follows the Supreme Court's tradition in overruling cases of drawing a distinction between constitutional decisions (which are the vast majority of reversals) and statutory decisions. Justice Douglas explains the judicial attitude toward overruling constitutional cases in *Smith v. Allwright*, 321 U.S. 649 (1944): "In constitutional questions, where correction depends upon amendment and not upon legislative action, this Court throughout its history has freely exercised its power to reexamine the basis of its constitutional decisions" (665). And, undoubtedly, as an originalist and a textualist, Justice Scalia would agree with Justice Douglas's statement five years later that "[a] judge looking at a constitutional decision may have compulsions to revere past history and accept what was once written. But he remembers above all else that it is the Constitution which he swore to support and defend, not the gloss which his predecessors may have put on it" (1949, 736). Unsurprisingly, Justice Scalia admitted in his dissent in *Lawrence v. Texas*, 539 U.S. 558 (2003) that "I do not myself believe in rigid adherence to stare decisis in constitutional cases" (587). In his majority opinion in *U.S. v. Dixon*, 509 U.S. 688 (1993), he noted that while stare decisis is the "preferred course" in constitutional adjudication, "when governing decisions are unworkable or are badly reasoned, 'this Court has never felt constrained to follow precedent'" (712; quoting *Payne v. Tennessee*, 501 U.S. 808, 827 [1991], in turn, quoting *Smith v. Allwright*, at 665).

Overruling statutory cases is a different matter. In his dissenting opinion in *Hohn v. United States*, 524 U.S. 236 (1998), Justice Scalia approvingly quotes *Patterson v. McLean Credit Union*, 491 U.S. 164, 172–73 (1989), urging, "The burden borne by the party advocating abandonment of an established precedent is greater where the Court is asked to overrule a point of statutory construction" (258–59). He quotes *Patterson* again in *Quill Corp. v. North Dakota Tax Collector*, urging, "We have long recognized that the doctrine of *stare decisis* has 'special force' where 'Congress remains free to alter what we have done'" (quoting 172–73, at 320). In *Quill* he argues against overruling *National Bellas Hess, Inc. v. Department of Revenue of Ill.*, 386 U.S. 753 (1967), because "Congress has the final say over regulation of interstate commerce, and it can change the rule of *Bellas Hess* by simply saying so" (320).

Justice Scalia's frequent reliance on error as a key reason for overruling suggests that the overruled courts were wrong because they misinterpreted the law. The implication is that they did not understand the law, so perhaps they were not as perceptive or as knowledgeable as they should be. Justice Scalia does not go into the shortcomings of his fellow justices to explain this lack of knowledge, but allows the implication to stand.

Of course it is possible to explain error in a way that deflects criticism from the overruled judges. For example, in an early admiralty jurisdiction case, *The Propeller Genesee Chief*, 53 U.S. (12 How.) 443 (1851), Chief Justice Taney described its troubled precedent, *The Thomas Jefferson*, as "an erroneous decision into which the [precedent] court fell" (456). That "accident" (a "falling") was caused by a setting where steamships were rare, and the Court was blind to problems presented by a narrowly interpreted common-law rule limiting its jurisdiction to tidewater. Thus, as Kenneth Burke would say, the *scene* of the precedent court's decision controlled his erroneous *act* (Burke [1945] 1969, 3), and the court could be forgiven.

Justice Scalia's failure to provide some explanation for why his predecessors made erroneous decisions is a weakness in his rhetoric of overruling. It leaves the impression that the Court is not infrequently a poor interpreter of the law, a fallible institution which nonetheless wields enormous powers. In fairness, Justice Scalia did not always forgive himself for error either, though in one instance he stood ready to correct it. In *Michigan v. Bay Mills Indian Community*, 134 S. Ct. 2024 (2014), which involved the regulation of casino gambling by Indian tribes, Scalia dissented from a position he had previously taken, noting that its "error has grown more glaringly obvious" over the years and that he should be able to "clean up a mess that I helped make" in establishing the problematic precedent (2045).

Justice Scalia's Appeal to the Present in Overruling Cases

The appeal to the present is concerned with doing justice in the instant case. One key concern in that vein is not hurting individuals who relied on prior interpretations of law. This is of particular note in cases involving property rights. As Justice Kagan noted recently in *Kimble et al. v. Marvel Entertainment*, 576 U.S. ___, 135 S. Ct. 2401 (2015): "[W]e have often recognized that in . . . 'cases involving property and contract rights,' considerations favoring stare decisis are 'at their acme.' E.g., *Payne*, 501 U. S., at 828; *Khan*, 522 U. S., at 20. That is because parties are especially likely to rely on such precedents when ordering their affairs" (slip op. at 9). Indeed, she calls the principle of not unsettling property rights a "superpowered form of *stare decisis*" (slip op. at 10). In this spirit of not unsettling property law, Justice Scalia insists in

Quill, "Having affirmatively suggested that the 'physical presence' rule could be reconciled with our new jurisprudence, we ought not visit economic hardship upon those who took us at our word" (321).

Because significant economic interests may build upon particular interpretations of law, that reliance is paramount in considering overruling. On the other hand, different kinds of reliance may be less compelling. For example, even though *Hubbard v. United States* involved the interpretation of a federal statute (which Justice Scalia urged could be corrected by Congress as needed), he concurred in the overruling of *United States v. Bramblett*, 348 U.S. 503 (1955), for its misinterpretation of 18 USCS § 1001 in part because

> preserving justifiable expectations . . . is not much at risk here. Those whose reliance on *Bramblett* induced them to tell the truth to Congress or the courts, instead of lying, have no claim on our solicitude. Some convictions obtained under *Bramblett* may have to be overturned, and in a few instances wrongdoers may go free who could have been prosecuted and convicted under a different statute if *Bramblett* had not been assumed to be the law. I count that a small price to pay for the uprooting of this weed. (717)

Likewise, in his majority opinion in *United States v. Gaudin*, he was less concerned that there had been reliance over a precedent involving a procedural rule because it "does not serve as a guide to lawful behavior" (521).

One of the most unusual claims of a reliance interest invoked by Justice Scalia involves not the reliance of citizens, but of Congress. Dissenting from *Hohn v. United States*, he argues, "While there is scant reason for denying *stare decisis* effect to *House*, there is special reason for according it: the reliance of Congress upon an unrepudiated decision central to the procedural scheme it was creating. Section 102 of AEDPA [the Antiterrorism and Effective Death Penalty Act of 1996] continues a long tradition of provisions enacted by Congress that limit appellate review of petitions" (261). After reviewing that long tradition, he concludes, "Quite obviously, with *House* on the books—neither overruled nor even *cited* in the later opinions that the Court claims 'disregarded' it—Congress presumably anticipated that § 102 of AEDPA would be interpreted in the same manner" (262). Although Justice Scalia's juxtaposition of "Quite obviously" with the more guarded "presumably" appear to waffle on the certainty he attributes to this reliance, he obviously thought that reliance important enough to dissent on behalf of that concern.

Generally, then, Justice Scalia is concerned about the present only where there are significant reliance interests guiding either economic decisions or congressional legislation. He does not use present concerns to support overruling—suggesting that the law ought to be refashioned in light of a pitiable litigant, for example, caught up in an unforeseen consequence of law's trajectory. Indeed, his justifications for overrulings where such issues arise return to the past, where there is error, with little explanation as to why the prior Court made that error.

Justice Scalia's Appeal to the Future in Overruling Cases

The concern over the future is about the consequences of the ruling for cases that might arise later. For example, in his majority opinion in *Crawford v. Washington*, 541 U.S. 36 (2004), he complained that *Ohio v. Roberts*, 448 U.S. 56 (1980), was poorly crafted to avoid violations of the Confrontation Clause, because

> [d]espite the plurality's speculation in *Lilly*, 527 U.S., at 137, 144 L. Ed. 2d 117, 119 S. Ct. 1887, that it was "highly unlikely" that accomplice confessions implicating the accused could survive *Roberts*, courts continue routinely to admit them [listing multiple cases]. One recent study found that, after *Lilly*, appellate courts admitted accomplice statements to the authorities in 25 out of 70 cases—more than one-third of the time. Kirst, Appellate Court Answers to the Confrontation Questions in *Lilly v. Virginia*, 53 Syracuse L. Rev. 87, 105 (2003). Courts have invoked *Roberts* to admit other sorts of plainly testimonial statements despite the absence of any opportunity to cross-examine. (63)

Thus, the consequences of *Roberts* were problematic in terms of how appellate courts were interpreting rules concerning accomplice confessions. Obviously, the *Roberts* Court created a bad precedent, and the *Lilly* Court misdiagnosed its impact. Other than lacking majority agreement (whereby more minds than in a "plurality" might have reached a better conclusion), Justice Scalia does not account for *Lilly*'s poor decision-making.

In his concurrence in *Hubbard v. United States*, Justice Scalia insists "that *Bramblett* has unacceptable consequences," chief among them the that fact "that so many Courts of appeal have strained so mightily to discern an exception that the statute does not contain . . . [demonstrating] how great a potential for mischief federal judges have discovered in the mistaken reading of 18 U.S.C.S." (716). Likewise, in his concurrence in the Double Jeopardy case of *Hudson, Baresel, and Rackley v. United States*, 522 U.S. 93 (1997), he "wholly agree[d] with the Court's conclusion that [*United States v.*] *Halper*'s test for whether a sanction is 'punitive' was ill-considered and unworkable" (106).

Justice Scalia has occasionally forgiven the Court for decisions with bad consequences. For example, in *Hubbard v. United States*, he explains that the precedent's bad consequences had not been foreseeable: "The reason here [for overruling], as far as I am concerned, is the demonstration, *over time*, that *Bramblett* has unacceptable consequences, which can be judicially avoided (absent overruling) only by limiting *Bramblett* in a manner that is irrational or by importing exceptions with no basis in law" (716; emphasis added). He adds that "so many Courts of appeal have strained so mightily to discern an exception that the statute does not contain . . . [demonstrating] how great a potential for mischief federal judges have discovered in the mistaken reading of 18 U.S.C.S. § 1001, a potential we did not fully appreciate when *Bramblett* was decided" (716). Not only does Justice Scalia identify with the precedent Court (as "we"), he forgives them for not "fully appreciat[ing]" the "potential for mischief" that would arise from their interpretation of the statute.

In a statutory case involving the Armed Career Criminal Act, Justice Scalia rejected as unconstitutionally vague a provision "which imposes an increased prison term upon a defendant with three prior convictions for a 'violent felony,' § 924(e)(1), a term defined by § 924(e)(2)(B)s residual clause to include any felony that 'involves conduct that presents a serious potential risk of physical injury to another'" (*Johnson v. United States*, 135 S. Ct. 2551, 2553 [2015]). Again he emphasized that the bad consequences of previous interpretations were not foreseeable, urging, "It has been said that the life of the law is experience. Nine years' experience trying to derive meaning from the residual clause convinces us that we have embarked upon a failed enterprise" (2560). Again, he implicates himself as among the "we [who] have embarked on a failed enterprise." His emphasis on experience as revealing these problems implies that the precedent Court could only discover what he knows with the benefit of time.

Perhaps because the future is unknown, Justice Scalia found the means to forgive some precedent Courts for their errors. Indeed, he is much more forgiving when considering the future than when considering the past or present.

Conclusion

My division of Justice Scalia's overruling discourse into arguments addressing the past, present, and future is meant to highlight how these competing concerns played out in his judicial practices. It also emphasizes that even an originalist such as Justice Scalia cannot look to the past alone to decide whether to overrule a precedent. However, my division of these three concerns in the preceding analysis draws attention away from the power of overruling discourse that combines two or more temporal concerns, as we see in Justice Scalia's majority opinion in *United States v. Gaudin*:

We do not minimize the role that stare decisis plays in our jurisprudence. See *Patterson v. McLean Credit Union*, 491 U.S. 164, 172, 105 L. Ed. 2d 132, 109 S. Ct. 2363 (1989). That role is somewhat reduced, however, in the case of a procedural rule such as this, which does not serve as a guide to lawful behavior. See *Payne v. Tennessee*, 501 U.S. 808, 828, 115 L. Ed. 2d 720, 111 S. Ct. 2597 (1991). It is reduced all the more when the rule is not only procedural but rests upon an interpretation of the Constitution. See ibid. And we think stare decisis cannot possibly be controlling when, in addition to those factors, the decision in question has been proved manifestly erroneous, and its underpinnings eroded, by subsequent decisions of this Court. *Rodriguez de Quijas v. Shearson/American Express, Inc.*, 490 U.S. 477, 480–481, 104 L. Ed. 2d 526, 109 S. Ct. 1917 (1989); *Andrews v. Louisville & Nashville R. Co.*, 406 U.S. 320, 32 L. Ed. 2d 95, 92 S. Ct. 1562 (1972). (521)

Here we have concerns over the past ("an interpretation of the Constitution"; "manifestly erroneous") and the present ("a procedural rule . . . which does not serve as a guide to lawful behavior"). In *United States v. Dixon*, Justice Scalia speaks to the past and the future in declaring, "We do not lightly reconsider a precedent, but, because *Grady* contradicted an 'unbroken line of decisions,' [past] contained 'less than accurate' historical analysis [past], and has produced 'confusion,' [future] we do so here" (711; citations omitted).

It is unsurprising that Justice Scalia invokes the past, the present, and the future in overruling cases—those are the rhetorical options available to any appellate justice. Given his originalist and textualist philosophy, it is also unsurprising that he cites error more frequently than any other ground to support overruling, as that involves a misunderstanding of "the law laid down" in the past. At the same time, he stands ready to dismiss mistakes where there is understandable and consequential reliance on prior decisions, which he believes is most pressing in property cases (as do more liberal justices, such as Justice Kagan), of some concern when Congress appears to have relied on the Court's interpretation in writing legislation, and of no concern where rules of procedure, which are not "guide[s] to law behavior" (*United States v. Gaudin*, 521), are involved. He also shows tolerance for overruling where a rule proves unworkable over time, not wanting to burden the High Court, lower courts, or the public with bad rules, which are like "weeds" (see *Hubbard v. United States*, 717).

Generally, then, Justice Scalia's rhetoric of overruling tended to find plenty of errors sufficient to support overruling, some reliance interests, and some concerns over the consequences of problematic rules. These could be variously emphasized, combined, and even used to make arguments on either side. The substantive nature of these arguments means that more or less weight could be given to particular temporal concerns, and their relevance to resolving cases highlighted through strategic constructions (such as an error being characterized as "clear").

Regarding the second rhetorical task of overruling—supporting the Court's image by offering some explanation of the error in a prior decision—Justice Scalia practically ignored it. An exception is his recognition that the operation of rules laid down by courts is not always foreseeable. This is a problem for one of the most powerful courts on earth, exercising as it does judicial review over the constitutionality of legislation. This incredible power makes significant rhetorical demands on the Court's ethos, which the Court itself typically seeks to maintain (Rountree 1995). But Justice Scalia occasionally has shown a lack of concern for maintaining that reputation. For example, following the Court's controversial decision in *Bush v. Gore*, 531 U.S. 98 (2000), he gave a speech suggesting that the High Court's reputation was something to be *used* more than *protected*, insisting, "The Court's reputation [is not] some shiny piece of trophy armor. . . . It's working armor and meant to be used and sometimes dented in the service of the public" (quoted in Rosen 2007, 215). As I have argued previously, the *Bush* decision put serious dents in the High Court reputation (Rountree 2007).

Finally, Justice Scalia's sharp-tongued style does not lend itself to forgiving the errors of his predecessors (or even his fellow justices). Stephen A. Newman worries that Justice Scalia's frequent use of "inflammatory words" and arguments "undermine[s] the legitimacy and stature of the judicial branch of government" (2006–7, 908–9). Whatever the reasons for his rhetorical approach to overruling, Justice Scalia often throws out the institutional baby with the bathwater.

References

Barrett, Amy Coney. 2017. "Originalism and Stare Decisis." *Notre Dame Law Review* 92, no. 5, 1921–44.

Blaustein, Albert P., and Andrew H. Field. 1958. "'Overruling' Opinions in the Supreme Court." *Michigan Law Review* 57, no.2, 152–94.

Burke, Kenneth. (1945) 1969. Berkeley: University of California Press.

DiStanisloa, P. Thomas, III. 2017. "The Highest Court: A Dialogue between Justice Louis Brandeis and Justice Antonin Scalia on Stare Decisis." *University of Richmond Law Review* 51:1149–73.

Douglas, William O. "Stare Decisis." 1949. *Columbia Law Review* 49, no. 6, 735–58.

Jonsen, Albert R. and Stephen Toulmin. 1988. *The Abuse of Casuistry: A History of Moral Reasoning.* Berkeley: University of California Press.

Langford, Catherine L. 2018. *Textual Tales: Justice Antonin Scalia and Constitutional Interpretation.* Tuscaloosa: University of Alabama Press.

Lewis, Ovid C. 1968. "The High Court: Final . . . but Fallible." *Case Western Reserve Law Review* 19:528–643.

Newman, Stephen A. 2006–7. "Political Advocacy on the Supreme Court: The Damaging Rhetoric of Antonin Scalia." *New York Law School Law Review* 51:907–26.

Rosen, Jeffrey. 2007. *The Supreme Court: The Personalities and Rivalries That Defined America.* New York: Holt.

Rountree, Clarke. 2007. *Judging the Supreme Court: Constructions of Motives in Bush v. Gore.* East Lansing: Michigan State University Press.

———. 1995. "On the Rhetorical Analysis of Judicial Discourse and More: A Response to Lewis." *Southern Communication Journal* 61, no. 2, 166–73.

Scalia, Antonin. 1989. "Originalism: The Lesser Evil." *University of Cincinnati Law Review* 57: 849–65.

———, and Bryan A. Garner. 2012. *Reading Law: The Interpretation of Legal Texts.* St. Paul, MN: Thompson/West.

Scordato, Marin Roger. 2008. "Reflections on the Nature of Legal Scholarship in the Post-Realist Era." *Santa Clara Law Review* 48:353–440.

Senior, Jennifer. 2013. "In Conversation: Antonin Scalia." *New York Magazine*, October 6. Online at http://nymag.com/news/features/antonin-scalia-2013–10/.

Supreme Court Decisions Overruled by Subsequent Decision. 2016. Washington, DC: U.S. Government Printing Office. Downloaded from https://www.gpo.gov/fdsys/pkg/GPO-CONAN -REV-2016/pdf/GPO-CONAN-REV-2016-13.pdf on 27 May 2017.

Wetlaufer, Gerald B. 1990. "Rhetoric and Its Denial in Legal Discourse." *Virginia Law Review* 76:1545–97.

Notes

Introduction

1. Aristotle, *On Rhetoric* 36.1355a, trans. George A. Kennedy (Oxford: Oxford University Press, 1991).

2. Justice Elena Kagan, *In Memorium: Justice Antonin Scalia*, 130 Harv. L. Rev. 5, 8 (2106). *See also* William N. Eskridge Jr., *All About Words: Early Understandings of the "Judicial Power" in Statutory Interpretation, 1776–1806*, 101 Columbia L. Rev. 990, 1090 (2001) ("We are all textualists.").

3. Antonin Scalia, *The Rule of Law as a Law of Rules*, 56 U. Chi. L. Rev. 1175, 1178 (1989).

Chapter 1

This chapter was first published in *Jahrbuch des öffentlichen Rechts der Gegenwart* 65 (2017): 765.

1. 135 S. Ct. 2480, 2496 (2015).

2. *Id.* at 2496, 2499, 2500, and 2501.

3. See, for example, Michigan v. Bryant, 562 U.S. 344, 389–94 (2011) (Scalia, dissenting) (calling an opinion by Justice Sotomayor using factual distinctions to limit the scope of one of his own decisions in an earlier Confrontation Clause case "a gross distortion of the facts [and] the law," "utter nonsense," and "unprincipled").

4. William Shakespeare, *Macbeth* 1.1.5.

5. 517 U.S. 620 (1996); 135 S. Ct. 2584 (2015).

6. Among other examples of this phenomenon is one I have discussed extensively in prior work: Scalia's observation in his lone dissent in *U.S. v. Virginia*, a case mandating the admission of women to the hitherto all-male Virginia Military Institute (VMI) that, going beyond the less rigorous "standard elaboration of intermediate scrutiny," Justice Ginsburg's majority opinion held that "VMI's single-sex composition is unconstitutional because there exist several women (or, one would have to conclude under the Court's reasoning, a single woman) willing and able to undertake VMI's program," so that, as a constitutional rule, "a sex-based classification is invalid unless it relates to characteristics that hold true in every instance"; see United States v. Virginia, 518 U.S. 515, 572–74 (1996) (Scalia, J., dissenting). For further discussion, see Mary Anne Case,

"'The Very Stereotype the Law Condemns:' Constitutional Sex Discrimination Law as a Quest for Perfect Proxies," 85 Cornell L. Rev. 1447 (2000).

7. Bowers v. Hardwick, 478 U.S. 186 (1986).

8. Romer, 517 U.S. at 640 (Scalia, dissenting) (quoting Padula v. Webster, 261 U.S. App. D.C. 365, 822 F.2d 97). Of course, there are many problems with Scalia's logic here—for example, that it is not sodomy, but same-sex desire, which is the behavior that defines the class of homosexuals. For further discussion, see Mary Anne Case, "Couples and Coupling in the Public Sphere: A Comment on the Legal History of Litigating for Lesbian and Gay Rights," 79 Virginia Law Review 1643 (1993).

9. Because the language of Amendment 2 was so sweeping in its potential negative effects on gays, lesbians, and bisexuals, advocates and scholars have long argued that "no group, even of the most heinous felons convicted under the most unimpeachable of criminal laws, could constitutionally have the protection of the laws removed from them on so wholesale a basis as that found in Amendment 2" (Mary Anne Case, "Of 'This' and 'That' in Lawrence v. Texas," 2003 S. Ct. Rev 75, 93 [2004]).

10. 539 U.S. 558 (2003).

11. Lawrence, 539 U.S. at 576.

12. *Id.* at 578.

13. *Id.* at 604 (Scalia, dissenting) (emphasis in original).

14. U.S. v. Windsor, 133 S. Ct. 2675, 2696 (2013).

15. *Id.* at 2709 (Scalia, dissenting). On the day it decided *Windsor*, the Court declined an opportunity to hold that there was a more general federal constitutional right to same-sex marriage, holding that the proponents of California's Proposition 8, which had amended the state constitution to eliminate same-sex marriage, lacked standing to appeal because the state of California had accepted the trial court's decision to strike down Proposition 8. See Hollingsworth v. Perry, 133 S. Ct. 2652 (2013).

16. Windsor, 133 S. Ct. at 2710.

17. *Id.* at 2696 ff. (Roberts, dissenting).

18. Lawrence, 539 U.S. at 601 (Scalia dissenting) (noting that O'Connor's "reasoning leaves on pretty shaky grounds state laws limiting marriage to opposite-sex couples" because it was hard to claim that "'preserving the traditional institution of marriage' is a legitimate state interest," as O'Connor did, when "preserving the traditional sexual mores of our society" no longer seemed to be a legitimate basis for upholding sodomy laws).

19. Windsor, 133 S. Ct. at 2709–10 (Scalia, dissenting) (citations omitted).

20. They also took up other arguments in his dissent. See, for example, Kitchen v. Herbert, at 755 F.3d 1193, 1220 (10th Cir. 2104).

21. See, for example, Kitchen v. Herbert, 961 F. Supp. 2d 1181, 1194 (D. Utah 2013) ("The court agrees with Justice Scalia's interpretation of *Windsor*").

22. Garrett Epps, "American Justice 2014: Nine Clashing Visions on the Supreme Court" (Philadelphia: University of Pennsylvania Press, 2014), Kindle edition at location 720. Although other U.S. Supreme Court Justices, such as Oliver Wendell Holmes, are known for their influential dissents, in each case these other dissenters were sketching out an affirmative vision of what the result should be, whereas Scalia depicted what was, for him, a nightmare vision.

23. Obergefell, 135 S. Ct. at 2593.

24. *Id.* at 2602. Cf. Windsor, 133 S. Ct. at 2710 (Scalia, dissenting) ("[DOMA] *This state law* tells those couples, and all the world, that their otherwise valid ~~marriages~~ *relationships* are unworthy of ~~federal~~ *state* recognition. This places same-sex couples in an unstable position of being

in a second-tier ~~marriage~~ *relationship*. The differentiation demeans the couple, whose moral and sexual choices the Constitution protects, see *Lawrence*").

25. Scalia has often said he writes his dissents, not for his colleagues or lower-court judges, but for law students, and implicit in that choice of audience may be a desire to write colorfully enough to attract their attention and that of casebook editors, who decide what snippets of opinions to include in the materials presented to students.

26. Though it contained far fewer excoriating adjectives than many of his later dissents, his dissent criticizing Justice O'Connor's concurring opinion in the abortion case of Webster v. Reproductive Health Services, 492 U.S. 490 (1989) for declining to reconsider the holding of Roe v. Wade, 410 US 113 (1973) was widely seen at the time as crossing an established line of civility and, in retrospect, as perhaps contributing to her joining a plurality explicitly reaffirming Roe a few years later in Planned Parenthood v. Casey, 505 U.S. 833 (1992), exactly the opposite of the result he had hoped for.

27. Linda Greenhouse, "Justice Scalia Objects," *New York Times*, March 9, 2011, online at http://opinionator.blogs.nytimes.com/2011/03/09/justice-scalia-objects/?_r=0.

28. 505 U.S. 1003 (1992).

29. 541 U.S. 36 (2003). Justice Sotomayor's distinguishing of *Crawford* to allow the admission into evidence of statements made by a dying person led to Scalia's excoriation of her opinion in *Michigan v. Bryant*, quoted above in note 6 above.

30. In his *Lucas* dissent, 505 U.S. at 1036, Justice Blackmun critically described this practice of Scalia's as follows:

"Today the Court launches a missile to kill a mouse. . . . [I]t ignores its jurisdictional limits, remakes its traditional rules of review, and creates simultaneously a new categorical rule and an exception (neither of which is rooted in our prior case law, common law, or common sense)."

31. Antonin Scalia, "The Rule of Law as a Law of Rules," 56 U. of Chicago L. Rev. 1175 (1989).

32. He seems to have attributed the same commitment to categorical rules to God; see "Transcript of Oral Argument," Holt v. Hobbs, 135 S. Ct. 853 (2015) (No. 13–6827), 2014 WL 5398229, at *5.

33. Scalia, "Rule of Law," 1178.

34. As he said with respect to a famous contracts case, "If you think it is terribly important that the case came out wrong, you are not yet thinking like a lawyer—or at least not like a common lawyer. That is really secondary. Famous old cases are famous, you see, not because they came out right, but because the rule of law they announced was the intelligent one"; see Antonin Scalia, "Common-Law Courts in a Civil-Law System: The Role of United States Federal Courts in Interpreting the Constitution and Laws," The Tanner Lectures on Human Values (Princeton University, 1995), at 82. The Tanner Lectures were subsequently published in book form, with several commentaries, as *A Matter of Interpretation: Federal Courts and the Law* (Princeton, NJ: Princeton University Press, 1997).

35. See Herrera v. Collins, 506 U.S. 390, 428 (1992) (Scalia, concurring).

36. For further discussion, see Mary Anne Case, "Are Plain Hamburgers Now Unconstitutional? The Equal Protection Component of Bush v. Gore as a Chapter in the History of Ideas about Law," 70 U. of Chicago L. Rev. 55 (2003).

37. Scalia, "Common-Law Courts," 100.

38. *Id.* at 88.

39. *Id.*

40. *Id.* at 85. There is an important distinction Scalia sometimes elides between arriving at the "most desirable resolution" in "the case at hand" and arriving at "the best rule of law to govern" it. Elsewhere, Scalia observes that "sticking close to those facts, not relying upon overarching generalizations, and thereby leaving considerable room for future judges is thought to be the genius of the common law" (Scalia, "Rule of Law," 1177). This is not the methodology used by Scalia, whose goal is always to constrain the discretion of future judges, including himself (see *Id.* at 1179), through the formulation, wherever possible, of a rule which rises above individual factual considerations.

41. Of course, as explained in note 44, one can engage in broken-field running around prior precedent merely to score a goal in the case at hand, not to formulate a general rule governing a class of cases, but, like Procrustes, Scalia wants an iron bed ready to house, not just this evening's visitors, but a host of guests yet to arrive.

42. I might also call it fancy dancing, to use a differently gendered metaphor, occupying a middle ground between admiration and condemnation.

43. See Gitlow v. N.Y., 268 U.S. 252 (1925).

44. See McDonald v. Chicago, 561 U.S. 742 (2010).

45. Lochner v. N.Y., 198 U.S. 45 (1905) was among the earliest and most prominent of a series of cases, since overruled, constitutionalizing aspects of freedom of contract.

46. 410 U.S. 113 (1973).

47. Scalia, "Common-Law Courts," 99.

48. *Id.*

49. McDonald v. Chicago, 561 U.S. 742 (2010). During the oral argument of *McDonald*, Scalia even waved away the possibility of shifting incorporation to a potentially more secure textual foundation, that of the Privileges and Immunities Clause of the Fourteenth Amendment, leading some conservative legal academics to accuse him of betraying his principles. See Josh Blackman and Ilya Shapiro, "Is Justice Scalia Abandoning Originalism?" *DC Examiner*, March 9, 2010, online at https://www.cato.org/publications/commentary/is-justice-scalia-abandoning-originalism.

50. Scalia, "Common-Law Courts," 85.

51. *Id.* at 99.

52. For another example, see R.A.V. v. City of St. Paul, 505 U.S. 377 (1992).

53. Emp't Div., Dep't of Human Res. of Or. v. Smith, 494 U.S. 872(1990).

54. *Id.* at 874.

55. 374 U.S. 398 (1963). Sherbert lost her job when, as a Seventh-day Adventist, she refused to work on her Saturday sabbath; state law explicitly protected those who were Sunday observers.

56. Reynolds v. United States, 98 U.S. 145 (1878).

57. Because Utah was then a territory of the federal government, *Reynolds*, unlike *Smith*, was indeed a First Amendment case in the strict sense.

58. Smith, 440 U.S. at 879 (quoting U. S. v. Lee).

59. Reynolds v. United States, 98 U.S. at 167–68, quoted in Smith, 440 U.S. at 879.

60. Smith, 440 U.S. at 879.

61. 310 U.S. 586 (1940). Compare Scalia's reliance in *R.A.V.* on Beauharnais v. Illinois, 343 U.S. 250 (1952), a case whose holding concerning racial hate speech had similarly been left behind by subsequent doctrinal developments. See 505 U.S at 382.

62. W. Va. State Bd. of Educ. v. Barnette, 319 U.S. 624, 642(1943).

63. Michael McConnell, John H. Garvey, and Thomas C. Berg, *Religion and the Constitution*, 2d ed. (New York: Aspen, 2006), 144.

64. Barnette, 319 U.S at 627, n. 3.

65. See United States v. Lee, 455 U.S. 252, 263, n. 3 (1982). *Lee*, like *Reynolds*, did not involve incorporation, but federal action, and hence the First Amendment proper. It is noteworthy that all of the cases Scalia had to distinguish heroically in order to establish that the general rule was the one he quoted from *Lee* did involve incorporation of the First Amendment against the states.

66. See Wisconsin v. Yoder, 406 U.S. 205 (1972).

67. Legislatures had previously granted, and the Court had applied, statutory accommodations.

68. Smith, 440 U.S. at 879.

69. *Id.* at 883.

70. Troxel v. Granville, 530 U.S. 57, 92 (2000) (Scalia, dissenting) ("Only three holdings of this Court rest in whole or in part upon a substantive constitutional right of parents to direct the upbringing of their children—two of them from an era rich in substantive due process holdings that have since been repudiated. See Meyer v. Nebraska . . . [1923]; Pierce v. Society of Sisters . . . [1925]; Wisconsin v. Yoder . . . [1972]").

71. See Kissinger v. Bd of Trustees of Ohio State Univ., 5 F.3d 177, 180 (6th Cir. 1993).

72. McConnell, Garvey, and Berg, *Religion and the Constitution*, 145. Unlike many other academic commentators, I have always thought that *Smith* was correctly decided, that the passage of RFRA in response to *Smith* was a mistake, and that the problem with Scalia's opinion in *Smith* was not the categorical rule he announced, but the fancy dancing he engaged in to leave no previously decided case behind in affirming that rule. I would have overruled *Yoder*, which I thought wrongly decided from the start. See Mary Anne Case, "Why 'Live-And-Let-Live' Is Not a Viable Solution to the Difficult Problems of Religious Accommodation in the Age of Sexual Civil Rights," 88 U.S.C. L. Rev. 463, 469 (2015).

73. 42 U.S.C. §§ 2000bb (b) (1).

74. See City of Boerne v. Flores, 521 U.S. 507 (1997).

75. Smith, 440 U.S. at 888–89 (citations omitted).

76. See, for example, Zubik v. Burwell, 136 S. Ct. 1557 (2016).

77. Burwell v. Hobby Lobby Stores, Inc., 134 S. Ct. 2751, 2804 (2014) (Ginsburg, dissenting).

78. Sebelius v. Hobby Lobby Stores, Inc., 2014 U.S. Trans. LEXIS 47 at *7.

79. Smith, 440 U.S. at 890.

80. Obergefell, 135 S. Ct at 2626 (Scalia, dissenting).

81. He did not expect or welcome RFRA, saying at oral argument in Holt v. Hobbs, 13–6827 at 26, "Bear in mind, I would not have enacted this statute."

82. Lamb's Chapel v. Center Moriches Union Free School District, 508 U.S. 384, 398 (1993) (Scalia, concurring in the judgment) (referring to the Lemon test for the Establishment Clause).

Chapter 2

1. Antonin Scalia, "Common-Law Courts in a Civil-Law System," in *A Matter of Interpretation* (Princeton, NJ: Princeton University Press, 1997), 3.

2. Scalia, "Common-Law Courts," 4 (my emphasis).

3. Scalia, "Common-Law Courts," 7.

4. See Victoria Nourse, *Misreading Law, Misreading Democracy* (Cambridge, MA: Harvard University Press, 2016).

5. 508 U.S. 223, 241, 1993.

6. 18 U. S. C. § 924 (c) (1) (2006).

7. *Id.* at 242 (emphasis added).

8. *Id.* at 242, n. 1 (emphasis added).

9. 508 U.S. at 242, n. 1.

10. See Scott Soames, "Deferentialism," *Fordham Law Review* 82 (2013): 101–22; reprinted in Soames, *Analytic Philosophy in America* (Princeton, NJ: Princeton University Press, 2014), 320–41. See also Scott Soames, "Deferentialism, Living Originalism, and the Constitution," in *The Nature of Legal Interpretation: What Jurists Can Learn about Legal Interpretation from Linguistics and Philosophy*, ed. Brian Slocum (Chicago: University of Chicago Press, 2017).

11. Scalia, "Common-Law Courts," 16. Hereafter cited parenthetically by page no. in the text.

12. Scalia, quoting Joel Prentice Bishop, in *Commentaries on the Written Laws and Their Interpretation* (Boston: Little, Brown, & Co. 1882), 57–58 (Scalia's emphasis).

13. 588 US 50 (2010).

14. 588 U.S. 310, (2010) (my emphasis).

15. 530 U.S. 703 (2000) (Scalia's emphasis).

16. Id.

17. 491 US 397 (1989).

18. 505 US 377 (1992).

19. 564 US 76 (2011).

20. See Soames, "Deferentialism."

21. See William Baude, "Is Originalism Our Law?" *Columbia Law Review* 115 (2015): 2349.

22. See section 5 of Scott Soames, "Reply to Rosen," in Brian Slocum, *The Nature of Legal Interpretation: What Jurists Can Learn about Legal Interpretation from Linguistics and Philosophy* (Chicago: University of Chicago Press, 2017), 272–81.

Chapter 3

1. Morrison v. Olson, 487 U.S. 654, 699 (1988) (Scalia, J. dissenting). I refer to this case as *Olson* to avoid confusion with another famous Supreme Court case, *Morrison v. United States.*

2. Theoretical linguists call this "entextualization." See Mertz 2007, 45.

3. In *Olson*, Justice Scalia wrote, "To repeat, Article II, § 1, cl. 1, of the Constitution provides: 'The executive Power shall be vested in a President of the United States.' As I described at the outset of this opinion, this does not mean *some of* the executive power, but *all of* the executive power." *Morrison*, 487 U.S. at 705 (Scalia, J. dissenting).

4. The statute specifies that "[i]f the Attorney General, upon completion of a preliminary investigation under this chapter, determines that there are no reasonable grounds to believe that further investigation is warranted," he may close the matter (28 U.S.C. § 592).

5. U.S. Const. art. II, § 2.

6. See Calabresi and Yoo 2008, 174–89, 278–90 (discussing Andrew Johnson and Franklin Roosevelt, respectively).

7. U.S. Const. art. II, §. 2.

8. My own view is that if Congress did not prescribe a good-faith limit, the Supreme Court would have to invent one: arbitrary or purposeless dismissals (ones not in good faith or for purely political reasons [e.g., party loyalty]) would violate due process.

9. *Morrison*, 487 U.S. at 705 (Scalia, J. dissenting).

10. A president who does not have a good enough lawyer to find a "good-faith" reason to remove an "independent agent" is not a very savvy president, has a terrible lawyer, or is picking a political fight.

11. Gormley 2001, 104–5; O'Sullivan 1996, 471–73.

12. See Nourse 2016, 108–113; (discussing this in the context of the health care case, *King v. Burwell*); Nourse, 2017.

13. West Virginia University Hospitals, Inc. v. Casey, 499 U.S. 83 (1991).

14. U.S. Const. Art. II, sec. 1.

15. Chabris and Simons 2009, 8; Kahneman 2011, 23–24.

16. Kahneman 2011, 13, 402–3.

17. Chugh and Bazerman 2007, 1.

18. Hofstadter and Sander 2013, 293.

19. Chugh and Bazerman, "Bounded Awareness," 1; Tor and Bazerman 2003, 353.

20. Tor and Bazerman 2003, 353.

21. Mikhail 2015, 1073–75.

22. Grice 1975, 41.

23. Wilson and Sperber 2012, 60, 177.

24. Allott and Shaer, 2017.

25. Endicott 2000.

26. See Nourse 2018.

27. *Morrison*, 487 U.S. at 705 (Scalia, J. dissenting).

28. Manning 2011, 1939–46.

Chapter 4

1. 283 U.S. 25, 26 (1931).

2. In contrast, the *McBoyle* case involved a criminal statute prohibiting the interstate transportation of stolen vehicles. Excluding airplanes from the definition of *vehicle* would narrow the scope of the criminal provision.

3. For an example of such a case, see http://www.nydailynews.com/news/crime/bicyclist-pleads-guilty-vehicular-manslaughter-article-1.1408495.

Chapter 5

1. See Holmes 1899, 419 ("Yet in fact we do not deal differently with a statute from our way of dealing with a contract. We do not inquire what the legislature meant; we ask only what the statute means.")

2. United States v. Carroll Towing Co., 159 F.2d 169, 173 (2d. Cir. 1947).

3. Hotchkiss v. National City Bank, 200 F. 287, 203 (S.D.N.Y. 1911).

4. TKO Equip. Co. v. C & G Coal Co., 863 F.2d 541, 545 (7th Cir. 1988) (citation omitted).

5. I personally am less concerned than was Scalia about the increased risks of intellectual corruption when one engages in individualized inquiry into the enactment of laws and the evils they were enacted to address. See Solan 2010. Nonetheless, the goal of achieving an evidence-based law of statutory interpretation is worth taking seriously at face value, regardless of one's predispositions.

6. Antonin Scalia, "Common-Law Courts in a Civil-Law System: The Role of United States Federal Courts in Interpreting the Constitution and Laws, in *A Matter of Interpretation: Federal Courts and the Law* (Princeton, NJ: Princeton University Press, 1997), 16.

7. 490 U.S. 504 (1989).

8. 490 U.S. at 528 (Scalia, J. concurring in the judgment).

9. Smith v. United States, 508 U.S. 223, 241 (1993) (Scalia, J. dissenting) (citations omitted).

10. 508 U.S. at 242 (Scalia, J., dissenting).

11. 153 U.S. 457 (1892).

12. *Id.* at 458.

13. *Id.* at 459.

14. *Id.* at 463.

15. 501 U.S. 380 (1991).

16. Emphasis mine in both excerpts.

17. 412 U.S. 755 (1973).

18. *Id.* at 504 (Scalia, J., dissenting).

19. *Id.* at 405 (citing Holmes 1899).

20. For different perspectives, compare Lynch, Coley, and Medin 2000; Prinz 2000; Armstrong, Gleitman, and Gleitman 1983; and Rosch 1975.

21. 504 U.S. 374 (1992).

22. *Id.* at 383.

23. United States v. Mead Corp, 533 U.S. 218, 241 (2001) (Scalia, J., dissenting).

24. Holloway v. United States, 526 U.S. 1, 20 (1999) (Scalia, J., dissenting).

25. BFP v. Resolution Trust Corp., 511 U.S. 531, 539–40 (1994).

26. 135 S. Ct. 2480 (2015).

27. *Id.* at 2489.

28. *Id.*

29. 499 U.S. 83, 101 (1991).

30. 490 U.S. at 528 (Scalia, J., concurring in the judgment).

Chapter 6

This chapter is based on a longer article that first appeared in the *Notre Dame Law Review*'s 2017 Federal Courts Issue honoring Justice Scalia ("Justice Scalia's Unfinished Business in Statutory Interpretation: Where Textualism's Formalism Gave Up," *Notre Dame Law Review* 92, no. 5 [2017]: 2053–76).

1. See Gregory v. Ashcroft, 501 U.S. 452, 469 (1991) (federalism); Whitman v. Am. Trucking Ass'ns, Inc., 531 U.S. 457, 468 (2001) (elephants in mouseholes); MCI Telecomms. Corp. v. AT&T Co., 512 U.S. 218, 234 (1994) (major questions); Morrison v. Nat'l Austl. Bank Ltd., 561 U.S. 247 (2010) (extraterritoriality).

2. In contrast, many state courts have actually attempted to doctrinalize interpretive methodology.

3. See, for example, United States v. Hayes, 555 U.S. 415, 429 (2009).

4. Abramski v. United States, 134 S. Ct. 2259, 2272 n. 10 (2014) (arguing about what triggers the lenity canon); *id.* at 2281 (Scalia, J., dissenting) (same).

5. *Id.* at 2281 (Scalia, J., dissenting); Bond v. United States, 134 S. Ct. 2077, 2095 (2014) (Scalia, J., concurring).

6. United States v. Lockhart, 136 S. Ct. 958, 962 (2016); Barnhart v. Thomas, 540 U.S. 20, 26 (2003).

7. See Bond v. United States, 134 S. Ct. 2077 (2014); Morrison v. Nat'l Austl. Bank, 561 U.S. 247 (2010).

8. Al-Bihani v. Obama, 619 F.3d. 1 (2010.

9. 29 U.S.C. § 1144(a), (b) (2) (A) (2006) (mandating preemption of state law except for "saving" areas of state law that relate to insurance). This clause alone has decided hundreds, if not thousands, of cases.

10. See Moses H. Cone Mem'l Hosp. v. Mercury Constr. Corp., 460 U.S. 1 (1983); Morrison v. Nat'l Austl. Bank Ltd., 561 U.S. 247, 255 (2010); United States v. Wells Fargo Bank, 485 U.S. 351, 357 (1988); Hagen v. Utah, 510 U.S. 399, 411 (1994); Marrama v. Citizens Bank of Mass., 549 U.S. 365, 367 (2007); Landgraf v. USI Film Prods., 511 U.S. 244, 287–88, 290–94 (1994) (Scalia, J., concurring); Smith v. Wade, 461 U.S. 30, 48–49 (1983).

11. Morrison v. Nat'l Austl. Bank Ltd., 561 U.S. 247, 255 (2010) (presumption against extraterritoriality); MCI Telecomms. Corp. v. AT&T Co., 512 U.S. 218 (1994) (creating the "major questions" rule).

12. 135 S. Ct. 2480 (2015).

13. Lockhart v. United States, 136 S. Ct. 958, 962 (2016).

14. 135 S. Ct. at 2492.

15. 136 S. Ct. at 962

16. *Id*. at 970.

Chapter 7

1. Prince, "1999," from the album *1999* (Warner Bros. Records, 1982).

2. Mitchell Berman argues for such a characterization of Justice Scalia: "Hubris, overconfidence, arrogance, dogmatism—these constitute one cluster of vices. They do not entail that the possessor of such defects of character be sarcastic, caustic, or disrespectful of others. Regrettably, however, Scalia fell victim to these vices too. . . . The dogmatism and incivility that Scalia displayed throughout his career are, in my judgment, two very serious defects of judicial character" (Berman 2017, 803, 805). Jeffrey M. Shaman and Marie A. Failinger catalogue the many examples of Justice Scalia's acerbic rhetoric (Shaman 2012; Failinger 2003). Additionally, Stephen A. Newman summarizes that Justice "Scalia's inflammatory words in opinion after opinion, often attacking the motives and honesty of other Justices, make him seem more like a partisan political figure than a judge" (Newman 2006, 909). Finally, Erwin Chemerinsky argues that Justice Scalia's outrageous rhetoric corrupts law students (Chemerinsky 2000, 399).

3. 272 U.S. 52 (1926) (declaring unconstitutional congressional attempts to restrict the president's executive authority to remove executive officers).

4. Indeed, he admits that even he would be hard-pressed to approve public flogging as a punishment (Scalia 1989a, 861).

5. 487 U.S. 266 (1988).

6. *Id*. at 273–74 (discussing Fallen v. U.S., 378 U.S. 139 [1964]).

7. *Id*. at 274 ("To the extent that these cases state the general rule in civil appeals, we do not disturb them. But we are persuaded that this general rule should not apply here.").

8. *Id*. at 276 (Scalia, J., dissenting).

9. *Id*. at 280.

10. *Id*.

11. *Id*. at 274–75.

12. *Id*. at 269–70. Reasons for delay between receipt and formal filing may be anything from an unexplained delay by the Clerk, Deloney v. Estelle, 661 F.2d 1061, 1062–63 (5th Cir. 1981), to the failure by the appellant to include the applicable filing fee with the notice, Parissi v. Telechron, Inc., 349 U.S. 46, 47 (1955).

13. In my experience, particularly with filings that were time-sensitive, lawyers ensure that papers are delivered personally to the Clerk for formal filing, and the delivery would include a copy for simultaneous stamping and return to the file. In this setting, "filing with the Clerk" entailed "filing by the Clerk."

14. Houston v. Lack, 487 U.S. at 282 (Scalia, J., dissenting).

15. See, for example, Boumediene v. Bush, 553 U.S. 723, 739–52 (2008), in which Justice Kennedy describes the history of the Great Writ. In this case Justice Scalia dissented with regard to extension of the writ to an alien held outside the jurisdiction of the United States.

16. Torres v. Oakland Scavenger Co., 487 U.S. 312 (1988).

17. *Id.* at 319 (Scalia, J., concurring in the judgment).

18. *Id.*

19. See, for example, United States v. Taylor, 487 U.S. 326, 344–45 (1988) (Scalia, J., concurring in part). ("Both of these points seem so utterly clear from the text of the legislation that there is no justification for resort to the legislative history. . . . This text is eminently clear, and we should leave it at that.")

20. *Id.* at 345.

21. U.S. Dept. of Justice v. Julian, 486 U.S. 13, 16–17 (1988) (Scalia, J., dissenting) (criticizing majority for failing to read the two laws harmoniously). Justice Scalia asserted personal indifference to the rule in question: "I have no idea whether [limiting to personal review] is sound, and neither does the Court. But the issue was obviously addressed by Congress, and resolved in favor of restricted access. We should not frustrate that disposition, unless FOIA unavoidably so requires" (*Id.* at 17).

22. *Id.* at 22–23.

23. John Doe Agency v. John Doe Corp., 493 U.S. 146, 160–64 (1989).

24. Bowen v. Massachusetts, 487 U.S. 913, 930 (Scalia, J., dissenting).

25. District of Columbia v. Heller, 554 U.S. 570, 635 (2008).

26. Justice Scalia opened the door to endless contextual litigation in the following statement: "Although we do not undertake an exhaustive historical analysis today of the full scope of the Second Amendment, nothing in our opinion should be taken to cast doubt on long-standing prohibitions on the possession of firearms by felons and the mentally ill, or laws forbidding the carrying of firearms in sensitive places such as schools and government buildings, or laws imposing conditions and qualifications on the commercial sale of arms" (*Id.* at 626–27).

27. *Id.* at 635.

28. Schmuck v. U.S., 489 U.S. 705, 722 (1989) (Scalia, J., dissenting).

29. *Id.* at 723 ("This federal statute is not violated by a fraudulent scheme in which, as at some point, a mailing happens to occur—nor even by one in which a mailing predictably and necessarily occurs. The mailing must be in furtherance of the fraud.")

30. *Id.* at 724–25.

31. *Id.* at 725.

32. Skinner v. Railway Labor Exec. Assn., 489 U.S. 602 (1989).

33. Nat'l Treasury Employees Union v. von Raab, 489 U.S. 656, 679 (1989) (Scalia, J., dissenting).

34. *Id.* at 681.

35. *Id.* at 681, 683, 686–87.

36. *Id.* at 684.

37. District of Columbia v. Heller, 554 U.S. 570 (2008). For my critiques of Justice Scalia's majority opinion, see Mootz 2017 and Mootz 2010.

Chapter 8

1. "Senate battle over Supreme Court nominee Neil Gorsuch has been relatively mild, but that's about to change." Online at http://www.latimes.com/politics/la-na-pol-gorsuch-senate-battle-20170318-story.html.

2. "Confirmation Hearing on the Nomination of Hon. Sonia Sotomayor, to Be an Associate Justice of the Supreme Court of the United States," 432. Online at https://www.gpo.gov/fdsys/pkg/CHRG-111shrg56940/pdf/CHRG-111shrg56940.pdf.

3. "Confirmation Hearing," 68.

4. *Rhetorical hermeneutics* names a theory of interpretation focused on the persuasive and figurative nature of making sense of texts and contexts. See Mailloux 2017; cf. Mootz 2010.

5. See John Paul II, *Evangelium Vitae*, online at http://w2.vatican.va/content/john-paul-ii/en/encyclicals/documents/hf_jp-ii_enc_25031995_evangelium-vitae.html.

6. Fish 2015, 178. The quotations in this and the next two paragraphs originally appeared in Fish's *New York Times* blog on 9 April 2006 ("Why Scalia Is Right") and 11 April 2006 ("How Scalia Is Wrong"), both of which are reprinted in Fish 2015.

7. See Fish 1989; 1999.

8. See Mailloux 1989, chap. 6; and Mailloux 2006, chap. 5.

9. Originalism remains rhetorically prominent in that game after Justice Scalia's death; see Lawrence B. Solum, "Statement of Lawrence B. Solum: Hearings on the Nomination of the Honorable Neil M. Gorsuch to Be an Associate Justice of the Supreme Court of the United States" (March 22, 2017). Online at http://dx.doi.org/10.2139/ssrn.2939019. Cf. Gorsuch 2016.

10. Atkins v. Virginia, 536 U.S. 304 (2002) (Scalia, J., dissenting).

11. Roper v. Simmons, 543 U.S. 551 (2005) (Scalia, J., dissenting).

12. See, for example, "Scalia: Non-Originalists Are 'Idiots,'" Associated Press, 14 February 2006, online at http://www.foxnews.com/story/2006/02/14/scalia-non-originalists-are-idiots (cited in Fish 2015, 179, n. 1).

13. See Dorf 2012, "The Undead Constitution," and Murphy 2014, "The Dead Constitution Tour," for examples of the circulation of this Scalia metaphor in academic and popular culture.

Chapter 9

1. This is my understanding. The German Constitutional Court is an example, perhaps, though note that there are many (related) institutional differences as well, including an "institutionalized bias against personalized judicial opinions" (Kommers and Miller 2012, 29).

2. For one recent survey, see Asenas and Johnson 2017.

3. King v. Burwell, 135 S. Ct. 2480 (2014).

4. This is Canon 26 in Scalia and Garner's work on the canons (Scalia and Garner 2012). I discuss these issues at much greater depth in Gamage and Shanske 2014.

5. Canon 24 ("Whole-Text Canon"); Canon 37 ("Absurdity Doctrine"); see also Canon 27 ("Harmonious-Reading Canon"); Canon 4 ("Presumption Against Ineffectiveness").

6. Scalia is also at great pains to emphasize that he authored decisions in which the results were not consistent with his presumed politics. See Scalia and Garner 2012, 17.

7. On this, see, generally, Eskridge 2013.

8. And these points are the ones that the majority counters in footnotes.

9. King v. Burwell, 135 S. Ct. 2480, 2497 (2015).

10. *Id.* at 2500 (Scalia, J., dissenting).

11. *Id.* at 2503 (Scalia, J., dissenting).

12. *Id.* at 2505. (Scalia, J., dissenting).

13. Aristotle, *Rhetoric*, 1.1.3, 1345a11–16. See also Burnyeat 1996.

14. A fair reading of his first partial term suggests that he might be, which, if sustained, makes the question posed here more urgent. See Greenhouse 2017.

15. Thanks to Carlton Larson for this point.

16. See, for example, AT&T Mobility LLC v. Concepcion, 563 U.S. 333, 348–52 (2011).

17. See, for example, Printz v. United States, 521 U.S. 898, 918 (1997).

18. See, for example, Employment Div., Dep't of Human Res. of Oregon v. Smith, 494 U.S. 872, 885 (1990).

19. Including that surely Scalia's interpretive method, at least as applied by Scalia, would have provided unpopular groups, such as criminal defendants, with many fewer rights to protect.

20. Scalia is worth citing at length on this point:

It is, in other words, an additional advantage of the unitary Executive that it can achieve a more uniform application of the law. Perhaps that is not always achieved, but the mechanism to achieve it is there. The mini-Executive that is the independent counsel, however, operating in an area where so little is law and so much is discretion, is intentionally cut off from the unifying influence of the Justice Department, and from the perspective that multiple responsibilities provide. What would normally be regarded as a technical violation (there are no rules defining such things), may in his or her small world assume the proportions of an indictable offense. What would normally be regarded as an investigation that has reached the level of pursuing such picayune matters that it should be concluded, may to him or her be an investigation that ought to go on for another year. How frightening it must be to have your own independent counsel and staff appointed, with nothing else to do but to investigate you until investigation is no longer worthwhile—with whether it is worthwhile not depending upon what such judgments usually hinge on, competing responsibilities. And to have that counsel and staff decide, with no basis for comparison, whether what you have done is bad enough, willful enough, and provable enough, to warrant an indictment. How admirable the constitutional system that provides the means to avoid such a distortion. And how unfortunate the judicial decision that has permitted it. (Morrison v. Olson, 487 U.S. 654, 732 [1988] [Scalia, J., dissenting])

21. See Shapiro 2007.

22. American Trucking Assns. v. Mich. Pub. Svc. Comm'n, 545 U.S. 429, 439, 125 S. Ct. 2419 (Scalia, J., concurring in judgment).

23. The role of judgment is further evidenced by the slightly different perspective taken by Justice Thomas; he is not committed to uphold dormant Commerce Clause precedents on the ground of stare decisis.

24. 135 S. Ct. 1787 (2015).

25. *Id.* at 1808–09.

26. See, for example, *Id.* at 1811 ("Maryland's refusal to give residents full tax credits against income taxes paid to other States has its disadvantages. It threatens double taxation and encourages residents to work in Maryland. But Maryland's law also has its advantages. It allows the State to collect equal revenue from taxpayers with equal incomes, avoids the administrative burdens of verifying tax payments to other States, and ensures that every resident pays the State at least

some income tax. Nothing in the Constitution precludes Maryland from deciding that the benefits of its tax scheme are worth the costs.") (Scalia, J. dissenting).

27. For evidence that Scalia believed in something like this, see the last quoted passage from
his dissent in *King v. Burwell.*

28. The classic cite is to *Bickel* 1962, 16.

29. Habermas 2001, 778 ("The two principles stand in a reciprocal relationship of material
implication.").

30. See Asenas and Johnson 2017.

31. See Carugati, Hadfield, and Weingast 2015, 316. ("Lanni points to openness as evidence of
the ad hoc and unpredictable nature of the Athenian legal regime. Conversely, we see openness
as a source of robustness—a means whereby the Athenians established a robust legal order that
was both common knowledge and incentive compatible for enforcers.")

Chapter 10

1. 531 U.S. 98 (2000).

2. See, for example, King v. Burwell, 135 S. Ct. 2480, 2496 (Scalia, J., dissenting).

3. See, e.g., Agency for International Development v. Alliance for Open Society International, Inc., 133 S. Ct. 2321, 2334 (2013) (Scalia, J. dissenting).

4. See, for example, Allentown Mack Sales and Service, Inc. v. N.L.R.B, 522 U.S. 359, 376
(1998) (Scalia, J., writing for the Court and criticizing the dissent's interpretation).

5. See, for example, American Express Co. v. Italian Colors Restaurant, 133 S. Ct. 2304, 2309
(2013) (Scalia, J., writing for the Court).

6. See, for example, Anza v. Ideal Steel Supply Corp., 547 U.S. 451, 462 (2006) (Scalia, J., concurring).

7. See, for example, Chisom v. Roemer, 501 U.S. 380, 409 (1991) (Scalia, J. dissenting).

8. See, for example, Abramski v. United States, 134 S. Ct. 2259, 2283 (2014) (Scalia, J., dissenting).

9. See, for example, City of Columbus v. Ours [*sic*] Garage and Wrecker Service, Inc., 536 U.S.
424, 435 (2002) (Scalia, J., dissenting).

10. See, for example, Daniels v. United States, 532 U.S. 374, 381 (2001) (Scalia, J., concurring
in part).

11. 531 U.S. at 119 and n. 4 (Rehnquist, C. J., concurring).

12. The methods employed here are common in the field of stylometrics. For the technical
details and for copies of our code and data, see dataverse, online at https://github.com/mjockers
/no_reasonable_person.

13. For documentation of the numbers of opinions cited in this and later paragraphs, see our
Appendix, online at https://github.com/mjockers/no_reasonable_person.

14. 486 U.S. 281, 324 n. 2 (1988).

15. 135 S. Ct. 2480, 2505 (2015).

16. 4 Wheat. 122, 203 (1819).

17. Texas Monthly, Inc. v. Bullock, 489 U.S. 1, 45 (1989) (Scalia, J., dissenting).

18. Green v. Bock Laundry Machine Co., 490 U.S. 504, 527 (1989) (Scalia, J., concurring in
the judgment).

19. King v. Burwell, 135 S. Ct. 2480, 2505 (2015) (Scalia, J., dissenting).

20. United States v. Granderson, 511 U.S. 39, 59 (1994) (Scalia, J., concurring in the judgment).

21. United States v. X-Citement Video, Inc., 513 U.S. 64, 82 (1994) (Scalia, J., dissenting).

22. King v. Burwell, 135 S. Ct. at 2505 (Scalia, J., dissenting).

23. Green v. Bock Laundry, 490 U.S. 504, 527–28 (Scalia, J., concurring in the judgment).

24. Liteky v. United States, 510 U.S. 540, 550 (1994) (Scalia, J., writing for the Court).

25. Dewsnup v. Timm, 502 U.S. 410, 427 (1992) (Scalia, J., dissenting).

26. 489 U.S. 1 (1989).

27. 543 U.S. 551 (2005).

28. 517 U.S. 620 (1996).

29. 554 U.S. 570 (2008).

30. 135 S. Ct. 2480 (2015).

31. *Id.* at 2492 (quoting United Sav. Assn. of Tex. v. Timbers of Inwood Forest Associates, Ltd., 484 U.S. 365, 371 (1988).)

32. *Id.* at 2495 (quoting Whitman v. American Trucking Assns., Inc., 531 U.S. 457, 468 [2001]).

Chapter 11

1. Steven Calabresi, in a *USA Today* article on February 24, 2016, is quoted describing Justice Scalia as "the most important justice in American history—greater than former Chief Justice John Marshall himself." For those (myself included) who would consider this evaluation far too generous, one might note that the comment was made right after Justice Scalia's death, and by one of his former law clerks.

2. 491 U.S. 110 (1989).

3. 505 U.S. 833 (1992).

4. 517 U.S. 620 (1996).

5. 539 U.S. 558 (2003).

6. 133 S. Ct. 2552 (2013).

7. 133 S. Ct. 2675 (2013).

8. See, for example, *Michael H.*, 491 U.S. at 120, 127 n. 6, 129 n. 7, 130.

9. *Id.* at 127 n. 6.

10. 410 U.S. 113 (1973).

11. *Casey*, 505 U.S. at 982 (Scalia, J., dissenting).

12. *Id.* at 1000–01 (emphasis in original).

13. From the cases mentioned in this chapter, one might get an impression of Justice Scalia as a strong advocate of an old-fashioned sort of judicial restraint (Thayer 1893). The regular refrain of his opinions in these cases is that the Supreme Court (and the other federal courts) should leave controversial issues to the people, that granting constitutional rights to parents, same-sex couples, and those seeking abortions is a mistake and contrary to the principles of government established by the Constitution. However, any such understanding of Justice Scalia's legal world-view would be partial and distorted. Justice Scalia had far less trouble with taking issues away from the people and from the States where he believed that there was express language protecting the constitutional right in question, even if the meaning and application of the right were far from self-evident. See, for example, *District of Columbia v. Heller*, 554 U.S. 570 (2008) (in Opinion written by Scalia, Court holds that 2nd Amendment protects individual gun ownership, over strong dissent and seemingly contrary precedent). And even regarding claims under the substantive due process clause, a clause and approach Justice Scalia sharply criticized on a number of occasions (in the cases covered in this chapter, and elsewhere), his view seemed to change when the right in question was one he favored. See *McDonald v. City of Chicago*, 561 U.S.

742, 791 (2010) (Scalia, J., concurring) (approving the application of the 2nd Amendment to the States under the Due Process clause of the Fourteenth Amendment).

14. *Romer*, 517 U.S. at 636 (Scalia, J., dissenting).

15. *Id*. (citing *Romer*, 517 U.S. at 634).

16. That such means might have been (at least at the time, or at least prior to *Romer*) "unimpeachable under any constitutional doctrine hitherto pronounced," *id*. at 636 (Scalia, J., dissenting), is beside the point.

17. In his dissenting opinion in *Lawrence v. Texas*, Justice Scalia mentions in passing that four persons were *executed* in what would become the United States during the colonial period. *Lawrence v. Texas*, 539 U.S. 558, 597 (Scalia, J., dissenting); see also Bearok and Cameron 2016.

18. *Lawrence v. Texas*, 539 U.S. at 603 (Scalia, J., dissenting).

19. *Romer*, 517 U.S. at 636, 638, 639 (Scalia, J., dissenting) (emphasis in original); see also *id*. at 637 ("'special rights'"); *id*. at 640, 641, 647 ("special protection"); *id*. at 641 ("special favor and protection"); *id*. at 644 ("favored status"); *id*. at 653 ("preferential treatment").

20. *Id*. at 637 (quoting *id*. at 629 [Majority Opinion]).

21. When referring to a long-term, same-sex, committed relationship, he places "life partner" in quotation marks, *id*. at 638 (Scalia, J., dissenting), implying a certain disdain for the lifestyle.

22. *Lawrence v. Texas*, 539 U.S. at 602 (Scalia, J., dissenting).

23. *Id*. at 636, 638 (emphasis in original).

24. *Id*. at 602.

25. 347 U.S. 483 (1954).

26. 163 U.S. 537 (1896).

27. 198 U.S. 45 (1905). See Snyder and Barrett 2012.

28. 25 U.S.C. §§ 1901–1963.

29. *Adoptive Couple v. Baby Girl*, 133 S. Ct. 2552, 2572 (2013) (Scalia, J., dissenting).

30. *Windsor*, 133 S. Ct. at 2697 (Scalia, J., dissenting); cf. *Morrison v. Olson*, 587, U.S. 654, 699 (1988) (Scalia, J., dissenting) ("That is what this suit is about. Power.").

31. *Windsor*, 133 S. Ct. at 2697 (Scalia, J., dissenting).

32. See *id*. at 2698–2705.

33. *Id*. at 2708

34. *Id*. at 2709. "It is hard to admit that one's political opponents are not monsters, especially in a struggle like this one, and the challenge in the end proves more than today's Court can handle." *Id*. at 2711.

35. *Id*. at 2693 (Opinions for the Court).

36. *Id*. at 2707 (Scalia, J., dissenting).

37. See, e.g., Schleiermacher 2012, 56–59); Foucault 1984, 60–61.

Chapter 12

1. Philip Bobbitt, *Constitutional Interpretation* (Oxford: Blackwell, 1991), 31: "A single modality cannot be both comprehensive and determinate. If it is determinate—does not generate contradictory outcomes—then there will be some cases it cannot decide; specifically, it will not be able to legitimate the particular method associated with that modality. If the scheme is comprehensive, it will generate inconsistent outcomes; specifically, it will be indeterminate as to which of the conventional modalities is to be applied." Cass R. Sunstein, in "Second Amendment Minimalism" (*Harvard Law Review* 122 [2008]: 246), says that "*Heller* is the most explicitly and self-consciously originalist opinion in the history of the Supreme Court."

I don't like the term *originalism*, but won't fight that battle here. I don't like it because it doesn't have a contrary; the opposition is defined by its opposition to originalism and not by anything of its own. "Living constitutionalism" is not a doctrine or a method, but a collection of citations from decisions one doesn't like. The contrast is polemical rather than substantive.

2. These two relations between method and result are parallel to the two relations between justice and law. Law can be measured by its ability to lead to justice. Or justice can be defined as the result of legal process. These two alternatives are marked out, maybe for the first time, in Plato's *Euthyphro*. Neither by itself is sustainable. Law as subordinate to justice becomes instrumental. Justice subordinate to law cannot command the allegiance of any but initiates into the law. My focus on the two directions of inference would be usefully complicated if we moved from Scalia's assertion of a single "method" of interpretation to a consideration of plural legitimate modes or styles of interpretation, or even methods in the plural. But that's an argument for another day. On the madness of following out a single method, regardless of where it leads, see Philip Bobbitt, "Constitutional Fate," *Texas Law Review* 38 (1980): 695–775 at 726: "No sane judge or law professor can be committed solely to one approach. Because there are many facets to a single constitutional problem and . . . many functions performed by a single opinion, the jurist or commentator uses different approaches, as a carpenter uses different tools, and often many tools, in a single project."

3. Kahn, Paul W., *Making the Case: The Art of the Judicial Opinion* (New Haven, CT: Yale University Press, 2016), 3: "There is a certain irony here: the more objective a judge thinks the law, the more likely he is to believe that judicial authority runs to the individual. A claim of legal objectivity is likely, therefore, to lead to dissensus, not unity, among judges" (136–37). "Legal procedure is not like a laboratory protocol: follow it and you are likely to reach the truth of the matter. Rather, it operates as a restraint on power: follow it and the state is less likely to abuse its immense power. Procedure is not about scientific method but about safeguarding a host of other values ranging from fairness to finality. Most of the time, a liberal state puts the worry about power ahead of the worry about truth."

4. J. Finnis and M. Nussbaum, "Is Homosexual Conduct Wrong? An Exchange," *New Republic*, November 15, 1993, 12. Online at http://ezproxy.lib.utexas.edu/login?url=http://search.proquest.com.ezproxy.lib.utexas.edu/docview/1301074465?accountid=7118.

Heller is not the only case where the Court is divided on whether a preamble is an operative part of a law or not, although it is the only case where the preamble in question is in the Constitution. For another example, see Webster, Attorney General of Missouri, et al. v. Reproductive Health Services et al., 492 U.S. 490; 109 S. Ct. 3040; 106 L. Ed. 2d 410; 1989 U.S. LEXIS 3290; 57 U.S.L.W. 5023.

5. Arguably, there's one more preamble. Article I, Section 8: "To promote the Progress of Science and useful Arts, by securing for limited Times to Authors and Inventors the exclusive Right to their respective Writings and Discoveries; . . ." I owe this citation to Sandy Levinson.

6. The "prefatory clause" becomes a "prologue" at 2790, n. 4.

7. I suggest that the Second Amendment has, and the rest of the Bill of Rights does not have, a preamble, to indicate the place of that amendment in the Constitution. It is the only amendment which amends a specific clause in the original Constitution. Scalia does not look to the Preamble to the Constitution but at how preambles to statutes are treated. "In America the settled principle of law is that the preamble cannot control the enacting part of the statute in cases where the enacting part is expressed in clear, unambiguous terms."

8. The only jazz singer I know to have sung the verse is Karin Allyson. See https://www.youtube.com/watch?v=zRBTTgTxqJE.

9. For details, see Eugene Garver, "At the Intersection of Politics and Religion: Posting the Ten Commandments," *Law, Culture, and the Humanities* 3 (2007): 205–24.

10. Similarly 603: "That of the nine state constitutional protections for the right to bear arms enacted immediately after 1789 at least seven unequivocally protected an individual citizen's right to self-defense is strong evidence that that is how the founding generation conceived of the right." Only if there is such a thing as "the right," and Scalia leans on the definite article (627–28): "It may be objected that if weapons that are most useful in military service—M-16 rifles and the like—are banned, then the Second Amendment's right is completely detached from the prefatory clause. But as we have said, the conception of the militia at the time of the Second Amendment's ratification was the body of all citizens capable of military service, who would bring the sorts of lawful weapons that they possessed at home to militia duty. It may well be true today that a militia, to be as effective as militias in the 18th century, would require sophisticated arms that are highly unusual in society at large. Indeed, it may be true that no amount of small arms could be useful against modern-day bombers and tanks. But the fact that modern developments have limited the degree of fit between the prefatory clause and the protected right cannot change our interpretation of the right."

11. "Though Justice Scalia himself remarkably conceded that individual 'self-defense had little to do with the [arms-bearing] right's codification' in the Second Amendment, he nevertheless confidently concluded that self-defense was 'the central component of the right itself' (*Heller* 128 S. Ct. at 2801) because the Amendment was 'widely understood to codify a pre-existing right, rather than to fashion a new one' (at 2804). In essence, he relied on the Second Amendment's text to bridge the wide gap in his historical evidence: 'The very text of the Second Amendment *implicitly* recognizes the pre-existence of the right . . .' (2797). Hence the Amendment's reference to '*the* [pre-existing] right' rather than to *a* [wholly novel] right." Thus Scalia in *Heller* quotes J. Bishop, *Commentaries on Written Laws and Their Interpretation*: "It is nothing unusual in acts . . . for the enacting part to go beyond the preamble; the remedy often extends beyond the particular act or mischief which first suggests the necessity of the law."

12. Stevens (688): "The preamble thus both sets forth the object of the Amendment and informs the meaning of the remainder of the text. Such text should not be treated as mere surplusage."

13. "In their full context, words mean what they conveyed to reasonable people at the time they were written" (Antonin Scalia, and Bryan A. Garner, *Reading Law: The Interpretation of Legal Texts* [St. Paul, MN: Thomson/West, 2012], 16). I wonder if a Christian would agree that the meaning of what Christians call the Old Testament is what its words "conveyed to reasonable people at the time they were written." In a longer version of this paper, I discuss Spinoza's account of the meaning of the Bible, an account which includes what the prophets meant, what the Bible means, and what the Bible means to its readers.

14. Stevens therefore criticized Scalia's opinion for not considering the preamble first. Scalia replies (578 n. 4): "If a prologue can be used only to clarify an ambiguous operative provision, surely the first step must be to determine whether the operative provision is ambiguous. It might be argued, we suppose, that the prologue itself should be one of the factors that go into the determination of whether the operative provision is ambiguous—but that would cause the prologue to be used to produce ambiguity rather than just to resolve it." Why that last sentence is supposed to be a *reductio ad absurdum* I do not know.

15. Scalia, in *Reading Law*, says, "In their full context, *words* mean what they conveyed to reasonable people at the time they were written" (16; emphasis mine). It makes a large difference whether this commits Scalia to the doctrine that words are the unit of meaning or whether

by "words" he means language. A dictionary might supply a list of tools, but words function as tools only when they are used. My own attempt to make sense of the *Charmides* can be found in "*Charmides* and the Virtue of Opacity: An Early Chapter in the History of the Individual," *Review of Metaphysics* 71, no. 3 (2018): 469–500.

16. Charles Fried's "Judgment" begins with this quotation from Montaigne's "On Experience": "Who would not say that glosses increase doubt and ignorance, since there is no book to be found, whether human or divine, with which the world busies itself, whose difficulties are cleared up by interpretation? The hundredth commentator hands it on to his successor thornier and rougher than the first one had found it. When do we agree and say, 'There has been enough about this book; henceforth there is nothing more to say about it?'" (Michel de Montaigne, *Complete Essays*, trans. Frame [Stanford, CA: Stanford University Press, 1958], 815–17). See Charles Fried, "Judgment," *Lewis & Clark Law Review* 15 (2011): 1025–46. "I cannot determinate the relevant facts until I know the law, but I cannot know the law until I know which facts are relevant. ... The successful opinion does not just persuade us to obey; rather, it persuades us to hold ourselves *accountable* for the law that it sets forth" (Kahn, *Making the Case*, 14, 51). See also page 118: "The rhetorical task of the opinion is to narrow the gap between the interpretation and the text that is the object of interpretation. To be fully persuaded is to think there is no gap at all: the opinion tells us what the law means."

17. Antonin Scalia, *A Matter of Interpretation: Federal Courts and the Law*, edited by Amy Gutmann (Princeton, NJ: Princeton University Press, 1997), 38).

18. There are musical performances that are accurately called inimitable. There are, more to the point, musical compositions that are so tied to their circumstances of production that further interpretation takes genius or talent as great as that of the composer. Mose Allison's songs are almost never, and should never, be performed by anyone else, and not because his talent is superior to other musicians. I once asked a very good pianist in a bar to play "Waltz for Debby," and he said that no one but Bill Evans should try to play it. I think he was wrong, but not in principle. It's hard to see why someone would try to sing "Strange Fruit" after Billy Holiday's version; it would be too much like Martin Short's pretending to be Jerry Lewis singing "Blowing in the Wind." My teacher recently set me to learning "Thou Swell," but once I heard Betty Carter I saw no reason to try to sing it. But as with the pianist and "Waltz for Debby," that could be my limitation.

19. A parallel, even farther afield, comes in Reviel Netz's treatment of Greek mathematics. "Mathematical texts start, most commonly, with some piece of prose preceding the sequence of proved results. Often, this is developed into a full 'introduction,' usually in the form of a letter" (*The Transformation of Mathematics in the Early Mediterranean World: From Problems to Equations* [Cambridge: Cambridge University Press, 2004], 94). And such "second-order" language can occur within the body of the mathematical text, as the preamble to the Second Amendment occurs within the Bill of Rights. "Only such an interest can explain such notorious definitions as *Elements* VII.1. 'A unit is that by virtue of which each of the things that exist is called one.' No use can be made of such definitions in the course of the first-order, demonstrative discourse. Such definitions belong to the second-order discourse alone." Still more closely parallel to the preamble to the Second Amendment is this: "Most commonly, definitions do not settle linguistic usage but geometrical propriety; they set out when a property, independently understood, is considered to hold."

20. Paul W. Kahn, *Legitimacy and History: Self-Government in American Constitutional Theory* (New Haven, CT: Yale University Press, 1992).

21. 17 U.S. at 40

Chapter 13

1. 505 U. S. 833 (1992), at 1001.

2. 60 U.S. 393 (1857), at 426.

3. Antonin Scalia, "Common-Law Courts in a Civil-Law System," in Scalia 1997, 14. Scalia is quoting here from Henry M. Hart and Albert M. Sacks, *The Legal Process*, ed. William N. Eskridge and Philip P. Frickey (St. Paul, MN: Foundation Press, 1995), 1169. Some of my thinking about textualism has been inspired by John Harrison, "Rules and Words" (unpublished MS presented to the Virginia Law School Workshop, spring 2004).

4. Scalia and Garner 2012, 16.

5. In my discussion of *Heller* here, I draw on an earlier analysis included in my article, "Law and Humanities: Two Attempts," *B.U. L. Rev.* 1437 (2013).

6. District of Columbia v. Heller, 128 S. Ct. 2783, 2788.

7. This point has been made by Reva Siegel, among others, who shows that the controversies that set the context of Scalia's "originalist" reading of the Second Amendment in fact derive from twenty-first-century political controversies over gun use/gun control. See Siegel 2008, 191.

8. After writing this essay, I was given the opportunity to read Eugene Garver's "Guns and Preludes," chapter 12 in this volume, and found myself in full agreement with his keen analysis of the role of preambles and with his critique of originalism.

9. "Brief for Professors of Linguistics and English," Dennis E. Baron, Ph.D., Richard W. Bailey, Ph.D. and Jeffrey P. Kaplan, Ph.D. in support of Petitioners. No. 07–290, at 2. The professors note in passing that we should not worry about the punctuation of the Amendment, since eighteenth-century usage regarded commas more as breathing marks than logical breaks (at 5, n. 2).

10. Pearson 1912, 152.

11. Wilkinson 2009, 253; Posner 2008.

12. National Rifle Association of America et. al v. City of Chicago, Illinois and Village of Oak Park, Illinois. 567 F.3d. (7th cir. (Ill), 2009, at 3.

13. Carroll 1960, 186.

14. Post 2004.

15. "gobbledy-gook"; see Glossip v. Gross, 576 U. S. ___ (2015), Justice Scalia concurring.

16. I have discussed this case in a short essay; see Brooks 2016, 1–7.

17. Scott v. Harris, 550 U.S. 372 (slip opinion), at 2.

18. The effect of viewing the video by a sample of 1,350 Americans and the diverse cognitive biases revealed in their interpretations have been well studied; see Kahan, Hoffman, and Braman 2009. While the aim of the authors of that article are different from mine, we agree that the single interpretation claim put forth by the Court majority is untenable.

19. de Man 1982.

20. Ryan 2011, 27.

21. But I think Ryan's "what the Constitution actually means" does not do justice to Jack Balkin's more subtle argument about "framework originalism." See Balkin 2011.

Chapter 14

1. *McCullen v. Coakley*, 134 S. Ct. 2518 (2014).

2. *Id.* at 2541 (Scalia, J., concurring in judgment).

3. *Id.* at 2541 (Scalia, J., concurring in judgment) (citing *Hill v. Colorado*, 530 U.S. 703 (2000); *Madsen v. Women's Health Center, Inc.*, 512 U.S. 753 (1994).

4. *See Madsen v. Women's Health Center, Inc.*, 512 U.S. 753, 785 (1994) (Scalia, J., concurring in judgment in part and dissenting in part); *Hill v. Colorado*, 530 U.S. 703, 741 (2000) (Scalia, J., dissenting). See also *Janklow v. Planned Parenthood*, 517 U.S. 1174, 1179 (1996) (Scalia, J., dissenting from the denial of certiorari).

5. *See Planned Parenthood v. Casey*, 505 U.S. 833, 995–96 (1992) (Scalia, J., dissenting) ("*Roe* fanned into life an issue that has inflamed our national politics in general, and has obscured with its smoke the selection of Justices to the Court in particular").

6. According to the National Abortion Federation (NAF), there have been eleven murders of abortion providers and twenty-six attempted murders since the early 1990s. The NAF also has documented more than two hundred bombings and arsons directed at reproductive health facilities since the 1970s. (National Abortion Federation 2017).

7. In terms of legislation, the most significant national victory for the pro-choice movement was likely the enactment of the Freedom of Access to Clinic Entrances (FACE) Act in 1994. *See* 18 U.S.C. § 248. This law criminalized interference by force, threat, or intimidation with people seeking reproductive health services and created a much-utilized civil cause of action.

8. *Frisby v. Schultz*, 487 U.S. 474 (1988).

9. *Madsen v. Women's Health Center*, 512 U.S. 753 (1994).

10. *Schenck v. Pro-Choice Network of Western NY*, 519 U.S. 537 (1997).

11. *Hill v. Colorado*, 530 U.S. 703 (2000).

12. *McCullen v. Coakley*, 134 S. Ct. 2518 (2014).

13. See, for example, cases described in note 28.

14. See generally *Frisby*, 487 U.S. at 757–76.

15. *Id.*, 487 U.S. at 784–85 (Scalia, J., dissenting)

16. See generally *Schenck*, 519 U.S. at 361–95.

17. See *Hill*, 530 U.S. at 742 (Scalia, J., dissenting) (italics in original).

18. *Madsen*, 512 U.S. at 785 (Scalia, J., dissenting) (quoting *Thornburgh v. American College of Obstetricians and Gynecologists*, 476 U.S. 747, 814 [1986] [O'Connor, J., dissenting]).

19. *Id.* (Scalia, J., dissenting).

20. *Hill*, 530 U.S. at 741–42 (Scalia, J., dissenting).

21. *Id.* at 753 (Scalia. J., dissenting).

22. *Id.* at 654 (Scalia, J., dissenting).

23. *Id.* at 745 (Scalia, J., dissenting).

24. *Stenberg v. Carhart*, 530 U.S. 914 (2000).

25. *Hill*, 530 U.S. at 763 (Scalia, J., dissenting).

26. In discourse, "prejudice" does not have an inherently negative connotation as "all understanding inevitably involves some prejudice." In this sense, "prejudice" merely reflects how prior beliefs and values shape a discursive actor's sense of "precedent." (Gadamer 2004, 272–73).

27. *Hill*, 530 U.S. at 757 (Scalia, J., dissenting).

28. *See Bray v. Alexandria Women's Clinic*, 506 U.S. 263 (1993) (rejecting claim that abortion protesters violated section 1985 (3) by obstructing access to abortion clinics); *Scheidler v. National Organization of Women*, 547 U.S. 9 (2006) (rejecting application of Hobbs Act to abortion protesters); *Scheidler v. National Organization of Women*, 537 U.S. 393 (2003) (generally rejecting application of Racketeering and Corrupt Influences Act (RICO) to abortion protesters). But see *National Organization of Women v. Scheidler*, 510 U.S. 249 (1994) (first case in series holding that RICO could apply to groups acting without an economic motive).

Chapter 15

Special thanks to Eric Nystrom for his patience, time, and expertise;
and many thanks to Laura Vleig for research assistance.

1. *Employment Division v. Smith*, 494 U.S. 872, 879 (1990) (quoting *Reynolds v. United States*, 98 U.S. 145, 166–67 [1879]).

2. *United States v. Lee*, 55 U.S. 252, 263 (Stevens, J., concurring).

3. *Smith*, 494 U.S. at 878–79. Unless otherwise noted, the use of italics in quotations from the *Smith* opinion indicates that emphasis has been added.

4. *Id.* at 879.

5. *Id.* at 879 (quoting *Lee*, 455 U.S. at 263 n. 3 [Stevens, J., concurring]).

6. *Id.* at 881.

7. *Id.* at 884.

8. *Id.* at 885.

9. *Id.* at 889.

10. *Id.* at 890.

11. *Burwell v. Hobby Lobby Stores, Inc.*, 134 S. Ct. 2751, 2785 (2014).

12. Credit for all data compilation and resulting images goes to Professor Eric Nystrom. I am responsible for all misinterpretations and errors in using the data and images. For other computational analyses of the legal "vitality" of precedent, see Nelson and Hinkle 2015, and Hinkle 2015.

13. Both the choice of treatment category and the determination that a later case relied on the portion of the precedent case represented in a particular headnote are decisions made by editors at Shepard's and LexisNexis. The treatment categories and headnote designations are useful proxies for content-analysis coding.

14. Recent study confirms that Supreme Court precedents depreciate quickly and that most variables have little effect on the rate of depreciation (Black and Spriggs 2013, 327–28).

15. For comparison, the balance of negative and positive citations is similar to the balance over time for *Regents of the University of California v. Bakke*, 438 U.S. 265 (1978) and less positive than the balance for *District of Columbia v. Heller*, 554 U.S. 570 (2008).

16. This is in line with findings in other citation studies: precedent has more power vertically than stare decisis does horizontally (Nelson and Hinkle 2015).

17. Citations to headnote 10 were omitted from the line graph for readability.

18. As one outgrowth of the work reported in this chapter, Professor Nystrom and I have begun work on an expanded project that will explore the body of Justice Scalia's majority opinions. This project will allow us to study the connections between rhetorical methods and opinion influence in a context less affected by individual circumstances surrounding an opinion.

19. Many lawsuits that do not rely on the First Amendment's Free Exercise Clause make essentially the same claim under the statutory alternatives.

20. *Smith*'s history includes a statutory override as well as a subsequent overruling of the override on constitutional grounds. One study has shown that statutory overrides have less effect than might be expected on future citations to the original opinion. (Broughman and Widiss 2017).

Contributors

BRIAN H. BIX
Law School and Philosophy Department
University of Minnesota
Minneapolis, MN 55455

LINDA L. BERGER
William S. Boyd School of Law
University of Nevada, Las Vegas
Las Vegas, NV 89154-1003

PETER BROOKS
Program in Law and Public Affairs
Princeton University
Princeton, NJ 08544-1013

MARY ANNE CASE
University of Chicago Law School
Chicago, IL 60637

EUGENE GARVER
Saint John's University
Collegeville, MN 56321

ABBE R. GLUCK
Yale University Law School
New Haven, CT 06520

MATTHEW L. JOCKERS
College of Arts & Sciences
University of Nebraska–Lincoln
Lincoln, NE 68588-0312

STEVEN MAILLOUX
Department of English
Loyola Marymount University
Los Angeles, CA 90045

FRANCIS J. MOOTZ III
McGeorge School of Law
University of the Pacific–Sacramento
Sacramento, California 95817

FERNANDO NASCIMENTO
University of Pittsburgh School of Law
Pittsburgh, PA 15260

VICTORIA F. NOURSE
Georgetown Law Center
Washington, DC 20001

CLARKE ROUNTREE
Department of Communication Arts
University of Alabama in Huntsville
Huntsville, AL 35899

DARIEN SHANSKE
School of Law and Department of Political Science
University of California–Davis
Davis, CA 95616

BRIAN G. SLOCUM
McGeorge School of Law
University of the Pacific–Sacramento
Sacramento, CA 95817

SCOTT SOAMES
School of Philosophy
University of Southern California
Los Angeles, CA 90089-0451

LAWRENCE M. SOLAN
Brooklyn Law School
Brooklyn, NY 11201

COLIN STARGER
University of Baltimore School of Law
Baltimore, MD 21201

GEORGE H. TAYLOR
University of Pittsburgh School of Law
Pittsburgh, PA 15260

Index of Cases

Index of Subjects